LINCOLN ON WAR

OTHER BOOKS BY HAROLD HOLZER

In Lincoln's Hand: His Original Manuscripts
with Commentary by Distinguished Americans
(coedited with Joshua Wolf Shenk)

The Lincoln Anthology:
Great Writers on His Life and Legacy from 1860 to Now
(editor)

Lincoln and New York
(editor)

The Lincoln Assassination: Crime and Punishment, Myth and Memory
(coedited with Craig L. Symonds and Frank J. Williams)

The New York Times Complete Civil War
(coedited with Craig L. Symonds)

Father Abraham: Lincoln and His Sons

Lincoln and Freedom: Slavery, Emancipation,
and the Thirteenth Amendment
(coedited with Sara Vaughn Gabbard)

Lincoln's White House Secretary:
The Adventurous Life of William O. Stoddard

Lincoln Revisited: New Insights from the Lincoln Forum
(coedited with John Y. Simon and Dawn Vogel)

Abraham Lincoln Portrayed in the Collections
of the Indiana Historical Society

The Emancipation Proclamation: Three Views—Social, Political,
Iconographic (with Edna Greene Medford and Frank J. Williams)

The Battle of Hampton Roads: New Perspectives on the USS Monitor
and CSS Virginia (coedited with Tim Mulligan)

Lincoln in the Times: *The Life of Abraham Lincoln as*
Originally Reported in the New York Times
(coedited with David Herbert Donald)

Lincoln at Cooper Union:
The Speech That Made Abraham Lincoln President

The President Is Shot! The Assassination of Abraham Lincoln

State of the Union: New York and the Civil War (editor)

The Lincoln Forum: Rediscovering Abraham Lincoln
(coedited with John Y. Simon)

*Abraham Lincoln the Writer: A Treasury of His Greatest Speeches
and Letters* (editor)

Lincoln Seen and Heard

Prang's Civil War Pictures: The Complete Battle Chromos of Louis Prang

The Union Image: Popular Prints of the Civil War North
(with Mark E. Neely, Jr.)

*Lincoln as I Knew Him: Gossip, Tributes, and Revelations from His Best
Friends and Worst Enemies* (editor)

The Lincoln Forum: Abraham Lincoln, Gettysburg and the Civil War
(coedited with John Y. Simon and William D. Pederson)

*The Union Preserved: A Guide to Civil War Records in
the New York State Archives* (editor)

The Lincoln Mailbag: America Writes to the President, 1860–1865
(editor)

Witness to War: The Civil War

The Civil War Era

Dear Mr. Lincoln: Letters to the President (editor)

Washington and Lincoln Portrayed: National Icons in Popular Prints

*The Lincoln-Douglas Debates:
The First Complete, Unexpurgated Text* (editor)

Mine Eyes Have Seen the Glory: The Civil War in Art
(with Mark E. Neely, Jr.)

Lincoln on Democracy (coedited with Mario Cuomo)

The Lincoln Family Album (with Mark E. Neely, Jr.)

The Confederate Image: Prints of the Lost Cause
(with Gabor S. Boritt and Mark E. Neely, Jr.)

The Lincoln Image: Abraham Lincoln and the Popular Print
(with Gabor S. Boritt and Mark E. Neely, Jr.)

LINCOLN
~ ON WAR ~

EDITED AND WITH AN INTRODUCTION BY
HAROLD HOLZER

ALGONQUIN BOOKS OF CHAPEL HILL   2011

Published by
Algonquin Books of Chapel Hill
Post Office Box 2225
Chapel Hill, North Carolina 27515-2225

a division of
Workman Publishing
225 Varick Street
New York, New York 10014

Library of Congress Cataloging-in-Publication Data
Lincoln, Abraham, 1809–1865.
[Selections. 2011]
Lincoln on war / edited and with an introduction by Harold Holzer. — 1st. ed.
p. cm.
Includes index.
ISBN 978-1-56512-378-6
1. Lincoln, Abraham, 1809–1865 — Military leadership — Sources.
2. United States — History — Civil War, 1861–1865 — Communications —
Sources.   3. United States — History — Civil War, 1861–1865 — Moral
and ethical aspects —Sources.   4. United States — History — Civil War,
1861–1865 — Campaigns —Sources.   5. Executive power — United States —
History — 19th century — Sources.   I. Holzer, Harold.   II. Title.
E457.92 2011
973.7 — dc22   2010044569

10 9 8 7 6 5 4 3 2 1

Frontispiece: Oil portrait of Abraham Lincoln by George Peter
Alexander Healy (1813–1894), ca. 1868. This painting was originally
owned by the president's son Robert T. Lincoln.
(*The White House Collection*)

To the Memory of Budge Weidman (1935–2010)
Like Lincoln, a beloved warrior

CONTENTS

LINCOLN ON WAR

ABRAHAM LINCOLN'S OFFICIAL White House portrait still dominates the State Dining Room.

The huge G. P. A. Healy canvas (see frontispiece), enshrined in an ornate gilt frame, idealizes Lincoln as a thoughtful statesman in repose. Clad in his customary black suit, he sits in a chair, alone in seeming isolation, leaning forward, his chin resting in his hand, thumb and forefinger encircling his face—looking inquisitive and engaged yet more passive than active. The pose seems almost to illustrate his overly modest 1864 confession: "I claim not to have controlled events, but confess plainly that events have controlled me."[1]

This is the Lincoln who looms over one of the mansion's largest and most famous public spaces, serving as the immutable backdrop for the great state occasions of the modern presidency. This is the Lincoln who implicitly consecrates all that occurs beneath his pacific gaze—transcending the secular and approaching the status of religious icon: the White House has even reproduced the image as a Christmas tree ornament!

What few of the dignitaries or tourists who gather beneath the picture realize, however, is that it is but a benign detail later extracted by artist Healy from a version that conveys a quite different meaning: a small group portrait called *The Peacemakers*, which hangs in one of the White House's private rooms, off limits and out of sight.

This more provocative rendition, actually the artist's original conception, shows Lincoln sitting in the identical pose, but aboard a riverboat, presiding over a March 1865 military summit at Hampton Roads, Virginia.[2] The artist clearly wants us to know that the storms of war are ebbing, for a symbolic rainbow can be seen bursting forth outside the ship-cabin window. But its title notwithstanding, the painting portrays Lincoln not as a "peacemaker" at all but rather as a warrior. For he is no longer alone. He is meeting with uniformed commanders Ulysses S. Grant, William Tecumseh Sherman, and David Dixon Porter. These are the very Union officers who had sacrificed thousands of troops, respectively, to the carnage of the Wilderness Campaign, led the devastating march through Georgia, and conducted the relentless naval assault on Vicksburg—all with Lincoln's encouragement or assent. The four men are peacemakers, all right, in the same way that guns are known as peacemakers: they have won the opportunity to pursue peace by waging ferocious war.

As these contrasting paintings remind us—one shows him pondering, the other commanding—Lincoln's image on matters military remains a bit fuzzy. Like the Healy paintings themselves, the larger impression is of a man of peace; the smaller, a man of war. Understandably, most modern Americans recall Lincoln as the era's quintessential civilian. But the fact remains that he was also an unrelenting warrior prepared to commit—even sacrifice—men and treasure in unprecedented numbers to secure the kind of peace worth having.[3] And the most powerful evidence of this focus comes from his own writings, words that counter the idealized image. Though often, and expertly, extracted and quoted, they have never until now been gathered in a single collection.

In many ways, Lincoln's words have been as imperfectly remembered as his image. The most famous invariably evoke peace and hope. "New birth of freedom," "the better angels of our nature," and "malice toward none" are the Lincolnian nuggets that come most quickly to mind: the timeless promises of the Gettysburg Address and the first and second inaugurals. But during his astonishingly productive and peerlessly influential political (and, in a sense, literary) career, Lincoln devoted far more energy, more time, and *more words* to the opposite subject: that of war. The fact that much of his output on this theme long remained private produced the same disorienting impact as the preferential treatment shown Healy's proudly displayed and intentionally generic copy portrait—at the expense of his more militaristic, and sequestered, original.

The Peacemakers by George Peter Alexander Healy (1813–1894), 1868. The painting depicts a council of war aboard the presidential vessel *River Queen,* docked at Union army headquarters, City Point, Virginia, on March 28, 1865. From left to right: General William T. Sherman, General Ulysses S. Grant, President Abraham Lincoln, and Admiral David Dixon Porter. *(The White House Collection)*

The tough reality can be found within Lincoln's language. During the final four years of his life—because the entire span of his presidency was enveloped by war—no other topic occupied him more exhaustively, or in turn called forth thoughts more inspiring, creative, daring, and occasionally irreverent, impatient, and desperate, than that which engaged him in his role as commander in chief of the United States Army and Navy.

Beginning with the onset of the war 150 years ago, in 1861, Lincoln used his pen as a major weapon in the arsenal he deployed in the fight to save the Union and, ultimately, to destroy slavery. His rare speeches to the public (for, as president, it should be noted, the famous orator seldom orated), his recorded statements to White House visitors, letters to the press, and remarks to troops en route to or returning from battlefields, along with his alternatively congratulatory and cajoling dispatches to commanders and politicians, constitute a remarkable archive of persuasion, morale building, political ingenuity, leadership skill, and most breathtaking of all, growing military sophistication. Abraham Lincoln, it might be said, came to deploy words as artillery, not merely to articulate overarching strategy and issue specific tactical orders but also to soften public opinion and stiffen military resolve to the bloody realities of prolonged hard fighting.[4]

True, more than one contemporary noted that Lincoln's Confederate counterpart, Jefferson Davis, a West Point graduate, Mexican War veteran, and former secretary of war, donned a spruce military uniform to appear majestically on the battlefield of Bull Run in 1861. "What a world of heroism in that act of our worthy President," one bedazzled Confederate government clerk marveled, proudly reporting that Davis had reached the field just in time to take personal command of his army's center column.[5] It hardly mattered to the court of public opinion that it later turned out that Davis had in fact arrived that day aboard a train, wearing civilian clothing, and well after the fighting was over. Unlike Lincoln, Davis was an instantly credible commander in chief because of his service in Mexico—in a war that young Congressman Lincoln had opposed. By contrast, Lincoln's lesser-known life story seemed inconsistent: a onetime volunteer soldier in a tinpot Indian war and an antiwar congressman thrust untested into the presidency.

Speaking of the Mexican-American War, few early biographies of Lincoln seemed to be complete without detailed reference to his dovish, and supposedly career-threatening, public stance against that conflict in late 1848 during his single term in the House of Representatives.[6] In Congress, as some of the speeches in this collection will attest, he did in fact daringly challenge the right of the president of the United States to commit troops to battle over unproven foreign aggression. On a more profound level, in a speech in the House of Representatives, Lincoln went so far as to question "[t]he exceeding brightness of military glory," which he darkly warned was an "attractive rainbow, that rises in showers of blood—that serpent's eye, that charms to destroy."[7] And yet to characterize Lincoln chiefly as an antiwar legislator who miraculously morphed into a ruthless wartime executive—a man who detested war but pursued it mercilessly when he had to—is to miss some of the crucial, subtler elements of his complicated political and personal evolution on matters military.

We should remember, first of all, that Lincoln's supposedly courageous and seemingly pacifistic opposition to the Mexican-American War in truth perfectly mirrored his Whig political party's unified opposition to Democratic president James Knox Polk's commitment of American troops—in a conflict initiated, most Northern Whigs charged, with an eye toward acquiring new slave territory to bolster the proslavery Democratic majority in Congress.

Lincoln was hardly the sole Whig to speak out in the House against the adventure. Representative Alexander H. Stephens of Georgia, for another, made a similar speech that brought tears to Lincoln's "old, withered, dry eyes," he appreciatively reported.[8] (Stephens would later become vice president of the Confederacy!) Nor did Lincoln bravely risk his political future by opposing the war, as some biographers have maintained. Voters did not return him to Congress, but by prearrangement he had agreed before accepting the nomination to serve only a single term in the House and to rotate his seat no matter what he accomplished (or how miserably he failed) in Washington. In advocating for peace, Lincoln acted more the antislavery man than the antiwar man. As suggested by a eulogy he offered for war hero Zachary Taylor just a few years later, brimming with enthusiastic accounts of Old Rough and Ready's valor in Mexico, Lincoln enjoyed a good soldier story as much as any man, even when it involved a war he opposed.

There is yet more to the full story of Lincoln's attitude toward war—principally the often ignored but lifelong appeal that things military held for this supposedly unmilitary man. Lincoln came of this interest naturally. Like most boys born during founding father Thomas Jefferson's presidency (even if in its very last weeks), young Abraham Lincoln was enraptured by the stories he heard, and later read, about the country's first war and the men who only thirty years earlier had so bravely fought it. "They were a forest of giant oaks . . .

pillars of the temple of liberty," he later said reverently of the veterans of the American Revolution. As a child he undoubtedly glimpsed some of those "giant oaks" for himself, perhaps when aging veterans gathered for their final Independence Day reunions, stuffed into their tattered, fading, but still evocative uniforms.

Lincoln could thus personally recall a time when "*living history was* to be found in every family—a history bearing the indubitable testimonies of its own authenticity, in the limbs mangled, in the scars of wounds received, in the midst of the very scenes related" by "a husband, a father, a son or a brother." Such "scenes of the revolution," he asserted, may have been fading "upon the memory of the world, and grow more and more dim by the lapse of time," but as he emphasized, they would never be "entirely forgotten."[9] He was certainly one of those who remembered. Lincoln never lost his respect for the descendants or relics of that struggle; to him, they were nothing less than sacred. The founders themselves Lincoln came to regard as "blessed fathers."[10]

The American Revolution, he learned as a child, and believed ever after, was provoked not by hate, revenge, or petty political disagreements but rather in pursuit of the "advancement of the noblest of causes— that of establishing and maintaining civil and religious liberty."[11] That was good enough for Lincoln—as the boy enraptured by war stories, and as the man leading a "good war" of his own to preserve what the founders had created. During his Indiana boyhood, Lincoln first read Mason Locke Weems's hagiographic and extraordinarily popular life of George Washington. "I remember all the accounts there given of the battle fields and struggles for the liberties of the country," he proudly testified years later. Speaking before the New Jersey state legislature en route to his inauguration in 1861, he confided that its stories "all fixed themselves on my memory . . . and you all know, for you have all been boys, how these early impressions last longer than any others." From that book, Lincoln came to realize that "there must have been something more than common that these men struggled for . . . something that held out a great promise to all the people of the world to all time to come."[12]

If fought for a noble purpose, he convinced himself, war was indeed worth waging. As a practical corollary matter, Lincoln long maintained that veterans deserved not only special honor but also special perquisites. In the Illinois state legislature in 1837, Lincoln proposed an amendment to a public revenue bill to allow surviving veterans of the Revolutionary War to lend out any part of their pensions without paying taxes.[13] A quarter of a century later, on Independence Day 1862, Lincoln, now president, welcomed a golden anniversary delegation of elderly War of 1812 veterans to the White House. Though he was too busy to prepare a formal speech for them, he still found time to greet them cordially and, not incidentally, confidently inferred from their arrival that they supported his fight to restore the Union for which they had fought fifty years earlier.[14]

Thus, long before he was himself compelled to manage the titanic civil war he came to office hoping his country might avoid, Lincoln was genuinely animated not only by the idea of justifiable wars like the Revolution and the War of 1812 (whose survivors he had personally seen straggling home from the Cumberland Trail near his Indiana childhood home), but by the very zeal for glory against which he later famously warned in his anti–Mexican War speech in Congress.

To the younger Lincoln, the appeal of military experience could be irresistible even when the cause seems less than noble to the modern reader. In 1832, at age twenty-three, he enlisted to fight with his local New Salem, Illinois, militia in a brief local war against the Indian chief Black Hawk, who had broken a recent treaty that sent him into exile and had menacingly reentered the state together with a band of armed Sac and Fox Indians. To his "own surprise," as he later put it, Lincoln's fellow volunteers promptly elected their tall, well-spoken comrade-in-arms as their company captain. For more than two decades, Lincoln would proudly recall that he "has not since had any success in life which gave him so much satisfaction" or "pleasure."[15]

It is true that Lincoln faced no real character-testing military action during the short-lived Black Hawk conflict (he merely "met the ordinary hardships of such an expedition, but was in no battle," he conceded). Nor did he learn there the finer points of command. It was even said that once after marching his men up to a fence and failing to recall the proper order for scaling it, he simply dismissed the company and shrewdly ordered them to reassemble ten minutes later on the other side.

Otherwise, Captain Lincoln occupied much of his time "at war" mediating disputes among his men and either racing or wrestling against his fellow recruits in athletic competitions—more often than not prevailing.[16] He encountered few Indians, though he once prevented fellow soldiers from pouncing on a confused and defenseless old brave who had wandered harmlessly into camp.

Lincoln remained realistic enough about his limited experience to turn it on its ear in order to mock Lewis Cass's run for the presidency in 1848. To the consternation of Whigs who had nominated authentic war hero Taylor, Democrats were attempting to portray their candidate as a military giant, too. Lincoln took to the floor of the House of Representatives to declare: "Mr. Speaker, did you know I am a military hero? Yes sir; in the days of the Black Hawk war, I fought, bled, and came away." He had been in no great battles, Lincoln cheerfully admitted, but had personally glimpsed at least one battlefield "very soon afterwards." Though he was certain he "did not break my sword, for I had none to break," he had "bent a musket pretty badly on one occasion." He had even led occasional "charges against the wild onions." He did not encounter any hostile Indians but "had a good many bloody struggles with the musquetoes; and, although I never fainted from loss of blood, I can truly say I was often very hungry."[17] One can just imagine Lincoln's customarily starchy fellow congressmen dissolved in laughter at this hilarious monologue. But the self-deprecating speech, delivered to focus scrutiny on the grandiose claims for Cass, hardly negates Lincoln's later expressions of genuine pride at his own limited military service.

In fact, when young Captain Lincoln's original thirty-day term of service in the Black Hawk War ended, and though most of his neighbors hastened home to resume their civilian lives, Lincoln reenlisted as a private—not once but three more times! In return for his extended service, he earned \$125 and some land in Iowa, but acquisitiveness alone cannot explain away the fact that he clearly *enjoyed* his life as a soldier, however uneventful. The inglorious conclusion to this, his only military experience—someone stole his horse, and Lincoln had to walk and canoe from Wisconsin Territory all the way back home to New Salem—could not dampen its warm memories. Unlike the American commander in chief with whom he is most often compared, Franklin D. Roosevelt, Lincoln never said, "I hate war." As he first experienced it, he rather liked it.

War might even upend a lifetime of political partisanship. Lincoln may have excoriated Democrat James Knox Polk over alleged American aggression against Mexico, but suddenly placed in Polk's shoes as commander in chief during the secession crisis, Lincoln could sound as bellicose as Polk and even cite former Democratic president Andrew Jackson, against whose policies he had all but built his own political career. Thus when Lincoln became president, he rejected an early proposal for conciliation over secession by exclaiming of his onetime political enemy (Jackson, not Black Hawk): "There is no . . . Jackson in that—no manhood or honor in that."[18] Old Hickory suddenly seemed exemplary enough to suit Lincoln when remembered for his tough and precedent-setting stand against South Carolina nullification. As chief executive, Lincoln even took to displaying a painting of the general-turned-president Jackson in his White House office. He kept it there throughout the war and perhaps cherished a remark that a journalist made upon viewing a recent painting of Lincoln: that he looked as if he boasted "enough of the General Jackson firmness to please the most ardent admirer of 'Old Hickory.' "[19]

Posturing and politics aside, Lincoln's wartime experience, if not quite Jacksonian, proved deeply significant to the young man. Back home, the men of his Black Hawk War company testified that their captain had shown himself "a kind hearted & noble man who did his duty well without fear[,] gold, favor or Affection. He had a somewhat good Eye for Military affairs, as said by Competent judges." Even back then, a New Salem friend marveled, "His heart & head

were large & Comprehensive enough to Command a Company—
regiment or other Core [*sic*] of men under any Circumstances."[20]

Time proved this judgment to be correct. In sum, Lincoln's attitude toward war did not shift as abruptly as some have suggested.
He was not simply a pro-peace Whig who turned into a ferocious
pro-war Republican when he saw his authority challenged. Such
assessments, all too common, begin Lincoln's extraordinary meta-
morphosis in the middle. His was a far more nuanced personal and
political journey, guided by history, values, experience, and sometimes political expediency.

And yet when he became commander in chief in March 1861, Lincoln
still knew next to nothing about military matters. As president-elect he
had exchanged a handful of letters with aged general in chief Winfield
Scott and sought updates from fellow Republicans already on the
ground in Washington. En route to the capital for his inauguration,
he struggled toward a coherent policy that was neither conciliatory
enough to legitimize secession, nor coercive enough to justify rebellion. Facing a crisis virtually from the moment he took office—
compelled immediately to decide whether or not to reenforce Fort
Sumter in Charleston harbor—he operated largely by instinct and
energy, throwing himself into exhausting meetings with generals,
studying maps, and bypassing Congress (then in recess) to order up
volunteers and a naval blockade. Above all, he successfully educated
himself, just as he had done years earlier with regard to the Bible,
Shakespeare, geometry, and the law: simply by reading voraciously.
As far as we know, Lincoln never opened Carl von Clausewitz's clas-
sic *On War* (it was not then available in English), but he subsequently
did borrow other military treatises from the Library of Congress,
consuming, for example, the essential handbook authored by his
own chief administrative general, Henry W. Halleck's *Elements of
Military Art and Science.*[21] In a way, as historian T. Harry Williams
has pointed out, he proved Clausewitz's argument that knowledge
of military affairs was less important as a qualification for a commander in chief than "a remarkable, superior mind and strength of

character."²² Searching for officers who were "zealous & efficient," he became more zealous and efficient than any of them.²³

To choose commanders and subordinates, Lincoln relied at first on his longtime knack for accurately evaluating men though not always with beneficial results; many among his initial roster of commanders disappointed him and hurt the Union cause. Undaunted, the president fired off suggestions, orders, and where necessary, dismissal notices. And he might use civilian means to military ends. He ingeniously commissioned inexperienced Democrats and flamboyant foreigners, for example, to raise their own companies of soldiers in an effort to widen support for the war even though most of these so-called political generals ultimately proved incompetent on the battlefield. In short, he learned as he went along. Words guided him, and in turn his own brilliantly crafted words began guiding others.

Though Lincoln quickly learned that war could be unrelenting, brutal, and destructive, he did not shrink from it. Instead he fought it aggressively—with words. He was no match for Jefferson Davis's superior experience or more martial bearing. But the president of the United States could turn a phrase far more adroitly than the president of the Confederate States—or just about anyone else of his time. And no weapons of war conquered more hearts and minds than the words of Abraham Lincoln. He may not have delivered many public orations from 1861 to 1865, but he made sure his words were fully deployed nationwide in letters published in the press, annual messages, and seemingly offhand but inspiring comments to visitors that were observed and reported by journalists. As he honed his skills as a communicator, he developed his skills as a commander. By war's end, no one doubted that Lincoln had been both its chief advocate and its chief administrator.

THIS COLLECTION ATTEMPTS to gather, present, and interpret Lincoln's most important (along with some of his most obscure but illuminating) words on this, the most engrossing theme of his beleaguered presidency and, ultimately, of the nation's imperiled existence.

It embraces the soaring, practical, comic, distraught, and hectoring. It covers strategy; tactics; the endless hiring, sustaining, motivating, and dismissal of commanders; the issue of military discipline; and a subject all too often overlooked by many Lincoln and Civil War aficionados: military technology. The first and only president to hold a federal patent for an invention, Lincoln became deeply interested in weapon development: torpedoes, balloon reconnaissance, machine guns, rifled cannons, and perhaps most important to the Union cause, ironclad warships—no matter how deadly. As he put it once to a critic who protested the harshness of the Union effort, a war to suppress so enormous a rebellion could simply not be waged with mere "elder squirts, charged with rose water."[24]

In examining Abraham Lincoln's chief speeches, letters, memoranda, orders, telegrams, and remarks in chronological order, readers will have the opportunity to experience fully, and in his very own words, his growth from eager young Indian war officer to politically motivated, middle-aged congressional dove, into surprisingly hardened and determined hawk. In this final iteration he expresses himself as increasingly willing to sacrifice life and treasure in unprecedented quantities, to risk wounding the pride of vain commanders, and even to mislead the public, if it means the preservation of an unbreakable union of states, the destruction of human slavery, and the restoration of America as an example to inspire the world— what Lincoln regarded as the central idea of what he so often called the "struggle."[25]

This book of course includes such masterpieces as his first and second inaugurals and his Gettysburg Address, along with his justly renowned letters of encouragement (and congratulations) to Generals Hooker, Grant, Sherman, and Sheridan. It also showcases his lesser-known, surprisingly rare, and enduringly fascinating public speeches on the war; his private memoranda and casual remarks on the progress of arms; his devout meditations on God's mysterious purposes in prolonging the war, often written out of the palpable depths of despair; his desperate telegrams to his commanders during and after battles; his irritable putdowns of dilatory or overly ambitious generals; his unabashedly partisan orders to give soldiers in the field the right to vote—presumably for him—in the 1864 presidential election; and his persistent defense of the society-altering recruitment of African American troops. Here, too, are examples of both his routine and rousing correspondence with his secretaries of war and the navy; the dry but history-altering proclamations (and more eloquent explanations) he issued to impose blockades, recruit troops, or quash civil liberties; and the long letters he cunningly crafted to individuals but designed as public messages (and released to the press) to rally the military and civilian population alike to fight on for union and freedom. Also, there are the letters he composed to failed commanders out of frustration, disappointment, and even fury and then filed away without sending—as if their writing alone had cooled his temper. Throughout the collection, Lincoln matures, the depth of feeling in his writing grows, and the increasingly tough words belie his increasingly soft image.

As he put it once, "[T]hose who make a causeless war should be compelled to pay the cost of it."[26] During his presidency, as this book will show, Lincoln made the foes of Union and freedom pay that cost dearly, using words to define what he called his "war power," a degree of unprecedented executive authority whose imposition still arouses legal and scholarly debate. In an altogether different mode, he also blessed the expansion of home-front charities aimed at caring for the troops, and advocated expanding the rights of minorities within the armed forces. He not only formally recruited the first organized "U.S. Colored Troops," he also eventually secured equal pay for black soldiers. He suspended the privileges of the writ of habeas corpus, passionately defending his authority to do so. But he also ordered the revocation of General Ulysses S. Grant's heinous General Order No. 11, which banned Jews "as a class" from his military department (though in this case, Lincoln preferred acting quietly, through intermediaries and *without* public words, in an effort to spare his most successful general from embarrassment).

In his voluminous correspondence—readers must remind themselves that this book presents only a fraction of the crushing paperwork that burdened Lincoln every single day of his presidency—he wrote to high officials and ordinary Americans alike, to rouse their spirits, inspire action, give thanks to God for military victories, appoint friends and friends' children to military posts and academies, and to "condole"[27] (as he once put it) the grieving parents, children, and siblings who had lost loved ones. He seldom took a day off. "I sincerely wish war was an easier and pleasanter business than it is," he lamented in late 1862, "but war does not admit of holy-days."[28]

A year before he ran for the presidency, Lincoln had told a Wisconsin audience that he sincerely yearned for a "world less inclined to wars, and more devoted to the arts of peace, than heretofore." Yet he soon found himself presiding over, and advocating through his outpouring of words, the largest, costliest, and deadliest war in world history. "War at best, is terrible," he conceded to an audience in Philadelphia in 1864, "and this war of ours, in its magnitude and in its duration, is one of the most terrible."[29] Before it was over, six hundred thousand young men lay dead—and the commander in chief himself had helped lead a naval expedition in Virginia and later exposed himself to Confederate sharpshooters at a Union fort in the suburbs of Washington. Lincoln did not think himself a brave man, yet he never lacked for either personal courage or the resolve, assurance, and breathtaking literary talent to use writing (what he once called "the great invention of the world"[30]) to compel his army, navy, and civilian constituency to keep fighting.

There have been many compendia of Lincoln's words, but this is the first to highlight exclusively his role as warrior in chief and military cheerleader in chief of a nation at war with itself. How better to understand his steely resolve or his manifest complexity? "Both parties deprecated war," Lincoln reminded America just six weeks before his death, recalling the tense days that had preceded secession and rebellion, "but one of them would *make* war rather than let the nation survive; and the other would *accept* war rather than let it perish. And the war came." Yet Lincoln was never willing to accept easy explanations—even his own. During that same extraordinary speech, he argued that both North and South were alike responsible for the devastating war that ensued, for both sections had tolerated the sin of slavery too long.[31] His words on war ultimately approached the sublime.

Why should we care today? For one thing, because Lincoln's written record on war is not merely a matter for history or historians. Modern commanders in chief, from Woodrow Wilson, Franklin D. Roosevelt, and Lyndon B. Johnson in the twentieth century, to George W. Bush and Barack Obama in the twenty-first, have routinely and repeatedly (if sometimes inappropriately) cited Lincoln's resolve, and quoted Lincoln's words (often unpersuasively), to justify wars of their own. As long as current and future presidents employ Abraham Lincoln as inspiration, it behooves the citizen to know his record well. And as the following pages will show, no leader in history better negotiated, or illuminated, the tension between organic belief and unexpected contingency. Using his own weapons—his words—Lincoln fought the Civil War as brilliantly as any general who ever took the field.

Let the chief author of that war (in more ways than one) speak for himself once again, in the words that he employed to justify, sustain, redefine, and consecrate it. Let him explain again in his own inimitable phrases why the honored dead of that war did not die "in vain"—but rather "gave their lives that that nation might live."[32]

NOTES

1. Lincoln to Albert G. Hodges, April 4, 1864, Roy P. Basler, ed., *The Collected Works of Abraham Lincoln*, 8 vols., hereinafter cited as *Collected Works of Lincoln* (New Brunswick, N.J.: Rutgers University Press, 1953–1955), 7:282.

2. Healy painted the small group portrait first, then extracted the Lincoln pose for a larger study—an unusual course for an artist. Lincoln's son liked the large picture so much he ordered a copy; today it hangs in the Newberry Library in Chicago. See Harold Holzer and Mark E. Neely Jr., *Mine Eyes Have Seen the Glory: The Civil War in Art* (New York: Orion Books, 1993), 155.

3. Two important, and excellent, 2008 books shed considerable light on Lincoln's military leadership. See James M. McPherson, *Tried by War:*

Abraham Lincoln as Commander in Chief (New York: Penguin Books, 2009), and Craig L. Symonds, *Lincoln and His Admirals: Abraham Lincoln, the U.S. Navy, and the Civil War* (New York: Oxford University Press, 2008). The two books shared the 2009 Lincoln Prize.

4. On his visits to federal encampments, Lincoln might be observed reviewing troops on horseback, sitting in the saddle so awkwardly that the bottom edges of his long underwear crept out visibly from below his trousers. To his soldiers, he understandably became "Father Abraham," not "General Lincoln." Yet shortly after the Union victory at Antietam in 1862, Lincoln embraced the opposite image, posing for photographer Alexander Gardner at the headquarters of General George B. McClellan. This time an artist's determination to create a military portrait held sway. While the results show the men standing before a tent, one can just make out, in the background, a perfectly sound-looking house that might as easily have served as the locale for the Lincoln-McClellan meeting (and photograph) had not Gardner likely determined that a picture made "on the field" would hold more appeal to the public. Whether consciously or not, the photo opportunity (a term not in use at the time, but entirely apt for this staged event) gave Lincoln another advantage: standing face-to-face with his diminutive commander, the six-foot-four-inch president, top hat adding another foot to his height, looks so much more imposing that there is little visual question of who is in charge. Lincoln must have relished the result. He kept one of the pictures taken that day for himself. See William C. Davis, *Lincoln's Men: How President Lincoln Became a Father to an Army and a Nation* (New York: Free Press, 1999), 141. For the Antietam photograph, see Charles Hamilton and Lloyd Ostendorf, *Lincoln in Photographs: An Album of Every Known Pose* (Norman: University of Oklahoma Press, 1963), 106–13. The portrait Lincoln retained showed him with General John McClernand and detective Allan Pinkerton. See Mark E. Neely Jr. and Harold Holzer, *The Lincoln Family Album*, rev. ed. (Carbondale: Southern Illinois University Press, 2006), 30.

5. John B. Jones, *A Rebel War Clerk's Diary at the Confederate States Capital,* 2 vols. (Philadelphia: J. B. Lippincott, 1866), 1:64.

6. See, for example, Albert J. Beveridge, *Abraham Lincoln 1809–1858,* 2 vols. (Boston: Houghton Mifflin, 1928), 1:433. For a modern historiographical analysis, see Daniel Walker Howe, "Abraham Lincoln's Opposition to the Mexican War," in *Lincoln's Legacy of Leadership,* ed. George A. Goethals and Gary L. McDonald, 87–99 (New York: Palgrave Macmillan, 2009).

7. *Collected Works of Lincoln,* 1:439.

8. Lincoln to William H. Herndon, February 2, 1848, ibid., 1:448. For

Stephens's words and Lincoln's reaction, see Ronald C. White Jr., *A. Lincoln: A Biography* (New York: Random House, 2009), 145–46.

9. Speech at the Young Men's Lyceum, Springfield, Illinois, January 27, 1838, *Collected Works of Lincoln*, 1:115.

10. From his speech in New Haven, March 6, 1860, ibid., 4:18.

11. Ibid.

12. Speech to New Jersey State Senate, Trenton, February 21, 1861, ibid., 4:235–36.

13. Text of an amendment offered on January 18, 1840, ibid., 1:183–84.

14. Ibid., 5:306.

15. Autobiographical sketch for the *Chicago Press & Tribune*, ca. June 1860, ibid., 4:64; autobiographical sketch for *Chester County* [Pennsylvania] *Times*, December 20, 1859, ibid., 3:512.

16. *Collected Works of Lincoln*, 4:64; George M. Harrison to William H. Herndon, January 29, 1867, in Douglas L. Wilson and Rodney O. Davis, *Herndon's Informants: Letters, Interviews, and Statements about Abraham Lincoln* (Urbana: University of Illinois Press, 1998), 553–56.

17. Speech in the U.S. House of Representatives, July 27, 1848, *Collected Works of Lincoln*, 1:510.

18. Remarks to a Baltimore delegation, April 22, 1861, ibid., 4:341.

19. *Boston Transcript*, July 14, 1860. Clipping copied in 1983 at the former Lincoln Museum, Fort Wayne, Indiana.

20. Mentor Graham, quoting "all in his Company & Regiment," in Wilson and Davis, eds., *Herndon's Informants*, 9.

21. For Clausewitz, see James M. McPherson, *Tried by War: Abraham Lincoln as Commander in Chief* (New York: Penguin Books, 2008), 6; for his book borrowing, see Earl Schenk Miers, ed., *Lincoln Day by Day: A Chronology, 1809–1865* (Washington, D.C.: Lincoln Sesquicentennial Commission, 1960), 3:88.

22. Carl von Clausewitz's *On War*, quoted in T. Harry Williams, *Lincoln and His Generals* (New York: Alfred A. Knopf, 1952), 7.

23. Letter to Secretary of War Simon Cameron, August 7, 1861, *Collected Works of Lincoln*, 4:475.

24. Letter to Cuthbert Bullitt, July 28, 1862, ibid., 5:346.

25. See, for example, his first annual message to Congress, December 3, 1861, ibid., 5:53. ("The struggle of today, is not altogether for today—it is for a vast future also.")

26. Letter to the House of Representatives, July 17, 1862, ibid., 5:329.

27. Lincoln actually used "condole" to acknowledge the loss of Chief Justice

Salmon P. Chase's sister in 1865. See Lincoln to Chase, January 2, 1865, ibid., 8:195.

28. Letter to Thomas H. Clay, October 8, 1862, ibid., 5:452.

29. Speech at the Wisconsin State Agricultural Society, Milwaukee, September 30, 1859, ibid., 3:481; Remarks at the Great Central Sanitary Fair, Philadelphia, June 16, 1864, ibid., 7:394.

30. Lecture on Discoveries and Inventions, February 11, 1859, ibid., 3:357.

31. Second Inaugural Address, March 4, 1865, ibid., 8:332.

32. Gettysburg Address, November 19, 1863, ibid., 7:23.

A NOTE ON THE TEXTS

THE OVERWHELMING MAJORITY of material on the following pages was written in Lincoln's own hand. The collection also includes official proclamations, which the president sometimes, but not always, drafted himself, but which expressed important wartime policy decisions; telegrams for which original manuscripts have in some cases vanished; and impromptu remarks recorded by and published in the press. On rare but irresistible occasions, the editor includes a reasonably authenticated conversation or overheard statement—particularly with regard to naval operations, since Lincoln devoted most of his oratory and correspondence to the land war and the records of his views on sea and river engagements and commanders remain scarce.

Except where indicated, all the presidential letters and speeches published on the following pages were written at or made from the White House.

It should be noted that notwithstanding his youthful immersion in Thomas Dilworth's *A New Guide to the English Tongue,* Abraham Lincoln never became a particularly good speller. He never learned how to spell *inauguration, dispatch, guarantee, privilege, position, installation, defense, partisan,* or a host of other words he nonetheless used with confident regularity (he could never even spell *Fort Sumter!*) He often put *e* before *i* or created fantastical combinations of letters to arrive at words like *previlege* and *magnificient.* The use of that technological alembic known as "spell check" easily revealed, and might just as easily have facilitated the correction of, all such mistakes, but the editor preferred to allow modern readers to see Lincoln's words exactly as he crafted them, his frequent misspellings intact—and the cautionary word *sic* employed only to acknowledge and clarify the most egregious of these. Some of these "*sic*" alerts are my own; others come from the authoritative texts published in *The Collected Works of Abraham Lincoln,* edited by Roy P. Basler in the 1950s, from which the overwhelming majority of material in this collection was obtained. To simplify this process for readers, I have not attempted to differentiate between my own editorial corrections and Basler's. I have, however, sparingly inserted additional bracketed explanatory text, chiefly to identify people and events not fully explained by Lincoln in his speeches, letters, and remarks.

In nearly all cases, Lincoln's words are printed as full, unabridged texts. Minor omissions (a word, a sentence, or rarely, a brief paragraph) are denoted with a conventional ellipsis. In the case of his longest speeches—principally his four annual messages to Congress—more extensive deletions were made to spare the reader from occasionally numbing detail about nonwar issues like revenues and continental expansion. These are clearly identified in each title ("From a speech" instead of "Speech"), with cuts indicated by a line of dots.

It is otherwise presumptuous, not to mention futile, to attempt to edit Abraham Lincoln.

LINCOLN ON WAR

Abraham Lincoln, ca. 1846, the year of his election to the House of Representatives, where he earned a reputation for his opposition to the Mexican-American War. Daguerreotype by Nicholas H. Shepherd, Springfield, Illinois. *(Library of Congress)*

THE EXCEEDING BRIGHTNESS

OF MILITARY GLORY

1832–1860

Together, these selected early letters and speeches from Abraham Lincoln's first three decades in public life document a truly remarkable personal and political evolution. During this period of individual and national growth, Lincoln emerged from obscurity, exulted in his brief experience in military service, then recast himself as a war critic, and finally morphed yet again into a resolute antislavery man. In what almost constituted successive fifteen-year cycles, he went from the eager volunteer in the Black Hawk War of 1832, to the virulently anti–Mexican War congressman of 1848, and finally to the presidential candidate and president-elect of 1860 prepared to accept war rather than let the union split and slavery spread. Over time, Lincoln also greatly refined his writing style, learning not only to purge his oratory of rhetorical excess but also to compose ostensibly private correspondence that when released to the press packed a powerful public wallop. In the writings that follow, Lincoln showed a taste—then a distaste for—and finally a resolve to endure, if required, the vicissitudes of war.

"THE SANGAMON COUNTY COMPANY, UNDER MY COMMAND"

Receipt for Weapons

NEW SALEM, ILLINOIS, APRIL 28, 1832

Biographers maintain that Captain Abraham Lincoln wrote this receipt after presenting his army quartermaster with an order from Brigadier Major John J. Hardin stating of his woefully undersupplied unit: "The Brigade Inspector having inspected Capt. Abram [sic] Lincoln's company, and mustered them into service, reported that thirty guns are wanting to arm the company completely. Quartermaster General Edwards will furnish the Captain with that number of arms." Adequately equipped at last, Lincoln's brief military career began. He later declared that being elected captain of volunteers "gave me more pleasure than any I have had since." Being on campaign—military, not political—left him feeling nothing less than "elated"—a valuable clue to his later interest in military affairs.

Received, April 28, 1832, for the use of the Sangamon County Company, under my command, thirty muskets, bayonets, screws and wipers, which I oblige myself to return upon demand.

A. LINCOLN, Capt.

"THE SILENT ARTILLERY OF TIME"

From an Address before the Young Men's Lyceum

SPRINGFIELD, ILLINOIS, JANUARY 27, 1838

Lincoln's first major political lecture was above all a ringing condemnation of violent "mobocratic spirit" and an appeal that "reverence for the laws" become the new "political religion of the nation." Importantly, Lincoln devoted some of this much-analyzed, and rather purple, early speech to an appreciation of George Washington and the heroes who had fought the Revolutionary War.

I do not mean to say, that the scenes of the revolution *are now or ever will be* entirely forgotten; but that like every thing else, they must fade upon the memory of the world, and grow more and more dim by the lapse of time. In history, we hope, they will be read of, and recounted, so long as the bible shall be read;—but even granting that they will, their influence *cannot be* what it heretofore has been. Even then, they *cannot be* so universally known, nor so vividly felt, as they were by the generation just gone to rest. At the close of that struggle, nearly every adult male had been a participator in some of its scenes. The consequence was, that of those scenes, in the form of a husband, a father, a son or a brother, a *living history was* to be found in every family—a history bearing the indubitable testimonies of its own authenticity, in the limbs mangled, in the scars of wounds received, in the midst of the very scenes related—a history, too, that could be read and understood alike by all, the wise and the ignorant, the learned and the unlearned. But *those* histories are gone. They *can* be read no more forever. They were a fortress of strength; but, what invading foemen could *never do*, the silent artillery of time *has done*; the levelling of its walls. They are gone. They *were* a forest of giant oaks; but the all-resistless hurricane has swept over them, and left only, here and there, a lonely trunk, despoiled of its verdure, shorn of its foliage; unshading and unshaded, to murmur in a few more gentle breezes, and to combat with its mutilated limbs, a few more ruder storms, then to sink, and be no more.

They *were* the pillars of the temple of liberty; and now, that they have crumbled away, that temple must fall, unless we, their descendants, supply their places with other pillars, hewn from the solid quarry of sober reason. Passion has helped us; but can do so no more. It will in future be our enemy. Reason, cold, calculating, unimpassioned reason, must furnish all the materials for our future support and defence.

"THE FIRST BLOOD SO SHED"

"Spot" Resolutions Introduced in the U.S. House of Representatives

WASHINGTON, DECEMBER 22, 1847

During his one and only term in Congress, Lincoln offered these politically risky resolutions questioning President Polk's claim that American blood had been shed by Mexicans on American soil—the alleged justification for the Mexican-American War. Lincoln demanded to know the exact "spot" where such an attack had taken place. Historians have been arguing ever since about whether or not this daring tactic did political harm to the young antiwar Whig. Lincoln himself thought they would "distinguish" him. But Democrats took to calling him "Benedict Arnold" or "Spotty Lincoln." Though Congress never adopted his "spot" resolutions, which were mainly aimed at providing copy to mail home to his Illinois district in reprints, Lincoln and his fellow House Whigs were successful in amending a congressional resolution of thanks to war hero Zachary Taylor by adding that his victory occurred "in a war unnecessarily and unconstitutionally begun by the President of the United States."

Whereas the President of the United States, in his message of May 11th. 1846, has declared that "The Mexican Government not only refused to receive him" (the envoy of the U.S.) "or listen to his propositions, but, after a long continued series of menaces, have at last invaded *our teritory,* and shed the blood of our fellow *citizens* on *our own soil*[.]"

And again, in his message of December 8, 1846 that "We had ample cause of war against Mexico, long before the breaking out of hostilities. But even then we forbore to take redress into our own hands, until Mexico herself became the aggressor by invading *our soil* in hostile array, and shedding the blood of our *citizens*[.]"

And yet again, in his message of December 7- 1847 that "The Mexican Government refused even to hear the terms of adjustment which he" (our minister of peace) "was authorized to propose; and finally, under wholly unjustifiable pretexts, involved the two countries in war, by invading the teritory of the State of Texas, striking the first blow, and shedding the blood of our *citizens* on *our own soil*[.]"

And whereas this House desires to obtain a full knowledge of all the facts which go to establish whether the particular spot of soil on which the blood of our *citizens* was so shed, was, or was not, *our own soil*, at that time; therefore

Resolved by the House of Representatives, that the President of the United States be respectfully requested to inform this House—

First: Whether the spot of soil on which the blood of our *citizens* was shed, as in his messages declared, was, or was not, within the teritories of Spain, at least from the treaty of 1819 until the Mexican revolution

Second: Whether that spot is, or is not, within the teritory which was wrested from Spain, by the Mexican revolution[.]

Third: Whether that spot is, or is not, within a settlement of people, which settlement had existed ever since long before the Texas revolution, until it's inhabitants fled from the approach of the U.S. Army.

Fourth: Whether that settlement is, or is not, isolated from any and all other settlements, by the Gulf of Mexico, and the Rio Grande, on the South and West, and by wide uninhabited regions on the North and East.

Fifth: Whether the *People* of that settlement, or a *majority* of them, or *any* of them, had ever, previous to the bloodshed, mentioned in his messages, submitted themselves to the government or laws of Texas, or of the United States, by *consent*, or by *compulsion*, either by accepting office, or voting at elections, or paying taxes, or serving on juries, or having process served upon them, or in *any other way*.

Sixth: Whether the People of that settlement, did, or did not, flee from the approach of the United States Army, leaving unprotected their homes and their growing crops, *before* the blood was shed, as in his messages stated; and whether the first blood so shed, was, or was not shed, within the *inclosure* of the People, or some of them, who had thus fled from it.

Seventh: Whether our *citizens,* whose blood was shed, as in his messages declared, were, or were not, at that time, *armed* officers, and *soldiers,* sent into that settlement, by the military order of the President through the Secretary of War—and

Eighth: Whether the military force of the United States, including those *citizens,* was, or was not, so sent into that settlement, after Genl. Taylor had, more than once, intimated to the War Department that, in his opinion, no such movement was necessary to the defence or protection of Texas.

"THE RIGHT TO RISE UP"

From a Speech to the U.S. House of Representatives on the War with Mexico

WASHINGTON, JANUARY 12, 1848

Just three weeks after introducing and explicating on his "spot" resolutions, Congressman Lincoln (not quite thirty-nine years old) again rose on the floor of the House to offer this carefully detailed but impassioned antiwar speech—in a sense, a lawyer's brief with a flourish. Though it failed to distinguish him in Washington and, worse, inflamed opposition at home, Lincoln proudly had it published as a pamphlet—his spelling errors intact—and distributed it widely to his Illinois Whig allies, asserting that it "condensed all I could" on the controversial issue of war and presidential power. That issue resurfaced again when Lincoln himself became president (with the onetime antiwar congressman now defending unchecked executive authority) and even continues to this day: consider the Bush-Obama era's still-unresolved battles over a chief executive's power in time of war.

Mr. Chairman:

Some, if not all the gentlemen on, the other side of the House, who have addressed the committee within the last two days, have spoken rather complainingly, if I have rightly understood them, of the vote

given a week or ten days ago, declaring that the war with Mexico was
unnecessarily and unconstitutionally commenced by the President.
I admit that such a vote should not be given, in mere party wantonness, and that the one given, is justly censurable, if it have no other,
or better foundation. I am one of those who joined in that vote; and
I did so under my best impression of the *truth* of the case. How
I got this impression, and how it may possibly be removed, I will
now try to show. When the war began, it was my opinion that all
those who, because of knowing too *little,* or because of knowing too
much, could not conscientiously approve the conduct of the President, in the beginning of it, should, nevertheless, as good citizens
and patriots, remain silent on that point, at least till the war should
be ended. Some leading democrats, including Ex President [Martin]
Van Buren, have taken this same view, as I understand them; and I
adhered to it, and acted upon it, until since I took my seat here; and
I think I should still adhere to it, were it not that the President and
his friends will not allow it to be so. Besides the continual effort of
the President to argue every silent vote given for supplies, into an
endorsement of the justice and wisdom of his conduct—besides that
singularly candid paragraph, in his late message in which he tells
us that Congress, with great unanimity, only two in the Senate and
fourteen in the House dissenting, had declared that, "by the act of
the Republic of Mexico, a state of war exists between that Government and the United States," when the same journals that informed
him of this, also informed him, that when that declaration stood
disconnected from the question of supplies, sixtyseven in the House,
and not fourteen merely, voted against it—besides this open attempt
to prove, by telling the *truth,* what he could not prove by telling the
whole truth—demanding of all who will not submit to be misrepre-
sented, in justice to themselves, to speak out—besides all this, one of
my colleagues (Mr. Richardson) [a Democrat elected to fill the seat
of Lincoln's lifelong political rival, Stephen A. Douglas—ed.] at a
very early day in the session brought in a set of resolutions, expressly
endorsing the original justice of the war on the part of the President.
Upon these resolutions, when they shall be put on their passage I

shall be *compelled* to vote; so that I can not be silent, if I would. Seeing this, I went about preparing myself to give the vote understandingly when it should come. I carefully examined the President's messages, to ascertain what he himself had said and proved upon the point. The result of this examination was to make the impression, that taking for true, all the President states as facts, he falls far short of proving his justification; and that the President would have gone farther with his proof, if it had not been for the small matter, that the *truth* would not permit him. Under the impression thus made, I gave the vote before mentioned. I propose now to give, concisely, the process of the examination I made, and how I reached the conclusion I did. The President, in his first war message of May 1846, declares that the soil was *ours* on which hostilities were commenced by Mexico; and he repeats that declaration, almost in the same language, in each successive annual message, thus showing that he esteems that point, a highly essential one. In the importance of that point, I entirely agree with the President. To my judgment, it is the *very point*, upon which he should be justified, or condemned. In his message of Decr. 1846, it seems to have occurred to him, as is certainly true, that title—ownership—to soil, or any thing else, is not a simple fact; but is a conclusion following one or more simple facts; and that it was incumbent upon him, to present the facts, from which he concluded, the soil was ours, on which the first blood of the war was shed.

. . . .

I am now through the whole of the President's evidence; and it is a singular fact, that if any one should declare the President sent the army into the midst of a settlement of Mexican people, who had never submited, by consent or by force, to the authority of Texas or of the United States, and that *there*, and *thereby*, the first blood of the war was shed, there is not one word in all the President has said, which would either admit or deny the declaration. This strange omission, it does seem to me, could not have occurred but by design. My way of living leads me to be about the courts of justice; and there, I have sometimes seen a good lawyer, struggling for his client's neck, in a desparate case, employing every artifice to work round, befog, and cover up, with many words, some point arising in the case, which he *dared* not admit, and yet *could* not deny. Party bias may help to make it appear so; but with all the allowance I can make for such bias, it still does appear to me, that just such, and from just such necessity, is the President's struggle in this case.

Some time after my colleague (Mr. Richardson) introduced the resolutions I have mentioned, I introduced a preamble, resolution, and interrogatories, intended to draw the President out, if possible, on this hitherto untrodden ground. To show their relevancy, I propose to state my understanding of the true rule for ascertaining the boundary between Texas and Mexico. It is, that *wherever* Texas was *exercising* jurisdiction, was hers; and *wherever Mexico* was exercising jurisdiction, was hers; and that *whatever* separated the actual exercise of jurisdiction of the one, from that of the other, was the true boundary between them. If, as is probably true, Texas was exercising jurisdiction along the western bank of the Nueces, and Mexico was exercising it along the eastern bank of the Rio Grande, then *neither* river was the boundary; but the uninhabited country between the two, was. The extent of our teritory in that region depended, not on any *treaty-fixed* boundary (for no treaty had attempted it) but on revolution. Any people anywhere, being inclined and having the power, have the *right* to rise up, and shake off the existing government, and form a new one that suits them better [a right Lincoln challenged years later as President when Texas and other states "rose up" against the Union—ed.]. This is a most valuable,—a most sacred right—a right, which we hope and believe, is to liberate the world. Nor is this right confined to cases in which the whole people of an existing government, may choose to exercise it. Any portion of such people that *can, may* revolutionize, and make their *own*, of so much of the teritory as they inhabit. More than this, a *majority* of any portion of such people may revolutionize, putting down a *minority*, intermingled with, or near about them, who may oppose their movement. Such minority, was precisely the case, of the tories of our own revolution. It is a quality of revolutions not to go by *old* lines, or *old* laws; but to break up both, and make new ones. As to the country now in question, we bought it of France in 1803, and sold it to Spain in 1819, according to the President's statements. After this, all Mexico, including Texas, revolutionized against Spain; and still later, Texas revolutionized against Mexico. In my view, just so far as she carried her revolution, by obtaining the *actual,* willing or unwilling, submission of the people, *so far,* the country was hers, and no farther. Now sir, for the purpose of obtaining the very best evidence, as to whether Texas had actually carried her revolution, to the place where the hostilities of the present war commenced, let the President answer the interrogatories, I proposed, as before mentioned, or some other similar ones. Let him answer, fully, fairly, and candidly. Let him answer with *facts,* and not with arguments. Let him remember he sits where Washington sat, and so remembering, let him answer, as Washington would answer. As a nation *should* not, and the Almighty *will* not, be evaded, so let him attempt no evasion—no equivocation. And if, so answering, he can show that the soil was ours, where the first blood of the war was shed—that it was not within an inhabited country, or, if within such, that the inhabitants had submitted themselves to the civil authority of Texas, or of the United States, and that the same is true of the site of Fort Brown, then I am with him for his justification. In that case I, shall be most happy to reverse the vote I gave the other day. I have a selfish motive for desiring that the President may do this. I expect to give some votes, in connection with the war , which, without his so doing, will be of doubtful propriety in my own judgment, but which will be free from the doubt if he does so. But if he *can* not, or *will* not do this—if on any pretence, or no pretence, he shall refuse or omit it, then I shall be fully convinced, of what I more than suspect already, that he is deeply conscious of being in the wrong—that he feels the blood of this war, like the blood of Abel, is crying to Heaven against him. That originally having some strong motive—what, I will not stop now to give my opinion concerning—to involve the two countries in a war, and trusting to escape scrutiny, by fixing the public gaze upon the exceeding brightness of military glory—that attractive rainbow, that rises in showers of blood—that serpent's eye, that charms to destroy—he plunged into it, and has swept, *on* and *on*, till, disappointed in his calculation of the ease with which Mexico might be subdued, he now finds himself, he knows not where. How like the half insane mumbling of a fever-dream, is the whole war part of his late message! At one time telling us that Mexico has nothing whatever, that we can get, but teritory; at another, showing us how we can support the war , by levying contributions on Mexico. At one time, urging the national honor, the security of the future, the prevention of foreign interference, and even, the good of Mexico herself, as among the objects of the war; at another, telling us, that "to reject indemnity, by refusing to accept a cession of teritory, would be to abandon all our just demands, and to wage the war , bearing all it's expenses, *without a purpose or definite object*[.]" So then, the national honor, security of the future, and every thing but teritorial indemnity, may be considered the *no-purposes,* and *indefinite,* objects of the war! But, having it now settled that teritorial indemnity is the only object, we are urged to seize, by legislation here, all that he was content to take, a few months ago, and the whole province of lower California to boot, and to still carry on the war—to take *all* we are fighting for, and *still* fight on. Again, the President is resolved, under all circumstances, to have full teritorial indemnity for the expenses of the war; but he forgets to tell us how we are to get the *excess,* after those expenses shall have surpassed the value of the *whole* of the Mexican teritory. So again, he insists that the separate national existence of Mexico, shall be maintained; but he does not tell us *how* this can be done, after we shall have taken *all* her teritory.

.   .   .   .

Again, it is a singular omission in this message, that it, no where intimates *when* the President expects the war to terminate. At it's beginning, Genl. [Winfield] Scott [a Mexican War hero and fellow Whig in politics—ed.] was, by this same President, driven into disfavor, if not disgrace, for intimating that peace could not be conquered in less than three or four months. But now, at the end of about twenty months, during which time our arms have given us the most splendid successes—every department, and every part, land and water, officers and privates, regulars and volunteers, doing all that men *could* do, and hundreds of things which it had ever before been thought men could *not* do,—after all this, this same President gives us a long message, without showing us, that, *as to the end,* he himself, has, even an immaginary [*sic*] conception. As I have before said, he knows not where he is. He is a bewildered, confounded, and miserably perplexed man. God grant he may be able to show, there is not something about his conscience, more painful than all his mental perplexity!

"No One Man Should Hold the Power"

Letter to William H. Herndon

WASHINGTON, FEBRUARY 15, 1848

Lincoln's young law partner, William H. Herndon, though an ardent Whig himself, warned the congressman that his antiwar stand meant "political suicide." Lincoln replied with a powerful attack on a president's power to make war—a power Lincoln would later assume for himself in putting down an internal rebellion. During this period, Lincoln was confronting issues that are still resonating in American political discourse 150 years later: the legitimacy of preemptive war, executive authority in wartime, and postwar exit strategy.

Dear William:

Your letter of the 29th. Jany. was received last night. Being exclusively a constitutional argument, I wish to submit some reflections upon it in the same spirit of kindness that I know actuates you. Let me first state what I understand to be your position. It is, that if it shall become *necessary, to repel invasion,* the President may, without violation of the Constitution, cross the line, and *invade* the territory of another country; and that whether such *necessity* exists in any given case, the President is to be the *sole* judge.

Before going further, consider well whether this is, or is not your position. If it is, it is a position that neither the President himself, nor any friend of his, so far as I know, has ever taken. Their only positions are first, that the soil was *ours* where hostilities commenced, and second, that whether it was rightfully *ours* or not, *Congress had annexed it,* and the President, for that reason was bound to defend it, both of which are as clearly proved to be false in fact, as you can prove that your house is not mine. That soil was not ours; and Congress did not annex or attempt to annex it. But to return to your position: Allow the President to invade a neighboring nation, whenever *he* shall deem it necessary to repel an invasion, and you allow him to do so, *whenever he may choose to say* he deems it necessary for such purpose—and you allow him to make war at pleasure. Study to see if you can fix *any limit* to his power in this respect, after you have given him so much as you propose. If, to-day, he should choose to say he thinks it necessary to invade Canada, to prevent the British from invading us, how could you stop him? You may say to him, "I see no probability of the British invading us" but he will say to you "be silent; I see it, if you dont."

The provision of the Constitution giving the war-making power to Congress, was dictated, as I understand it, by the following reasons. Kings had always been involving and impoverishing their people in wars, pretending generally, if not always, that the good of the people was the object. This, our Convention understood to be the most oppressive of all Kingly oppressions; and they resolved to so frame the Constitution that *no one man* should hold the power of bringing this oppression upon us. But your view destroys the whole matter, and places our President where kings have always stood. Write soon again.

Yours truly,
A. LINCOLN

"AS TO THE MEXICAN WAR"

From a Fragment on the Presidential Election of 1848

WASHINGTON, [MARCH ?] 1848

Lincoln wrote these notes to himself about the forthcoming presidential campaign after abandoning his longtime hero, civilian politician Henry Clay, to support General Zachary Taylor, a military hero, for the top spot on the Whig ticket because he seemed more electable than the thrice-defeated Clay. Despite Taylor's military credentials, Lincoln believed the Whig candidate must continue to oppose the Mexican War. Besides, the War was "substantially over," Lincoln wrote, by early March.

It appears to me that the national debt created by the war, renders a modification of the existing tariff indispensable; and when it shall be modified, I should be pleased to see it adjusted with a due reference to the protection of our home industry. The particulars, it appears to me, must and should be left to the untramelled discretion of Congress.

As to the Mexican war, I still think the defensive line policy the best to terminate it. In a final treaty of peace, we shall probably be under a sort of necessity of taking some teritory; but it is my desire that we shall not acquire any extending so far South, as to enlarge and agrivate the distracting question of slavery. Should I come into the presidency before these questions shall be settled, I should act in relation to them in accordance with the views here expressed.

Finally, were I president, I should desire the legislation of the country to rest with Congress, uninfluenced by the executive in it's origin or progress, and undisturbed by the veto unless in very special and clear cases.

"A WICKED AND UNCONSTITUTIONAL WAR"

From a Letter to Usher F. Linder

WASHINGTON, MARCH 22, 1848

Charleston, Illinois, attorney Usher F. Linder was one of many correspondents who cautioned Lincoln against extreme opposition to the Mexican War, worrying that the congressman would be accused of holding radical antislavery positions simply by supporting Zachary Taylor for the presidential nomination. In his reply, Lincoln reminded Democrat Linder, an old colleague from their days in the Illinois State Legislature, that even as he opposed the war he consistently voted to supply the troops in the field.

Friend Linder:

Yours of the 15th. is just received, as was a day or two ago, one from [Alexander] Dunbar on the same subject. Although I address this to you alone, I intend it for you Dunbar, and Bishop, and wish you to show it to them. In Dunbar's letter, and in Bishop's paper, it is assumed that Mr. [John J.] Crittenden's [U.S. senator from Kentucky—ed.] position on the war is correct. Well, so I think. Please wherein is my position different from his? Has *he* ever approved the President's conduct in the beginning of the war, or his mode or objects in prossecuting it? Never. He condemns both. True, he votes supplies, and so do I. What, then, is the difference, except that he is a great man and I am a small one?

Towards the close of your letter you ask three questions, the first of which is "Would it not have been just as easy to have elected Genl. Taylor without opposing the war as by opposing it?" I answer, I suppose it would, if we could do *neither*—could be *silent* on the question; but the Locofocos [radical urban Democrats, named for the self-igniting matches used to light candles—ed.] here will not let the whigs be *silent.* Their very first act in congress was to present a preamble declaring that war existed by the act of Mexico, and the whigs were obliged to vote on it—and this policy is followed up by them;

so that they are compelled to *speak* and their only option is whether they will, when they do speak, tell the *truth*, or tell a foul, villainous, and bloody falsehood. But, while on this point, I protest against your calling the condemnation of Polk "opposing the war." In thus assuming that all must be opposed to the war, even though they vote supplies, who do not not [*sic*] endorse Polk, with due deference I say I think you fall into one of the artfully set traps of Locofocoism.

Your next question is "And suppose we could succeed in proving it a wicked and unconstitutional war, do we not thereby strip Taylor and Scott of more than half their laurels?" Whether it would so strip them is not matter of demonstration, but of *opinion* only; and my opinion is that it would not; but as your opinion seems to be different, let us call in some others as umpire. There are in this H.R. [House of Representatives—ed.] some more than forty members who support Genl. Taylor for the Presidency, every one of whom has voted that the war was "unnecessarily and unconstitutionally commenced by the President" every one of whom has spoken to the same effect, who has spoken at all, and not one of whom supposes he thereby strips Genl. of any laurels. More than this; two of these, Col. [William T.] Haskell [congressman from Tennessee—ed.] and Major [John P.] Gaines [congressman from Kentucky—ed.], themselves fought in Mexico; and yet they vote and speak just as the rest of us do, without ever dreaming that they "strip" themselves of any laurels. There may be others, but Capt. Bishop is the only intelligent whig who has been to Mexico, that I have heard of taking different ground.

Your third question is "And have we as a party, ever gained any thing, by falling in company with abolitionists?" Yes. We gained our only national victory by falling in company with them in the election of Genl. Harrison. Not that we fell into abolition doctrines; but that we took up a man whose position induced them to join us in his election. But this question is not so significant as a *question*, as it is as a charge of abolitionism against those who have chosen to speak their minds against the President. As you and I perhaps would again differ as to the justice of this charge, let us once more call in our umpire. There are in this H.R. whigs from the slave states as follows: one from Louisiana, one from Mississippi, one from Florida, two from Alabama, four from Georgia, five from Tennessee, six from Kentucky, six from North Carolina, six from Virginia, four from Maryland and one from Delaware, making thirtyseven in all, and all slave-holders, every one of whom votes the commencement of the war "unnecessary and unconstitutional" and so falls subject to your charge of abolitionism!

"*En passant*" these are all *Taylor* men, except one in Tenn. two in Ky, one in N.C. and one in Va. Besides which we have one in Ills— two in Ia, three in Ohio, five in Penn. four in N.J. and one in Conn. While this is less than half the whigs of the H.R. it is three times as great as the strength of any other one candidate. . . .

Yours as ever,

A. LINCOLN

"YES, SIR, I AM A WAR HERO"

*From a Speech to the U.S. House of Representatives
on the Presidential Question*

WASHINGTON, JULY 27, 1848

---

*Lincoln's last, most overtly political—and most uproariously funny—
speech on the Mexican War was meant to excoriate Democratic presidential candidate Lewis Cass, whom some supporters characterized as
a military hero. Here he likens Cass's questionable military record to
his own experience in the Black Hawk conflict of 1832. Though he was
currently backing a genuine war veteran, Zachary Taylor, for the White
House, Lincoln also used this oration to warn yet again, and with unusual vehemence, against the pitfalls of the quest for military glory.*

Mr. Speaker, it is no business, or inclination of mine, to defend Martin Van Buren [former Democratic president of the United

States—ed.]. In the war of extermination now waging between him and his old admirers, I say, devil take the hindmost—and the foremost. But there is no mistaking the origin of the breach; and if the curse of "stinking" and "rotting" is to fall on the first and greatest violators of principle in the matter, I disinterestedly suggest, that the gentleman from Georgia, and his present co-workers, are bound to take it upon themselves.

But the gentleman from Georgia further says we have deserted all our principles, and taken shelter under Gen: Taylor's military coat-tail; and he seems to think this is exceedingly degrading. Well, as his faith is, so be it unto him. But can he remember no other military coat tail under which a certain other party have been sheltering for near a quarter of a century? Has he no acquaintance with the ample military coat tail of Gen: Jackson? Does he not know that his own party have run the five last Presidential races under that coat-tail? and that they are now running the sixth, under the same cover? Yes sir, that coat tail was used, not only for Gen: Jackson himself; but has been clung to, with the gripe [*sic*] of death, by every democratic candidate since. You have never ventured, and dare not now venture, from under it. Your campaign papers have constantly been "Old Hickories" with rude likenesses of the old general upon them; hickory poles, and hickory brooms, your never-ending emblems; Mr. Polk himself was "Young Hickory" "Little Hickory" or something so; and even now, your campaign paper here, is proclaiming that Cass and Butler are of the true "Hickory stripe." No sir, you dare not give it up.

Like a horde of hungry ticks you have stuck to the tail of the Hermitage lion to the end of his life; and you are still sticking to it, and drawing a loathsome sustenance from it, after he is dead. A fellow once advertised that he had made a discovery by which he could make a new man out of an old one, and have enough of the stuff left to make a little yellow dog. Just such a discovery has Gen: Jackson's popularity been to you. You not only twice made President of him out of it, but you have had enough of the stuff left, to make Presidents of several comparatively small men since; and it is your chief reliance now to make still another.

Mr. Speaker, old horses, and military coat-tails, or tails of any sort, are not figures of speech, such as I would be the first to introduce into discussions here; but as the gentleman from Georgia has thought fit to introduce them, he, and you, are welcome to all you have made, or can make, by them. If you have any more old horses, trot them out; any more tails, just cock them, and come at us.

I repeat, I would not introduce this mode of discussion here; but I wish gentlemen on the other side to understand, that the use of degrading figures is a game at which they may not find themselves able to take all the winnings. (We give it up). Aye, you give it up, and well you may; but for a very different reason from that which you would have us understand. The point—the power to hurt—of all figures, consists in the *truthfulness* of their application; and, understanding this, you may well give it up. They are weapons which hit you, but miss us.

MILITARY TAIL OF THE GREAT MICHIGANDER

But in my hurry I was very near closing on the subject of military tails before I was done with it. There is one entire article of the sort I have not discussed yet; I mean the military tail you democrats are now engaged in dovetailing onto the great Michigander. Yes sir, all his biographers (and they are legion) have him in hand, tying him to a military tail, like so many mischievous boys tying a dog to a bladder of beans. True, the material they have is very limited; but they drive at it, might and main. He *in*vaded Canada without resistance, and he *out*vaded it without pursuit. As he did both under orders, I suppose there was, to him, neither credit or discredit in them; but they [are made to] constitute a large part of the tail. He was not at Hull's surrender, but he was close by; he was volunteer aid to Gen: Harrison on the day of the battle of the Thames; and, as you said in 1840, Harrison was picking huckleberries [whortleberries] two miles off while the battle was fought, I suppose it is a just conclusion with you, to say Cass was aiding Harrison to pick huckleberries [picking whortleberries]. This is about all, except the mooted question of the broken sword. Some authors say he broke it, some say he threw it away, and some others, who ought to know, say nothing about it. Perhaps it would be a fair historical compromise to say, if he did not break it, he didn't do any thing else with it.

By the way, Mr. Speaker, did you know I am a military hero? Yes sir; in the days of the Black Hawk war, I fought, bled, and came away. Speaking of Gen: Cass' career, reminds me of my own. I was not at Stillman's defeat [the most infamous engagement of the war, May 14, 1832, in which white soldiers were repulsed by a small band of Indians—ed.], but I was about as near it, as Cass was to Hulls surrender [General William Hull surrendered Detroit to the British in 1812, and Cass, then his subordinate, had brought charges against him— ed.]; and, like him, I saw the place very soon afterwards. It is quite certain I did not break my sword, for I had none to break; but I bent a musket pretty badly on one occasion. If Cass broke his sword, the idea is, he broke it in de[s]peration; I bent the musket by accident. If Gen: Cass went in advance of me in picking huckleberries [whortleberries], I guess I surpassed him in charges upon the wild onions. If he saw any live, fighting indians, it was more than I did; but I had a good many bloody struggles with the musquetoes; and, although I never fainted from loss of blood, I can truly say I was often very hungry. Mr. Speaker, if I should ever conclude to doff whatever our democratic friends may suppose there is of black cockade federalism about me, and thereupon, they shall take me up as their candidate for the Presidency, I protest they shall not make fun of me, as they have of Gen: Cass, by attempting to write me into a military hero.

. . . .

THE WHIGS AND THE WAR

But, as Gen: Taylor is, par excellence, the hero of the Mexican war; and, as you democrats say we whigs have always opposed the war, you think it must be very awk[w]ard and embarrassing for us to go for Gen: Taylor. The declaration that we have always opposed the war, is true or false, accordingly as one may understand the term "opposing the war." If to say "the war was unnecessarily and un-constitutionally commenced by the President" be opposing the war, then the whigs have very generally opposed it. Whenever they have spoken at all, they have said this; and they have said it on what has appeared good reason to them. The marching [of] an army into the midst of a peaceful Mexican settlement, frightening the inhabitants away, leaving their growing crops, and other property to destruc-tion, to *you* may appear a perfectly amiable, peaceful, unprovoking procedure; but it does not appear so to *us*. So to call such an act, to us appears no other than a naked, impudent absurdity, and we speak of it accordingly. But if, when the war had begun, and had become the cause of the country, the giving of our money and our blood, in common with yours, was support of the war, then it is not true that we have always opposed the war. With few individual excep-tions, you have constantly had our votes here for all the necessary supplies. And, more than this, you have had the services, the blood, and the lives of our political bretheren in every trial, and on every field. The beardless boy, and the mature man—the humble and the distinguished, you have had them.

Through suffering and death, by disease, and in battle, they have endured, and fought, and fell with you. Clay and Webster each gave a son, never to be returned. From the state of my own residence, besides other worthy but less known whig names, we sent Marshall, Morrison, Baker, and Hardin; they all fought, and one fell; and in the fall of that one, we lost our best whig man. Nor were the whigs few in number, or laggard in the day of danger. In that fearful, bloody, breathless struggle at Buena Vista, where each man's hard task was to beat back five foes or die himself, of the five high officers who perished, four were whigs.

In speaking of this, I mean no odious comparison between the lion-hearted whigs and democrats who fought there. On other occasions, and among the lower officers and privates on *that* occasion, I doubt not the proportion was different. I wish to do justice to all. I think of all those brave men as Americans, in whose proud fame, as an American, I too have a share. Many of them, whigs and democrats, are my constituents and personal friends; and I thank them—more than thank them—one and all, for the high, imperishable honor they have confered on our common state.

But the distinction between the cause of the *President* in beginning the war, and the cause of the *country* after it was begun, is a distinction which you can not perceive. To you the President, and the country, seems to be all one. You are interested to see no distinction between them; and I venture to suggest that possibly your interest blinds you a little. We see the distinction, as we think, clearly enough; and our friends who have fought in the war have no difficulty in seeing it also. What those who have fallen would say were they alive and here, of course we can never know; but with those who have returned there is no difficulty. Col: Haskell, and Major Gaines, members here, both fought in the war; and one of them underwent extraordinary perils and hardships; still they, like all other whigs here, vote, on the record, that the war was unnecessarily and unconstitutionally commenced by the President. And even Gen: Taylor himself, the noblest Roman of them all, has declared that as a citizen, and particularly as a soldier, it is sufficient for him to know that his country is at war with a foreign nation, to do all in his power to bring it to a speedy and honorable termination, by the most vigorous and energetic opperations, without enquiring about it's justice, or any thing else connected with it.

Mr. Speaker, let our democratic friends be comforted with the assurance, that we are content with our position, content with our company, and content with our candidate; and that although they, in their generous sympathy, think we ought to be miserable, we really are not, and that they may dismiss the great anxiety they have on *our* account.

"ABSENCE OF EXCITEMENT AND ABSENCE OF FEAR"

From a Eulogy for Zachary Taylor

CHICAGO, ILLINOIS, JULY 25, 1850

Called on to eulogize President Zachary Taylor after his sudden death just sixteen months after assuming the presidency, ex-Congressman Lincoln managed to have it both ways: offering a thrilling and appreciative history of the old general's military triumphs (including those during a war that Lincoln had so passionately opposed) and then reminding his audience that the hero's greatest asset was coolness under pressure—a trait Lincoln would exhibit himself when he became commander in chief eleven years later.

General Zachary Taylor, the eleventh elected President of the United States, is dead. He was born Nov. 2nd, 1784 [actually November 24—ed.], in Orange county, Virginia; and died July the 9th 1850, in the sixty-sixth year of his age, at the White House in Washington City. He was the second son [in fact, the third—ed.] of Richard Taylor, a Colonel in the army of the Revolution. His youth was passed among the pioneers of Kentucky, whither his parents emigrated soon after his birth; and where his taste for military life, probably inherited, was greatly stimulated. Near the commencement of our last war with Great Britain, he was appointed by President Jefferson, a lieutenant in the 7th regiment of Infantry. During the war, he served under Gen. Harrison in his North Western campaign against the Indians; and, having been promoted to a captaincy, was intrusted with the defence of Fort Harrison, with fifty men, half of them unfit for duty. A strong party of Indians, under the Prophet, brother of Tecumseh, made a midnight attack on the Fort; but Taylor, though weak in his force, and without preparation, was resolute, and on the alert; and, after a battle, which lasted till after daylight, completely repulsed them. Soon after, he took a prominent part in the expedition under Major Gen. Hopkins against the Prophet's town; and,

on his return, found a letter from President Madison, who had succeeded Mr. Jefferson, conferring on him a major's brevet for his gallant defence of Fort Harrison.

After the close of the British war, he remained in the frontier service of the West, till 1818. He was then transferred to the Southern
frontier, where he remained, most of the time in active service till
1826. In 1819, and during his service in the South, he was promoted to
the rank of lieutenant colonel. In 1826 he was again sent to the North
West, where he continued until 1836. In 1832, he was promoted to
the rank of a colonel. In 1836 he was ordered to the South to engage
in what is well known as the Florida War. In the autumn of 1837, he
fought and conquered in the memorable battle of Okeechobee, one
of the most desperate struggles known to the annals of Indian warfare. For this, he was honored with the rank of Brigadier General;
and, in 1838 was appointed to succeed Gen. Jessup in command of
the forces in Florida. In 1841 he was ordered to Fort Gibson to take
command of the Second Military department of the United States;
and in September, 1844, was directed to hold the troops between
the Red River and the Sabine in readiness to march as might be indicated by the Charge of the United States, near Texas. In 1845 his
forces were concentrated at Corpus Christi.

In obedience to orders [a subtle reference to widespread opposition to the war at the time—ed.], in March 1846, he planted his troops
on the Rio Grande opposite Mattamoras. Soon after this, and near
this place, a small detachment of Gen. Taylor's forces, under Captain
Thornton, was cut to pieces by a party of Mexicans. Open hostilities
being thus commenced, and Gen. Taylor being constantly menaced
by Mexican forces vastly superior to his own, in numbers, his position became exceedingly critical. Having erected a fort, he might
defend himself against great odds while he could remain within it;
but his provisions had failed, and there was no supply nearer than
Point Isabel, between which and the new fort, the country was open
to, and full of, armed Mexicans. His resolution was at once taken.
He garrisoned Fort Brown, (the new fort) with a force of about four

hundred; and, putting himself at the head of the main body of his troops, marched forthwith for Point Isabel. He met no resistance on his march. Having obtained his supplies, he began his return march, to the relief of Fort Brown, which he at first knew, would be, and then knew had been besieged by the enemy, immediately upon his leaving it. On the first or second day of this return march, the Mexican General, Arista, met General Taylor in front, and offered battle. The Mexicans numbered six or eight thousand, opposed to whom were about two thousand Americans. The moment was a trying one. Comparatively, Taylor's forces were but a handful; and few, of either officers or men, had ever been under fire. A brief council was held; and the result was, the battle commenced. The issue of that contest all remember—remember with mingled sensations of pride and sorrow, that then, American valor and powers triumphed, and then the gallant and accomplished, and noble Ringgold fell.

The Americans passed the night on the field. The General knew the enemy was still in his fort; and the question rose upon him, whether to advance or retreat. A council was again held; and, it is said, the General overruled the majority, and resolved to advance. Accordingly in the morning, he moved rapidly forward. At about four or five miles from Fort Brown he again met the enemy in force, who had selected his position, and made some hasty fortification. Again the battle commenced, and raged till toward nightfall, when the Mexicans were entirely routed, and the General with his fatigued and bleeding, and reduced battalions marched into Fort Brown. There was a joyous meeting. A brief hour before, whether all *within* the fort had perished, all *without* feared, but none could tell— while the incessant roar of artillery, wrought those *within* to the highest pitch of apprehension, that their brethren *without* were being massacred to the last man. And now the din of battle nears the fort and sweeps obliquely by; a gleam of hope flies through the half imprisoned few; they fly to the wall; every eye is strained—it is—it is—the stars and stripes are still aloft! Anon the anxious brethren meet; and while hand strikes hand, the heavens are rent with a loud, long, glorious, gushing cry of victory! victory!! victory!!!

.   .   .   .

Gen. Taylor's battles were not distinguished for brilliant military manoeuvers; but in all, he seems rather to have conquered by the exercise of a sober and steady judgment, coupled with a dogged incapacity to understand that defeat was possible. His rarest military trait, was a combination of negatives—absence of *excitement* and absence of *fear*. He could not be *flurried,* and he could not be *scared.*

In connection with Gen. Taylor's military character, may be mentioned his relations with his brother officers, and his soldiers. Terrible as he was to his country's enemies, no man was so little disposed to have difficulty with his friends. During the period of his life, *duelling* was a practice not quite uncommon among gentlemen in the peaceful avocations of life, and still more common, among the officers of the Army and Navy. Yet, so far as I can learn, a *duel* with Gen. Taylor, has never been talked of.

He was alike averse to *sudden,* and to *startling* quarrels; and he pursued no man with *revenge*. A notable, and a noble instance of this, is found in his conduct to the gallant and now lamented Gen. Worth. A short while before the battles of the 8th and 9th of May, some questions of precedence arose between Worth, (then a colonel) and some other officer, which question it seems Gen. Taylor's duty to decide. He decided against Worth. Worth was greatly offended, left the Army, came to the United States, and tendered his resignation to the authorities at Washington. It is said, that in his passionate feeling, he hesitated not to speak harshly and disparagingly of Gen. Taylor. He was an officer of the highest character; and his word, on military subjects, and about military men, could not, with the country, pass for nothing. In this absence from the army of Col. Worth, the unexpected turn of things brought on the battles of the 8th and 9th. He was deeply mortified—in almost absolute desperation—at having lost the opportunity of being present, and taking part in those battles. The laurels won by his previous service, in his own eyes, seemed withering away. The Government, both *wisely* and *generously,* I think, declined accepting his resignation; and he returned to Gen. Taylor. Then came Gen. Taylor's *opportunity* for revenge. The battle of Monterey was approaching, and even at hand. Taylor *could* if he *would,* so place Worth in that battle, that his name would scarcely be noticed in the report. But no. He felt it was due to the service, to assign the real post of honor to some one of the best officers; he knew Worth was one of the best, and he felt that it was *generous* to allow him, then and there, to retrieve his secret loss. Accordingly he assigned to Col. Worth in that assault, what was *par excellence,* the post of honor; and, the duties of which, he executed so well, and so brilliantly, as to eclipse, in that battle, even Gen. Taylor himself.

As to Gen. Taylor's relations with his soldiers, details would be endless. It is perhaps enough to say—and it is far from the *least* of his honors that we can *truly* say—that of the many who served with him through the long course of forty years, all testify to the uniform kindness, and his constant care for, and hearty sympathy with, their every want and every suffering; while none can be found to declare, that he was ever a tyrant anywhere, in anything.

"THE RIGHT . . . TO REVOLUTIONIZE"

Resolutions in Support of Hungarian Freedom

SPRINGFIELD, ILLINOIS, JANUARY 9, 1852

Lincoln and his fellow Illinois progressives lionized the exiled Hungarian patriot Lajos Kossuth, then touring the American west in search of support for a new revolution against Austrian occupation of his beleaguered country. A group of local leaders invited Kossuth to Springfield and asked Lincoln to draft a set of resolutions spelling out their support. Typically, the ex-congressman, now busy with his private law practice, was cautious. His resolutions opposed tyranny but warned against foreign intervention. (He would make a similar case nine years later as president, in arguing that European powers should not intervene in the American Civil War by recognizing the Confederacy as a separate nation.) In 1852, however, Springfield's pro-interventionists won the day. The local Kossuth meeting reconvened and asked another delegate to compose amendments that made clear that nothing could ever restrain the United States from "interfering" in behalf of any people "struggling for liberty in any part of the world." This is Lincoln's original draft.

Whereas, in the opinion of this meeting, the arrival of Kossuth in our country, in connection with the recent events in Hungary, and with the appeal he is now making in behalf of his country, presents an occasion upon which we, the American people, cannot remain silent, without justifying an interference against our continued devotion to the principles of our free institutions, therefore,

Resolved, 1. That it is the right of any people, sufficiently numerous for national independence, to throw off, to revolutionize, their existing form of government, and to establish such other in its stead as they may choose.

2. That it is the duty of our government, to neither foment, nor assist, such revolutions in other governments.

3. That, as we may not legally or warrantably interfere abroad, *to aid,* so no other government may interfere abroad, *to suppress* such revolutions; and that we should at once, announce to the world, our determinations to insist upon this *mutuality* of non-intervention, as a sacred principle of the international law.

4. That the late interference of Russia in the Hungarian struggle was, in our opinion, such illegal and unwarrantable interference.

5. That to have resisted Russia in that case, or to resist any power in a like case, would be no violation of our own cherished principles of non-intervention, but, on the contrary, would be ever meritorious, in us, or any independent nation.

6. That whether we will, in fact, interfere in such case, is purely a question of policy, to be decided when the exigency arrives. [Lincoln always allowed for exigencies—ed.]

7. That we recognize Governor Kossuth of Hungary the most worthy and distinguished representative of the cause of civil and

religious liberty on the continent of Europe. A cause for which he and his nation struggled until they were overwhelmed by the armed intervention of a foreign despot, in violation of the more sacred principles of the laws of nature and of nations—principles held dear by the friends of freedom everywhere, and more especially by the people of these United States.

8. That the sympathies of the country, and the benefits of its position, should be exerted in favor of the people of every nation struggling to be free; and whilst we meet to do honor to Kossuth and Hungary, we should not fail to pour out the tribute of our praise and approbation to the patriotic efforts of the Irish, the Germans and the French, who have unsuccessfully fought to establish in their several governments the supremacy of the people.

9. That there is nothing in the past history of the British government, or in its present expressed policy, to encourage the belief that she will aid, in any manner, in the delivery of continental Europe from the yoke of despotism; and that her treatment of Ireland, of O'Brien, Mitchell, and other worthy patriots, forces the conclusion that she will join her efforts to the despots of Europe in suppressing every effort of the people to establish free governments, based upon the principles of true religious and civil liberty.

"WITH THE PURSE AND SWORD"

From a Speech at Galena, Illinois

JULY 23, 1856

Speaking at a rally for the new Republican Party's first presidential candidate, John C. Frémont, Lincoln began confronting the real possibility that opposition to slavery might lead to an attempt by Southerners to destroy the Union. Would the North respond with force? This is one of Lincoln's earliest ruminations on that explosive subject.

Do you say that such restriction of slavery would be unconstitutional and that some of the States would not submit to its enforcement? I grant you that an unconstitutional act is not a law; but I do not ask, and will not take your construction of the Constitution. The Supreme Court of the United States is a tribunal to decide such questions, and we will submit to its declarations [the next year, Lincoln in fact rejected the Supreme Court's *Dred Scott* decision—and did not "submit"—ed.]; and if you do also, there will be an end of the matter. Will you? If not, who are the disunionists, you or we? We, the majority, would not strive to dissolve the Union; and if any attempt is made it must be by you, who so loudly stigmatize us as disunionists. But the Union, in any event, won't be dissolved. We don't want to dissolve it, and if you attempt it, *we won't let you.* With the purse and sword, the army and navy and treasury in our hands and at our command, you *couldn't do it.* This Government would be very weak, indeed, if a majority, with a disciplined army and navy, and a well-filled treasury, could not preserve itself, when attacked by an unarmed, undisciplined, unorganized minority.

All this talk about the dissolution of the Union is humbug— nothing but folly. *We* WON'T dissolve the Union, and *you* SHAN'T.

"IF ONE PEOPLE WILL MAKE WAR UPON ANOTHER"

Fragment on Government

[APRIL 1, 1854?]

In this justly famous rumination on the proper role of government in society—still quoted by politicians today—Lincoln included the war power among government's "legitimate" objects. Though he later conceded that government could not assume "the duty of redressing or preventing all the wrongs in the world," Lincoln insisted it was always obliged to "redress all wrongs which are wrongs to the nation itself."

Government is a combination of the people of a country to effect certain objects by joint effort. The best framed and best administered governments are necessarily expensive; while by errors in frame and maladministration most of them are more onerous than they need be, and some of them very oppressive. Why, then, should we have government? Why not each individual take to himself the whole fruit of his labor, without having any of it taxed away, in services, corn, or money? Why not take just so much land as he can cultivate with his own hands, without buying it of any one?

The legitimate object of government is "to do for the people what needs to be done, but which they can not, by individual effort, do at all, or do so well, for themselves." There are many such things— some of them exist independently of the injustice in the world. Making and maintaining roads, bridges, and the like; providing for the helpless young and afflicted; common schools; and disposing of deceased men's property, are instances.

But a far larger class of objects springs from the injustice of men. If one people will make war upon another, it is a necessity with that other to unite and cooperate for defense. Hence the military department. If some men will kill, or beat, or constrain others, or despoil them of property, by force, fraud, or noncompliance with contracts, it is a common object with peaceful and just men to prevent it. Hence the criminal and civil departments.

"A House Divided against Itself Cannot Stand"

*From a Speech Accepting the Republican Designation
for U.S. Senate*

SPRINGFIELD, ILLINOIS, JUNE 16, 1858

Lincoln wrote this speech to launch his campaign against Stephen A. Douglas for the U.S. Senate. His closest political advisers, to whom he read the oration aloud before delivering it, warned him its implied prediction of national strife would forever cast him as a war-mongering radical, but Lincoln rejected their counsel and delivered it anyway. During the season of Lincoln-Douglas debates that followed, he was in fact compelled to explain—and in a sense, back away from—it repeatedly.

If we could first know *where* we are, and *whither* we are tending, we could then better judge *what* to do, and *how* to do it.

We are now far into the *fifth* year, since a policy was initiated, with the *avowed* object, and *confident* promise, of putting an end to slavery agitation.

Under the operation of that policy, that agitation has not only, *not ceased*, but has *constantly augmented*.

In *my* opinion, it *will* not cease, until a *crisis* shall have been reached, and passed.

"A House divided against itself cannot stand."

I believe this government cannot endure, permanently half *slave* and half *free*.

I do not expect the Union to be *dissolved*—I do not expect the house to *fall*—but I *do* expect it will cease to be divided.

It will become *all* one thing, or *all* the other.

Either the *opponents* of slavery, will arrest the further spread of it, and place it where the public mind shall rest in the belief that it is in the course of ultimate extinction; or its *advocates* will push it forward, till it shall become alike lawful in *all* the States, *old* as well as *new*—*North* as well as *South*.

"The Idea That I Withheld Supplies from the Soldiers"

Excerpt from the First Lincoln-Douglas Debate

OTTAWA, ILLINOIS, AUGUST 21, 1858

Unwaveringly opposed to slavery extension in any form, newly anointed Republican senatorial candidate Lincoln challenged incumbent Democratic senator Stephen A. Douglas to a series of debates, which attracted national attention. Their seven "joint meetings" focused primarily on the slavery issue, but Douglas missed no opportunity to condemn Lincoln's congressional record on war, charging in this opening debate that "he distinguished himself by . . . taking the side of the common enemy against his own country; and when he returned home he found that the indignation of the people followed him everywhere, and he was again submerged or obliged to retire into private life, forgotten by his former friends." The following is excerpted from Lincoln's indignant reply, which did little to affect the outcome: Douglas was reelected.

I think my friend, the Judge, is equally at fault when he charges me at the time when I was in Congress of having opposed our soldiers who were fighting in the Mexican war. The Judge did not make his charge very distinctly but I can tell you what he can prove by referring to the record. You remember I was an old Whig, and whenever the Democratic party tried to get me to vote that the war had been righteously begun by the President, I would not do it. But whenever they asked for any money, or land warrants, or anything to pay the soldiers there, during all that time, I gave the same votes that Judge Douglas did. [Loud applause.] You can think as you please as to whether that was consistent. Such is the truth; and the Judge has the right to make all he can out of it. But when he, by a general charge, conveys the idea that I withheld supplies from the soldiers who were fighting in the Mexican war, or did anything else to hinder the soldiers, he is, to say the least, grossly and altogether mistaken, as a consultation of the records will prove to him.

"THE TUG HAS TO COME"

Letter to Lyman Trumbull

SPRINGFIELD, ILLINOIS, DECEMBER 10, 1860

Though he lost to Stephen A. Douglas for the Senate in 1858, Lincoln defeated him for president two years later. Following Lincoln's election in November, Lyman Trumbull, Illinois' junior senator, peppered the new president-elect with reports on efforts in Washington to reach compromises on the slavery issue in order to prevent secession and war. Reluctant to see a lame-duck government make policy that would bind his administration, Lincoln reached an important decision: instruct fellow Republicans to resist any compromise that would include slavery extension, the threat of Southern armed resistance notwithstanding.

My dear Sir:

Let there be no compromise on the question of *extending* slavery. If there be, all our labor is lost, and, ere long, must be done again. The dangerous ground—that into which some of our friends have a hankering to run—is Pop[ular]. Sov[ereignty]. Have none of it. Stand firm. The tug has to come, & better now, than any time hereafter.

Yours as ever

A. LINCOLN.

"HOLD, OR RETAKE, THE FORTS"

Letter to Elihu B. Washburne

SPRINGFIELD, ILLINOIS, DECEMBER 21, 1860

Illinois congressman Elihu B. Washburne had written President-elect Lincoln on December 17 to warn him that President James Buchanan had left the federal forts in South Carolina, including Fort Sumter, all but defenseless. Lincoln relayed this reply to the old general. A day after writing it, Lincoln delivered substantially the same message to Major David Hunter: "If the forts fall, my judgment is that they are to be retaken." Still more than two months away from taking office, Lincoln was beginning to show the resolve he would demonstrate as commander in chief.

My dear Sir:

Last night I received your letter giving an account of your interview with Gen. [Winfield] Scott, and for which I thank you. Please present my respects to the General, and tell him, confidentially, I shall be obliged to him to be as well prepared as he can to either *hold*, or *retake*, the forts, as the case may require, and after the inaugeration.

Yours as ever

A. LINCOLN.

"GIVE THE UNION MEN A RALLYING CRY"

From a Letter to Lyman Trumbull

SPRINGFIELD, DECEMBER 24, 1860

As the tumultuous year of 1860 came to an end, General Winfield Scott informed President-elect Lincoln that as a gesture of conciliation, outgoing chief executive James Buchanan was considering altogether abandoning federal forts in South Carolina—a state that had just seceded from the Union. This was the "confidential" reaction Lincoln shared with the junior U.S. senator from Illinois, which he no doubt hoped would be shared with other power brokers. Here, the onetime antiwar congressman laid down the gauntlet: he would not conciliate the South by giving up federal military installations—even if it meant war.

Despaches [sic] have come here two days in succession, that the Forts in South Carolina, will be surrendered by the order, or consent at least, of the President.

I can scarcely believe this; but if it prove true, I will, if our friends at Washington concur, announce publicly at once that they are to be retaken after the inaugeration. This will give the Union men a rallying cry, and preparation will proceed somewhat on their side, as well as on the other.

Yours as ever
A. LINCOLN.

Abraham Lincoln in 1862, photograph by Mathew B. Brady, Washington.
(Library of Congress)

II

A PEOPLE'S CONTEST

1861–1862

When Abraham Lincoln spoke the final words of his inaugural address on March 4, 1861, a cannon roar erupted on Capitol Hill to salute the new president. The artillery salvo was the first, but not the last, gunfire that the country would hear over the next four tumultuous years. On his very first day of work in the White House, the new president faced an immediate and vexing military crisis: the threat of attack should he attempt to resupply Fort Sumter in Charleston Harbor, South Carolina—a port which, that state now maintained, belonged to the new Confederate States of America. Lincoln took that dare. Sumter was subsequently assaulted and soon abandoned, but the administration emerged armed with a new cause: the fight to preserve the union. No one, North or South, Lincoln admitted, expected the ensuing war to last as long, or cost as much in life and treasure, as it did.

During the next two years, Lincoln trained himself—much as he had educated himself as a lawyer—on military strategy and tactics. He appointed and dismissed an array of underachieving field commanders, brilliantly managed public opinion, and then redefined the war not only as a battle to restore the nation, but as one to eradicate slavery. In the following letters, memoranda, and speeches, Lincoln grows from masterful politician to masterful commander in chief. In the span of only twenty-four months, a politician becomes a leader.

"If We Surrender, It Is the End of Us"

Letter to James T. Hale

SPRINGFIELD, ILLINOIS, JANUARY 11, 1861

This letter went to the Republican congressman from Pennsylvania who had urged Lincoln to accept brokered congressional compromises on slavery that called for extension of the old Missouri Compromise line all the way to the Pacific Coast. As his reply shows, Lincoln remained adamantly opposed to slavery extension, even if it meant secession and war.

My dear Sir:

Yours of the 6th is received. I answer it only because I fear you would misconstrue my silence. What is our present condition? We have just carried an election on principles fairly stated to the people. Now we are told in advance, the government shall be broken up, unless we surrender to those we have beaten, before we take the offices. In this they are either attempting to play upon us, or they are in dead earnest. Either way, if we surrender, it is the end of us and of the government. They will repeat the experiments upon us *ad libitum*. A year will not pass, till we shall have to take Cuba as a condition upon which they will stay in the Union. They now have the Constitution, under which we have lived over seventy years, and acts of Congress of their own framing, with no prospect of their being changed; and they can never have a more shallow pretext for breaking up the government, or extorting a compromise, than now. There is, in my judgment, but one compromise which would really settle the slavery question, and that would be a prohibition against acquiring any more territory.

Yours very truly,

A. LINCOLN.

"THE WORDS 'COERCION' AND 'INVASION'"

From a Speech at Indianapolis, Indiana

FEBRUARY 11, 1861

All eyes—and ears—focused on the president-elect as he began his jour-ney to Washington for his March 4 inauguration. Lincoln was careful to say nothing controversial at his departure from Springfield. His first oration after leaving his hometown, however, excited much controversy. Speaking from the balcony of a hotel in Indianapolis, he seemed, at least to some, surprisingly eager to challenge the South to a confrontation as he questioned states' rights and stressed the national government's right to hold its forts. The Cleveland Plain Dealer *predicted that the South would regard this speech "as the tocsin of war," adding that Lincoln had "finally opened his mouth, and . . . got his foot in it." But the laughter that greeted some of Lincoln's points here indicates that many North-erners still considered Southern claims of independence to be a joke.*

The words "coercion" and "invasion" are in great use about these days. Suppose we were simply to try if we can, and ascertain what, is the meaning of these words. Let us get, if we can, the exact definitions of these words—not from dictionaries, but from the men who con-stantly repeat them—what things they mean to express by the words. What, then, is "coercion"? What is "invasion"? Would the marching of an army into South Carolina, for instance, without the consent of her people, and in hostility against them, be coercion or invasion? I very frankly say, I think it would be invasion, and it would be co-ercion too, if the people of that country were forced to submit. But if the Government, for instance, but simply insists upon holding its own forts, or retaking those forts which belong to it,—[cheers,]—or the enforcement of the laws of the United States in the collection of duties upon foreign importations,—[renewed cheers,]—or even the withdrawal of the mails from those portions of the country where the mails themselves are habitually violated; would any or all of these things be coercion? Do the lovers of the Union contend that they will resist coercion or invasion of any State, understanding that any or all of these would be coercing or invading a State? If they do, then it occurs to me that the means for the preservation of the Union they so greatly love, in their own estimation, is of a very thin and airy character. [Applause.] If sick, they would consider the little pills of the homoepathist as already too large for them to swallow. In their view, the Union, as a family relation, would not be anything like a regular marriage at all, but only as a sort of free-love arrangement,— [laughter,]—to be maintained on what that sect calls passionate attraction. [Continued laughter.] But, my friends, enough of this.

What is the particular sacredness of a State? I speak not of that position which is given to a State in and by the Constitution of the United States, for that all of us agree to—we abide by; but that position assumed, that a State can carry with it out of the Union that which it holds in sacredness by virtue of its connection with the Union. I am speaking of that assumed right of a State, as a primary principle, that the Constitution should rule all that is less than itself, and ruin all that is bigger than itself. [Laughter.] But, I ask, wherein does consist that right? If a State, in one instance, and a county in another, should be equal in extent of territory, and equal in the number of people, wherein is that State any better than the county? Can a change of name change the right? By what principle of original right is it that one-fiftieth or one-ninetieth of a great nation, by calling themselves a State, have the right to break up and ruin that nation as a matter of original principle? Now, I ask the question—I am not deciding anything—[laughter,]—and with the request that you will think somewhat upon that subject and decide for yourselves, if you choose, when you get ready,—where is the mysterious, original right, from principle, for a certain district of country with inhabitants, by merely being called a State, to play tyrant over all its own citizens, and deny the authority of everything greater than itself. [Laughter.] I say I am deciding nothing, but simply giving something for you to reflect upon; and, with having said this much, and having declared, in the start, that I will make no long speeches, I thank you again for this magnificent welcome, and bid you an affectionate farewell. [Cheers.]

"That Thing which They Struggled For"

Address to the New Jersey State Senate at Trenton

FEBRUARY 21, 1861

After spending days quelling the uproar caused by his nonconciliatory Indianapolis speech—at one point later in his journey he even denied that a crisis really existed—Lincoln seemed to find his rhetorical footing once he reached the scenes of the American Revolution: Trenton and, later, Philadelphia. In the New Jersey capital he gave two speeches. Addressing the upper house, the president-elect shared his innermost feelings about the struggles of George Washington and his army more than four score years earlier.

Mr. President and Gentlemen of the Senate of the State of New-Jersey:

I am very grateful to you for the honorable reception of which I have been the object. I cannot but remember the place that New-Jersey holds in our early history. In the early Revolutionary struggle, few of the States among the old Thirteen had more of the battle-fields of the country within their limits than old New-Jersey. May I be pardoned if, upon this occasion, I mention that away back in my childhood, the earliest days of my being able to read, I got hold of a small book, such a one as few of the younger members have ever seen, "Weem's [*sic*] Life of Washington." I remember all the accounts there given of the battle fields and struggles for the liberties of the country, and none fixed themselves upon my imagination so deeply as the struggle here at Trenton, New-Jersey. The crossing of the river; the contest with the Hessians; the great hardships endured at that time, all fixed themselves on my memory more than any single revolutionary event; and you all know, for you have all been boys, how these early impressions last longer than any others. I recollect thinking then, boy even though I was, that there must have been something more than common that those men struggled for. I am exceedingly anxious that that thing which they struggled for; that something even more than National Independence; that something that held out a great promise to all the people of the world to all time to come; I am exceedingly anxious that this Union, the Constitution, and the liberties of the people shall be perpetuated in accordance with the original idea for which that struggle was made, and I shall be most happy indeed if I shall be an humble instrument in the hands of the Almighty, and of this, his almost chosen people [a reference by the Bible-savvy Lincoln to the biblical Hebrews who freed themselves from slavery—ed.], for perpetuating the object of that great struggle. You give me this reception, as I understand, without distinction of party. I learn that this body is composed of a majority of gentlemen who, in the exercise of their best judgment in the choice of a Chief Magistrate, did not think I was the man. I understand, nevertheless, that they came forward here to greet me as the constitutional President of the United States—as citizens of the United States, to meet the man who, for the time being, is the representative man of the nation, united by a purpose to perpetuate the Union and liberties of the people. As such, I accept this reception more gratefully than I could do did I believe it was tendered to me as an individual.

"It May Be Necessary to Put the Foot Down Firmly"

From an Address to the New Jersey State Assembly

FEBRUARY 21, 1861

In the lower house of the New Jersey legislature only minutes after his rather amicable speech to the Senate, Lincoln abruptly shifted tone and indicated he would resist the secessionists. Was this, too, coercion—the back of the hand he had just seemed to extend? One eyewitness remembered that when the president-elect uttered the phrase "it may be necessary to put the foot down firmly," he brought his huge boot crashing to the floor with an audible and dramatic thud. With preinaugural oratory like this, Lincoln steeled the nation for armed resistance to secession and rebellion.

Mr. Speaker and Gentlemen:

I have just enjoyed the honor of a reception by the other branch of this Legislature, and I return to you and them my thanks for the reception which the people of New-Jersey have given, through their chosen representatives, to me, as the representative, for the time being, of the majesty of the people of the United States. I appropriate to myself very little of the demonstrations of respect with which I have been greeted. I think little should be given to any man, but that it should be a manifestation of adherence to the Union and the Constitution. I understand myself to be received here by the representatives of the people of New-Jersey, a majority of whom differ in opinion from those with whom I have acted. This manifestation is therefore to be regarded by me as expressing their devotion to the Union, the Constitution and the liberties of the people. You, Mr. Speaker, have well said that this is a time when the bravest and wisest look with doubt and awe upon the aspect presented by our national affairs. Under these circumstances, you will readily see why I should not speak in detail of the course I shall deem it best to pursue. It is proper that I should avail myself of all the information and all the time at my command, in order that when the time arrives in which I must speak officially, I shall be able to take the ground which I deem the best and safest, and from which I may have no occasion to swerve. I shall endeavor to take the ground I deem most just to the North, the East, the West, the South, and the whole country. I take it, I hope, in good temper—certainly no malice toward any section. I shall do all that may be in my power to promote a peaceful settlement of all our difficulties. The man does not live who is more devoted to peace than I am. [Cheers.] None who would do more to preserve it. But it may be necessary to put the foot down firmly. [Here the audience broke out into cheers so loud and long that for some moments it was impossible to hear Mr. L.'s voice.] He continued: And if I do my duty, and do right, you will sustain me, will you not? [Loud cheers, and cries of "Yes," "Yes," "We will."] Received, as I am, by the members of a Legislature the majority of whom do not agree with me in political sentiments, I trust that I may have their assistance in piloting the

President-elect Abraham Lincoln appears on the speaker's platform for a Washington's Birthday flag-raising ceremony at Independence Hall, Philadelphia, on February 22, 1861. He can be seen standing, hat in hand, above the white star at left, just above the giant flag that drapes the rostrum. *(Library of Congress)*

ship of State through this voyage, surrounded by perils as it is; for, if it should suffer attack now, there will be no pilot ever needed for another voyage.

"I WOULD RATHER BE ASSASSINATED"

Address at Independence Hall, Philadelphia, Pennsylvania

FEBRUARY 22, 1861

Hours before delivering this Washington's Birthday speech at the shrine of American freedom, Lincoln learned that a death threat awaited him in hostile Baltimore, Maryland. Some of his advisers urged him to hasten to Washington without any further public appearances, but Lincoln insisted on fulfilling his commitment at Independence Hall, where he raised a large American flag and delivered these defiant remarks inside—though few in the crowd realized that his life had actually been threatened.

I am filled with deep emotion at finding myself standing here in the place where were collected together the wisdom, the patriotism, the devotion to principle, from which sprang the institutions under which we live. You have kindly suggested to me that in my hands is the task of restoring peace to our distracted country. I can say in return, sir, that all the political sentiments I entertain have been drawn, so far as I have been able to draw them, from the sentiments which originated, and were given to the world from this hall in which we stand. I have never had a feeling politically that did not spring from the sentiments embodied in the Declaration of Independence. (Great cheering.) I have often pondered over the dangers which were incurred by the men who assembled here and adopted that Declaration of Independence—I have pondered over the toils that were endured by the officers and soldiers of the army, who achieved that Independence. (Applause.) I have often inquired of myself, what great principle or idea it was that kept this Confederacy so long together. It was not the mere matter of the separation of the colonies from the mother land; but something in that Declaration giving liberty, not alone to the people of this country, but hope to the world for all future time. (Great applause.) It was that which gave promise that in due time the weights should be lifted from the shoulders of all men, and that *all* should have an equal chance. (Cheers.) This is the sentiment embodied in that Declaration of Independence.

Now, my friends, can this country be saved upon that basis? If it can, I will consider myself one of the happiest men in the world if I can help to save it. If it can't be saved upon that principle, it will be truly awful. But, if this country cannot be saved without giving up that principle—I was about to say I would rather be assassinated on this spot than to surrender it. (Applause.)

Now, in my view of the present aspect of affairs, there is no need of bloodshed and war. There is no necessity for it. I am not in favor of such a course, and I may say in advance, there will be no blood shed unless it be forced upon the Government. The Government will not use force unless force is used against it. (Prolonged applause and cries of "That's the proper sentiment.")

My friends, this is a wholly unprepared speech. I did not expect to be called upon to say a word when I came here—I supposed I was merely to do something towards raising a flag. I may, therefore, have said something indiscreet, (cries of "no, no"), but I have said nothing but what I am willing to live by, and, if it be the pleasure of Almighty God, die by.

"THE MOMENTOUS ISSUE OF CIVIL WAR"

First Inaugural Address

WASHINGTON, MARCH 4, 1861

Long overshadowed by his more famous second inaugural address, Lincoln's first inaugural was unquestionably his most important speech to that date and one of the greatest of his career. Though Lincoln hoped it would allay fears among Southerners that he planned to end slavery where it currently and legally existed, the Richmond Times Dispatch *insisted that the speech "inaugurates civil war," declaring, "The sword is drawn and the scabbard thrown away." Even the pro-Union New York diarist George Templeton Strong, who believed the speech was generally "conciliatory" and "peaceable," admitted, "There's a clank of metal in it." Lincoln's final text was actually toned down from the more bellicose draft that he composed before heading to Washington in February. Lincoln initially proposed to conclude the talk with a dare: "Shall it be peace or a sword?"*

In compliance with a custom as old as the government itself, I appear before you to address you briefly, and to take, in your presence,

This is the way the North receives it.   THE PRESIDENT'S INAUGURAL,   This is the way the South receives it.
And

Lincoln as he seemed a few weeks into his presidency—portrayed as both a temperate goddess of justice and a grimacing god of war in "The President's Inaugural." This is the *New York Illustrated News'* visual response to Lincoln's half-belicose, half-conciliatory inaugural Address. *(Harold Holzer)*

the oath prescribed by the Constitution of the United States, to be taken by the President "before he enters on the execution of his office."

I do not consider it necessary, at present, for me to discuss those matters of administration about which there is no special anxiety, or excitement.

Apprehension seems to exist among the people of the Southern States, that by the accession of a Republican Administration, their property, and their peace, and personal security, are to be endangered. There has never been any reasonable cause for such apprehension. Indeed, the most ample evidence to the contrary has all the while existed, and been open to their inspection. It is found in nearly all the published speeches of him who now addresses you. I do but quote from one of those speeches when I declare that "I have no purpose, directly or indirectly, to interfere with the institution of slavery in the States where it exists. I believe I have no lawful right to do so, and I have no inclination to do so." Those who nominated and elected me did so with full knowledge that I had made this, and many similar declarations, and had never recanted them. And more than this, they placed in the platform, for my acceptance, and as a law to themselves, and to me, the clear and emphatic resolution which I now read:

"*Resolved,* That the maintenance inviolate of the rights of the States, and especially the right of each State to order and control its own domestic institutions according to its own judgment exclusively, is essential to that balance of power on which the perfection and endurance of our political fabric depend; and we denounce the lawless invasion by armed force of the soil of any State or Territory, no matter under what pretext, as among the gravest of crimes."

I now reiterate these sentiments: and in doing so, I only press upon the public attention the most conclusive evidence of which the case is susceptible, that the property, peace and security of no section are to be in anywise endangered by the now incoming Administration. I add too, that all the protection which, consistently with the Constitution and the laws, can be given, will be cheerfully given to all the States when lawfully demanded, for whatever cause—as cheerfully to one section as to another.

There is much controversy about the delivering up of fugitives from service or labor. The clause I now read is as plainly written in the Constitution as any other of its provisions:

"No person held to service or labor in one State, under the laws thereof, escaping into another, shall, in consequence of any law or regulation therein, be discharged from such service or labor, but shall be delivered up on claim of the party to whom such service or labor may be due." [Quoting the U.S. Constitution, article 4, section 2—ed.]

It is scarcely questioned that this provision was intended by those who made it, for the reclaiming of what we call fugitive slaves; and the intention of the law-giver is the law. All members of Congress swear their support to the whole Constitution—to this provision as much as to any other. To the proposition, then, that slaves whose cases come within the terms of this clause, "shall be delivered up," their oaths are unanimous. Now, if they would make the effort in good temper, could they not, with nearly equal unanimity, frame and pass a law, by means of which to keep good that unanimous oath?

There is some difference of opinion whether this clause should be enforced by national or by state authority; but surely that difference is not a very material one. If the slave is to be surrendered, it can be of but little consequence to him, or to others, by which authority it is done. And should any one, in any case, be content that his oath shall go unkept, on a merely unsubstantial controversy as to how it shall be kept?

Again, in any law upon this subject, ought not all the safeguards of liberty known in civilized and humane jurisprudence to be introduced, so that a free man be not, in any case, surrendered as a slave? And might it not be well, at the same time, to provide by law for the enforcement of that clause in the Constitution which guarranties that "The citizens of each State shall be entitled to all previleges and immunities of citizens in the several States"?

I take the official oath to-day, with no mental reservations, and with no purpose to construe the Constitution or laws, by any hyper-critical rules. And while I do not choose now to specify particular acts of Congress as proper to be enforced, I do suggest, that it will be much safer for all, both in official and private stations, to conform to, and abide by, all those acts which stand unrepealed, than to violate any of them, trusting to find impunity in having them held to be unconstitutional.

It is seventy-two years since the first inauguration of a President under our national Constitution. During that period fifteen differ-ent and greatly distinguished citizens, have, in succession, adminis-tered the executive branch of the government. They have conducted it through many perils; and, generally, with great success. Yet, with all this scope for precedent, I now enter upon the same task for the brief constitutional term of four years, under great and peculiar difficulty. A disruption of the Federal Union heretofore only menaced, is now formidably attempted.

I hold, that in contemplation of universal law, and of the Constitution, the Union of these States is perpetual. Perpetuity is implied, if not expressed, in the fundamental law of all national governments. It is safe to assert that no government proper, ever had a provision in its organic law for its own termination. Continue to execute all the express provisions of our national Constitution, and the Union will endure forever—it being impossible to destroy it, except by some action not provided for in the instrument itself.

Again, if the United States be not a government proper, but an association of States in the nature of contract merely, can it, as a contract, be peaceably unmade, by less than all the parties who made it? One party to a contract may violate it—break it, so to speak; but does it not require all to lawfully rescind it?

Descending from these general principles, we find the proposition that, in legal contemplation, the Union is perpetual, confirmed by the history of the Union itself. The Union is much older than the Constitution. It was formed in fact, by the Articles of Association in 1774. It was matured and continued by the Declaration of Independence in 1776. It was further matured and the faith of all the then thirteen States expressly plighted and engaged that it should be perpetual, by the Articles of Confederation in 1778. And finally, in 1787, one of the declared objects for ordaining and establishing the Constitution, was *"to form a more perfect union."*

But if destruction of the Union, by one, or by a part only, of the States, be lawfully possible, the Union is *less* perfect than before the Constitution, having lost the vital element of perpetuity.

It follows from these views that no State, upon its own mere motion, can lawfully get out of the Union,—that *resolves* and *ordinances* to that effect are legally void; and that acts of violence, within any State or States, against the authority of the United States, are insurrectionary or revolutionary [Lincoln originally wrote "treasonable"—ed.], according to circumstances.

I therefore consider that, in view of the constitution and the laws, the Union is unbroken; and, to the extent of my ability, I shall take care, as the constitution itself expressly enjoins upon me, that the laws of the Union be faithfully executed in all the states. Doing this I deem to be only a simple duty on my part; and I shall perform it, so far as practicable, unless my rightful masters, the American people, shall withhold the requisite means, or, in some authoritative manner, direct the contrary. I trust this will not be regarded as a menace, but only as the declared purpose of the Union that it *will* constitutionally defend, and maintain itself.

In doing this there needs to be no bloodshed or violence; and there shall be none, unless it be forced upon the national authority. The power confided to me, will be used to hold, occupy, and possess the property, and places belonging to the government, and to collect the duties and imposts; but beyond what may be necessary for these objects, there will be no invasion—no using of force against, or among the people anywhere. Where hostility to the United States, in any interior locality, shall be so great and so universal, as to prevent competent resident citizens from holding the Federal offices, there will be no attempt to force obnoxious strangers among the people for that object. While the strict legal right may exist in the government to enforce the exercise of these offices, the attempt to do so would be so irritating, and so nearly impracticable with all, that I deem it better to forego, for the time, the uses of such offices.

The mails, unless repelled, will continue to be furnished in all parts of the Union. So far as possible, the people everywhere shall have that sense of perfect security which is most favorable to calm thought and reflection. The course here indicated will be followed, unless current events, and experience, shall show a modification, or change, to be proper; and in every case and exigency, my best discretion will be exercised, according to circumstances actually existing, and with a view and a hope of a peaceful solution of the national troubles, and the restoration of paternal sympathies and, affections.

That there are persons in one section, or another who seek to destroy the Union at all events, and are glad of any pretext to do it, I will neither affirm or deny; but if there be such, I need address no word to them. To those, however, who really love the Union, may I not speak?

Before entering upon so grave a matter as the destruction of our national fabric, with all its benefits, it's memories, and it's hopes, would it not be wise to ascertain precisely why we do it? Will you hazard so desperate a step, while there is any possibility that any portion of the ills you fly from, have no real existence? Will you, while the certain ills you fly to, are greater than all the real ones you fly from? Will you risk the commission of so fearful a mistake?

All profess to be content in the Union, if all constitutional rights can be maintained. Is it true, then, that any right, plainly written in the Constitution, has been denied? I think not. Happily the human mind is so constituted, that no party can reach to the audacity of doing this. Think, if you can, of a single instance in which a plainly written provision of the Constitution has ever been denied. If, by the mere force of numbers, a majority should deprive a minority of any clearly written constitutional right, it might, in a moral point of view, justify revolution—certainly would, if such right were a vital one; but such is not our case. All the vital rights of minorities, and of individuals, are so plainly assured to them, by affirmations and negations guarranties and prohibitions, in the Constitution, that controversies never arise concerning them. But no organic law can ever be framed with a provision specifically applicable to every question which may occur in practical administration. No foresight can anticipate, nor any document of reasonable length contain express provisions for all possible questions. Shall fugitives from labor be surrendered by national or by State authority? The Constitution does not expressly say. *May* Congress prohibit slavery in the territories? The Constitution does not expressly say. *Must*

Congress protect slavery in the territories? The Constitution does not expressly say.

From questions of this class spring all our constitutional controversies, and we divide upon them into majorities and minorities. If the minority will not acquiesce [Lincoln originally wrote "submit"—ed.], the majority must, or the government must cease. There is no other alternative; for continuing the government, is acquiescence on one side or the other. If a minority, in such case, will secede rather than acquiesce, they make a precedent which, in turn, will divide and ruin them; for a minority of their own will secede from them, whenever a majority refuses to be controlled by such minority. For instance, why may not any portion of a new confederacy, a year or two hence, arbitrarily secede again, precisely as portions of the present Union now claim to secede from it. All who cherish disunion sentiments are now being educated to the exact temper of doing this. Is there such perfect identity of interests among the States to compose a new Union, as to produce harmony only, and prevent renewed secession? Plainly, the central idea of secession, is the essence of anarchy. A majority, held in restraint by constitutional checks, and limitations, and always changing easily, with deliberate changes of popular opinions and sentiments, is the only true sovereign of a free people. Whoever rejects it, does, of necessity, fly to anarchy or to despotism. Unanimity is impossible; the rule of a minority, as a permanent arrangement, is wholly inadmissable; so that, rejecting the majority principle, anarchy, or despotism in some form, is all that is left.

I do not forget the position assumed by some, that constitutional questions are to be decided by the Supreme Court; nor do I deny that such decisions must be binding in any case, upon the parties to a suit, as to the object of that suit, while they are also entitled to a very high respect and consideration, in all parallel cases, by all other departments of the government. And while it is obviously possible that such decision may be erroneous in any given case, still the evil effect following it, being limited to that particular case, with the chance that it may be over-ruled, and never become a precedent for other cases, can better be borne than could the evils of a different practice. At the same time the candid citizen must confess, that if the policy of the government, upon vital questions, affecting the whole people, is to be irrevocably fixed by decisions of the Supreme Court, the instant they are made, in ordinary litigation between parties, in personal actions, the people will have ceased, to be their own rulers, having, to that extent, practically resigned their government, into the hands of that eminent tribunal. Nor is there, in this view, any assault upon the Court, or the judges. It is a duty, from which they may not shrink, to decide cases properly brought before them; and it is no fault of theirs, if others seek to turn their decisions to political purposes.

One section of our country believes slavery is *right,* and ought to be extended, while the other believes it is *wrong,* and ought not to be extended. This is the only substantial dispute. The fugitive slave clause of the Constitution, and the law for the suppression of the foreign slave trade, are each as well enforced, perhaps as any law can ever be in a community where the moral sense of the people imperfectly supports the law itself. The great body of the people abide by the dry legal obligation in both cases, and a few break over in each. This, I think, cannot be perfectly cured; and it would be worse in both cases *after* the separation of the sections, than before. The foreign slave trade, now imperfectly suppressed, would be ultimately revived without restriction, in one section; while fugitive slaves, now only partially surrendered, would not be surrendered at all, by the other.

Physically speaking, we cannot separate. We cannot remove our respective sections from each other, nor build an impassable wall between them. A husband and wife may be divorced, and go out of the presence, and beyond the reach of each other; but the different parts of our country cannot do this. They cannot but remain face to face; and intercourse, either amicable or hostile, must continue between them. Is it possible then to make that intercourse more advantageous, or more satisfactory, *after* separation than *before*? Can aliens make treaties easier than friends can make laws? Can treaties be more faithfully enforced between aliens, than laws can among friends? Suppose you go to war, you cannot fight always; and when, after much loss on both sides, and no gain on either, you cease fighting, the identical old questions, as to terms of intercourse, are again upon you.

This country, with its institutions, belongs to the people who inhabit it. Whenever they shall grow weary of the existing government, they can exercise their *constitutional* right of amending it, or their *revolutionary* right to dismember, or overthrow it. I can not be ignorant of the fact that many worthy, and patriotic citizens are desirous of having the national constitution amended. While I make no recommendation of amendments, I fully recognize the rightful authority of the people over the whole subject, to be exercised in either of the modes prescribed in the instrument itself; and I should, under existing circumstances, favor, rather than oppose, a fair oppertunity being afforded the people to act upon it.

I will venture to add that, to me, the Convention mode seems preferable, in that it allows amendments to originate with the people themselves, instead of only permitting them to take, or reject, propositions, originated by others, not especially chosen for the purpose, and which might not be precisely such, as they would wish to either accept or refuse. I understand a proposed amendment to the constitution— which amendment, however, I have not seen, has passed Congress, [by inauguration day a proposed but ultimately unratified Thirteenth Amendment had indeed passed both houses—ed.] to the effect that the federal government, shall never interfere with the domestic institutions of the States, including that of persons held to service. To avoid misconstruction of what I have said, I depart from my purpose not to speak of particular amendments, so far as to say that, holding such a provision to now be implied Constitutional law, I have no objection to it's being made express, and irrevocable. [Lincoln in fact dutifully forwarded the little-known resolution to the states, but only a handful even took action; when a new Thirteenth Amendment passed Congress and was sent to the states four years later, it called instead for the total eradication of slavery—ed.]

The Chief Magistrate derives all his authority from the people,

and they have conferred none upon him to fix terms for the separation of the States. The people themselves can do this also if they
choose; but the executive, as such, has nothing to do with it. His duty
is to administer the present government, as it came to his hands, and
to transmit it, unimpaired by him, to his successor.

Why should there not be a patient confidence in the ultimate justice of the people? Is there any better, or equal hope, in the world? In
our present differences, is either party without faith of being in the
right? If the Almighty Ruler of nations, with his eternal truth and
justice, be on your side of the North, or on yours of the South, that
truth, and that justice, will surely prevail, by the judgment of this
great tribunal, the American people.

By the frame of the government under which we live, this same
people have wisely given their public servants but little power for
mischief; and have, with equal wisdom, provided for the return of
that little to their own hands at very short intervals.

While the people retain their virtue, and vigilance, no administration by any extreme of wickedness or folly, can very seriously
injure the government, in the short space of four years.

My countrymen, one and all, think calmly and *well*, upon this
whole subject. Nothing valuable can be lost by taking time. [Lincoln
added, then deleted, "Nothing worth preserving is either breaking
or burning"—ed.] If there be an object to *hurry* any of you, in hot
haste, to a step which you would never take *deliberately*, that object
will be frustrated by taking time; but no good object can be frustrated by it. Such of you as are now dissatisfied, still have the old
Constitution unimpaired, and, on the sensitive point, the laws of
your own framing under it; while the new administration will have
no immediate power, if it would, to change either. If it were admitted that you who are dissatisfied, hold the right side in the dispute,
there still is no single good reason for precipitate action. Intelligence,
patriotism, Christianity, and a firm reliance on Him, who has never
yet forsaken this favored land, are still competent to adjust, in the
best way, all our present difficulty.

In *your* hands, my dissatisfied fellow countrymen, and not in *mine,* is the momentous issue of civil war. The government will not assail *you.* [Lincoln deleted "unless you *first* assail it"—ed.] You can have no conflict, without being yourselves the aggressors. *You* have no oath registered in Heaven to destroy the government, while *I* shall have the most solemn one to "preserve, protect and defend" it. [Lincoln's original ending, here, was as follows: "*You* can forbear, the assault upon it; *I* can *not* shrink from the defense of it. With you, and now with *me,* is the solemn question of "Shall it be peace, or a sword?"—ed.]

I am loth to close. We are not enemies, but friends. We must not be enemies. Though passion may have strained, it must not break our bonds of affection. The mystic chords of memory, stretching from every battle-field, and patriot grave, to every living heart and hearthstone, all over this broad land, will yet swell the chorus of the Union, when again touched, as surely they will be, by the better angels of our nature.

"The Power Confided to Me"

Unsent Letter to Secretary of State William H. Seward

THE WHITE HOUSE, APRIL 1, 1861

Though they had held office less than a month, Secretary of State William H. Seward scolded Lincoln on April 1 in a memorandum entitled "Some thoughts for the President's consideration," charging the administration was "yet without a policy either foreign or domestic." Seward audaciously proposed that Gulf state federal forts be defended as a matter of patriotism and pro-Unionism but that Fort Sumter be abandoned because its reinforcement had been too closely tied to the slavery issue. Lincoln, who regarded the unsolicited advice as a bald play for political dominance of the new administration, decided that he must not let Seward "take the first trick." In this draft reply, he established a uniform policy of safeguarding federal property in all the seceded states—and also made clear that he, and no one else, would serve as commander in chief in case of war. History might have been altogether different had Seward seized policy-making power from Lincoln on this day. In the end, Lincoln did not even send this note to his secretary of state, although he may have shown it to him and taken it back. More likely, he made these points orally in person, deftly averting a showdown. Seward never questioned Lincoln's leadership again.

My dear Sir:

Since parting with you I have been considering your paper dated this day, and entitled "Some thoughts for the President's consideration." The first proposition in it is, "1st. We are at the end of a month's administration, and yet without a policy, either domestic or foreign."

At the *beginning* of that month, in the inaugeral, I said "The power confided to me will be used to hold, occupy and possess the property and places belonging to the government, and to collect the duties, and imposts." This had your distinct approval at the time; and, taken in connection with the order I immediately gave General Scott, directing him to employ every means in his power to strengthen and hold the forts, comprises the exact domestic policy you now urge, with the single exception, that it does not propose to abandon Fort Sumpter [*sic*].

Again, I do not perceive how the reinforcement of Fort Sumpter would be done on a slavery, or party issue, while that of Fort Pickens would be on a more national, and patriotic one.

The news received yesterday in regard to St. Domingo [Spanish colonists had occupied the island on March 16, and dispatched troops from Spain to support its annexation—ed.], certainly brings a new item within the range of our foreign policy; but up to that time we have been preparing circulars, and instructions to ministers, and the like, all in perfect harmony, without even a suggestion that we had no foreign policy.

Upon your closing propositions, that "whatever policy we adopt, there must be an energetic prossecution of it"

"For this purpose it must be somebody's business to pursue and direct it incessantly"

"Either the President must do it himself, and be all the while active in it, or"

"Devolve it on some member of his cabinet"

"Once adopted, debates on it must end, and all agree and abide[.]" I remark that if this must be done, *I* must do it. When a general line of policy is adopted, I apprehend there is no danger of its being changed without good reason, or continuing to be a subject of unnecessary debate; still, upon points arising in its progress, I wish, and suppose I am entitled to have the advice of all the cabinet.

Your Obt. Servt.
A. LINCOLN

"BEING *READY*"

Letter to Governor Andrew Curtin

APRIL 8, 1861

Lincoln wrote this famous alert to Governor Andrew Curtin of Pennsylvania a few days before Confederates began bombarding Fort Sumter. He was preparing the loyal states for an overt act of aggression from the South.

My dear Sir:

I think the necessity of being *ready* increases. Look to it.

Yours truly
A. LINCOLN

"CAUSE THE LAWS TO BE DULY EXECUTED"

Proclamation Calling the Militia and Convening Congress

APRIL 15, 1861

The firing on (and subsequent surrender of) Fort Sumter in mid-April left Lincoln no alternative but to call for seventy-five thousand volunteers to put down what he now concluded was a genuine rebellion. Skeptics argued that congressional approval was required for such a massive troop buildup, but with the House and Senate out of session, Lincoln confidently insisted he held the power to act in their absence. The president did call the Congress back for an extraordinary special session on Independence Day—but not for another three months.

By the President of the United States
A Proclamation.

Whereas the laws of the United States have been for some time past, and now are opposed, and the execution thereof obstructed, in the States of South Carolina, Georgia, Alabama, Florida, Mississippi, Louisiana, and Texas, by combinations too powerful to be suppressed by the ordinary course of judicial proceedings, or by the powers vested in the Marshals by law,

Now therefore, I, Abraham Lincoln, President of the United States, in virtue of the power in me vested by the Constitution, and the laws, have thought fit to call forth, and hereby do call forth, the militia of the several States of the Union, to the aggregate number of seventy-five thousand, in order to suppress said combinations, and to cause the laws to be duly executed, The details, for this object, will be immediately communicated to the State authorities through the War Department.

I appeal to all loyal citizens to favor, facilitate and aid this effort to maintain the honor, the integrity, and the existence of our National Union, and the perpetuity of popular government; and to redress wrongs already long enough endured.

I deem it proper to say that the first service assigned to the forces hereby called forth will probably be to re-possess the forts, places, and property which have been seized from the Union; and in every event, the utmost care will be observed, consistently with the objects aforesaid, to avoid any devastation, any destruction of, or interference with, property, or any disturbance of peaceful citizens in any part of the country.

And I hereby command the persons composing the combinations aforesaid to disperse, and retire peaceably to their respective abodes within twenty days from this date.

Deeming that the present condition of public affairs presents an extraordinary occasion, I do hereby, in virtue of the power in me vested by the Constitution, convene both Houses of Congress. Senators and Representatives are therefore summoned to assemble at their respective chambers, at 12 o'clock, noon, on Thursday, the fourth day of July, next, then and there to consider and determine, such measures, as, in their wisdom, the public safety, and interest may seem to demand.

In Witness Whereof I have hereunto set my hand, and cause the Seal of the United States to be affixed.

> Done at the City of Washington this fifteenth day of April in the year of our Lord One thousand, Eight hundred and Sixty-one, and of the Independence of the United States the Eighty-fifth.

By the President: ABRAHAM LINCOLN
WILLIAM H. SEWARD, Secretary of State.

"HELM, MIGHT BE APPOINTED"

Letter to Secretary of War Simon Cameron

APRIL 16, 1861

Benjamin Hardin Helm was married to Mary Lincoln's beloved half sister Emilie, and Lincoln hoped to lure him to federal service, as he indicated in this letter to his secretary of war. Instead, he took a commission in the Confederate Army. A brother-against-brother war thus became a brother-in-law against brother-in-law war for the beleaguered Lincoln family. On September 21, 1863, Brigadier General Helm was fatally wounded at the Battle of Chickamauga.

My dear Sir

Some time ago I requested that Ben. Hardin Helm, might be appointed a Pay-Master, which I still desire.

Next to this, for the sake of my friend, Major [David] Hunter [an officer who had served as a Lincoln bodyguard during the preinaugural journey—ed.], I especially wish Robert A. Kinzie [Hunter's brother-in-law—ed.] to be appointed a Pay-Master [a plum patronage job responsible for dispensing salaries to the troops; Kinzie was appointed per Lincoln's request on May 2—ed.]. This is not a formality, but an earnest reality.

Your Obt. Servt.

A. LINCOLN

"PREVENT EXIT AND ENTRANCE OF VESSELS"

Proclamation of a Blockade

APRIL 19, 1861

Five days after the surrender of Fort Sumter, at the suggestion of General Winfield Scott, President Lincoln declared a blockade against vessels leaving or entering the ports of belligerent Southern states. Although

such a move implicitly recognized the Confederacy as a foreign power,
Lincoln never acknowledged that the Rebels constituted a separate na-
tion. Employing several legal and military devices at once to put down
the unrest, he insisted he had total authority and that the Rebels had no
legal status. Lincoln extended the blockade to include North Carolina
and Virginia once those states seceded.

By the President of the United States of America:
A Proclamation.

Whereas an insurrection against the Government of the United
States has broken out in the States of South Carolina, Georgia, Alabama, Florida, Mississippi, Louisiana, and Texas, and the laws of the
United States for the collection of the revenue cannot be effectually
executed therein conformably to that provision of the Constitution
which requires duties to be uniform throughout the United States:

And whereas a combination of persons engaged in such insurrection, have threatened to grant pretended letters of marque to au-
thorize the bearers thereof to commit assaults on the lives, vessels,
and property of good citizens of the country lawfully engaged in
commerce on the high seas, and in waters of the United States: And
whereas an Executive Proclamation has been already issued, requir-
ing the persons engaged in these disorderly proceedings to desist
therefrom, calling out a militia force for the purpose of repressing
the same, and convening Congress in extraordinary session, to deliberate and determine thereon:

Now, therefore, I, Abraham Lincoln, President of the United
States, with a view to the same purposes before mentioned, and
to the protection of the public peace, and the lives and property of
quiet and orderly citizens pursuing their lawful occupations, until
Congress shall have assembled and deliberated on the said unlawful proceedings, or until the same shall have ceased, have further
deemed it advisable to set on foot a blockade of the ports within
the States aforesaid, in pursuance of the laws of the United States,
and of the law of Nations, in such case provided. For this purpose a

competent force will be posted so as to prevent entrance and exit of vessels from the ports aforesaid. If, therefore, with a view to violate such blockade, a vessel shall approach, or shall attempt to leave either of the said ports, she will be duly warned by the Commander of one of the blockading vessels, who will endorse on her register the fact and date of such warning, and if the same vessel shall again attempt to enter or leave the blockaded port, she will be captured and sent to the nearest convenient port, for such proceedings against her and her cargo as prize, as may be deemed advisable.

And I hereby proclaim and declare that if any person, under the pretended authority of the said States, or under any other pretense, shall molest a vessel of the United States, or the persons or cargo on board of her, such person will be held amenable to the laws of the United States for the prevention and punishment of piracy.

In witness whereof, I have hereunto set my hand, and caused the seal of the United States to be affixed.

> Done at the City of Washington, this nineteenth day of April, in the year of our Lord one thousand eight hundred and sixty-one, and of the Independence of the United States the eighty-fifth.

By the President: ABRAHAM LINCOLN
WILLIAM H. SEWARD, Secretary of State

"OUR MEN ARE NOT MOLES"

Remarks to a Delegation from Baltimore

APRIL 22, 1861

Lincoln made this irate reply to a group of Baltimore citizens sent by Mayor George W. Brown to protest the movement of Union troops through their city en route to the defense of Washington. An angry mob of secessionists had already attacked one such regiment, and now local leaders felt that the people were "exasperated . . . by the passage of troops," urging "no more be ordered to come." Equally exasperated, Lincoln wrote Mayor Brown and Maryland governor Thomas H. Hicks suggesting further provocation of civilians could be "avoided, unless they go out of their way to seek it." But to the committee that brought the message, Lincoln had a far sharper reply, as follows. In time of war, as Lincoln was making clear, national authority trumped states' rights.

You, gentlemen, come here to ask for peace on any terms, and yet have no word of condemnation for those who are making war on us. You express great horror of bloodshed, and yet would not lay a straw in the way of those who are organizing in Virginia and elsewhere to capture this city. The rebels attack Fort Sumter, and your citizens attack troops sent to the defense of the Government, and the lives and property in Washington, and yet you would have me break my oath and surrender the Government without a blow. There is no Washington in that—no Jackson in that—no manhood nor honor in that. I have no desire to invade the South; but I must have troops to defend this Capital. Geographically it lies surrounded by the soil of Maryland; and mathematically the necessity exists that they should come over her territory. Our men are not moles, and can't dig under the earth; they are not birds, and can't fly through the air. There is no way but to march across, and that they must do. But in doing this there is no need of collision. Keep your rowdies in Baltimore, and there will be no bloodshed. Go home and tell your people that if they will not attack us, we will not attack them; but if they do attack us, we will return it, and that severely.

"WHY DON'T THEY COME?"

Comments from a White House Window

APRIL 23, 1861

According to his assistant private secretary, John Hay, Lincoln blurted out these words at the end of a particularly nerve-racking day on April 23. After pacing anxiously for a half hour, the president, worried that troops from the North would not reach Washington in time to save it, "stopped and gazed long and wistfully out of the window down the Potomac in the direction of the expected ships; and unconscious of other presence in the room, at length broke out with irrepressible anguish" the following "repeated exclamation."

Why don't they come! Why don't they come!

"YOU ARE THE ONLY NORTHERN REALITIES"

Comments to Newly Arrived Massachusetts Volunteers

APRIL 24, 1861

Lincoln made these exasperated remarks to troops who had finally arrived to defend the capital.

I don't believe there is any North. The Seventh Regiment [then reportedly en route to Washington from New York—ed.] is a myth. *You* are the only Northern realities.

"Cruise upon the Potomac"

Letter to Secretary of the Navy Gideon Welles

APRIL 29, 1861

Intent on defending Washington from attack, Lincoln thought a navy warship could add an extra level of protection. Though he had never been at sea, Lincoln sensed from the first that the coming war would involve navies as well as armies.

Sir:

You will please to have as strong a War Steamer as you can conveniently put on that duty, to cruise upon the Potomac, and to look in upon, and, if practicable, examine the Bluff and vicinity, at what is called the White House, once or twice per day; and, in case of any attempt to erect a battery there, to drive away the party attempting it, if practicable; and, in every event to report daily to your Department, and to me.

Your Obt. Servt.

A. LINCOLN

Private note. The above order I make at the suggestion of General Scott, though the execution of it, I believe is substantially what you are already doing[.]

A. L.

"Suppression of Unlawful Violence"

Proclamation Calling for 60,034 Additional Volunteers

MAY 3, 1861

Though Congress had yet to meet in special session to address the national emergency, Lincoln acted just a few weeks after his initial militia proclamation to call for an additional 60,000 volunteers into military service. Under his authority, the federal army, long a force of modest

size, was rapidly growing into the most formidable on the planet. By
month's end, with men lured by both patriotism and good, regular pay,
it would boast 156,000 men, with another 25,000 in the navy.

By the President of the United States
A Proclamation.

Whereas existing exigencies demand immediate and adequate measures for the protection of the National Constitution and the preservation of the National Union by the suppression of the insurrectionary combinations now existing in several States for opposing the laws of the Union and obstructing the execution thereof, to which end a military force in addition to that called forth by my proclamation of the fifteenth day of April in the present year, appears to be indispensably necessary,

Now, therefore, I, Abraham Lincoln President of the United States, and Commander-in-Chief of the Army and Navy thereof, and of the Militia of the several States, when called into actual service, do hereby call into the service of the United States, forty-two thousand and thirty four volunteers, to serve for the period of three years, unless sooner discharged, and to be mustered into service as Infantry and cavalry. The proportions of each arm, and the details of enrollment and organization will be made known, through the Department of War.

And I also direct that the regular army of the United States be increased by the addition of eight regiments of infantry, one regiment of cavalry, and one regiment of artillery, making altogether a maximum aggregate increase of twenty-two thousand, seven hundred and fourteen officers and enlisted men; the details of which increase will also be made known through the Department of War.

And I further direct the enlistment for not less than one or more than three years, of eighteen thousand seamen, in addition to the present force, for the naval service of the United States. The details of the enlistment and organization will be made known through the Department of the Navy.

The call for volunteers hereby made, and the direction for the increase of the regular army, and for the enlistment of seamen hereby given, together with the plan of organization adopted for the volunteer and for the regular forces hereby authorized, will be submitted to Congress as soon as assembled.

In the meantime I earnestly invoke the cooperation of all good citizens in the measures hereby adopted, for the effectual suppression of unlawful violence, for the impartial enforcement of constitutional laws, and for the speediest possible restoration of peace and order and, with these, of happiness and prosperity throughout our country.

> In testimony whereof I have hereunto set my hand and caused the seal of the United States to be affixed. Done at the City of Washington this third day of May, in the year of our Lord one thousand eight hundred and sixty-one, and of the independence of the United States the eighty-fifth.

By the President: ABRAHAM LINCOLN
WILLIAM H. SEWARD, Secretary of State.

"GET THE GERMAN BRIGADE IN SHAPE"

Letter to Carl Schurz

MAY 13, 1861

To unite ethnic groups and loyal pro-war Democrats in defense of the Union, Lincoln commissioned officers such as Carl Schurz, a noted orator with almost no military experience but enormous influence among fellow German-born refugees from the European Revolutions of 1848. Few of the subsequently appointed Democrats (such as Generals Benjamin Butler and John McClernand) or émigrés (such as Schurz or fellow German generals Franz Sigel and Alexander Schimmelfennig) proved successful commanders. But Lincoln's savvy bow to his diverse

constituency indeed helped forge a broad Northern coalition to com-
bat the rebellion. Here, the same day as he asks his secretary of war
to commission Schurz "at once" and perhaps even assume command
at Fortress Monroe, Virginia, Lincoln invites Schurz to organize his
German-born troops. But professional West Point–trained command-
ers objected, so Lincoln consoled Schurz with a diplomatic appointment.
A year later, a still determined Schurz returned to take up command
of a unit of John C. Frémont's army, and later fought—without distinc-
tion—at the Battles of Chancellorsville and Gettysburg. However inept
on the battlefield, generals like Schurz kept Lincoln's pro-war coalition
alive and well.

Get the German brigade in shape, and at their request, you shall
be Brigadier General. Will write you at New-York. [The president
wrote three days later as promised to concede, "I have not succeeded . . . can not make it move smoothly just yet."—ed.]

A. LINCOLN

"I KNOW BUT LITTLE ABOUT SHIPS"

Letter to Secretary of the Navy Gideon Welles

MAY 14, 1861

In the weeks after the surrender of Fort Sumter, Lincoln scrambled
to build a navy—and staff it. Here he recommends a commission for
a Maine Republican who had little on his resume save for voting for
Lincoln at the Republican national convention the previous May. Sec-
retary of the Navy Gideon Welles, whom Lincoln soon took to calling
"Neptune," had been chief of the Bureau of Provisions and Clothing for
the navy during the Mexican War.

My dear Sir:
I know but little about ships; but I feel a good deal of interest for
George W. Lawrence, of Maine, who is a proficient in that line. I

believe it is settled that the Govt. has large use for all the barches [*sic*] of Maine; and I shall be glad if Mr. Lawrence can be engaged in it on fair terms to himself and to us.

Yours very truly

A. LINCOLN

"A TASTE ALTOGETHER MILITARY"

Condolence Letter to Ephraim D. and Phoebe Ellsworth

MAY 25, 1861

Ephraim Elmer Ellsworth was a former student at Lincoln's Springfield law office, who had already earned considerable fame as the spruce drillmaster of an elite unit of Zouaves—soldiers attired in brightly colored uniforms in the style of the French foreign legion. In February Ellsworth had accompanied the president-elect to Washington, acting as a bodyguard. On May 24, angered by the sight of a Confederate flag flying from atop a hotel in nearby Alexandria, Virginia—within clear sight of the White House—Ellsworth marched his soldiers across the Potomac River and hauled down the banner himself. On his way downstairs, the infuriated innkeeper shot him to death—making Ellsworth the first Union officer killed in the war. Devastated, Lincoln gave the young martyr a White House funeral, and sent this justly famous condolence letter to his grieving parents. Ellsworth's death was only a taste of the carnage yet to come.

My dear Sir and Madam,

In the untimely loss of your noble son, our affliction here, is scarcely less than your own. So much of promised usefulness to one's country, and of bright hopes for one's self and friends, have rarely been so suddenly dashed, as in his fall. In size, in years, and in youthful appearance, a boy only, his power to command men, was surpassingly great. This power, combined with a fine intellect, an indomitable energy, and a taste altogether military, constituted in him, as seemed to me, the best natural talent, in that department, I ever knew. And yet he was singularly modest and deferential in social intercourse. My acquaintance with him began less than two years ago; yet through the latter half of the intervening period, it was as intimate as the disparity of our ages, and my engrossing engagements, would permit. To me, he appeared to have no indulgences or pastimes; and I never heard him utter a profane, or an intemperate word. What was conclusive of his good heart, he never forgot his parents. The honors he labored for so laudably, and, in the sad end, so gallantly gave his life, he meant for them, no less than for himself.

In the hope that it may be no intrusion upon the sacredness of your sorrow, I have ventured to address you this tribute to the memory of my young friend, and your brave and early fallen child.

May God give you that consolation which is beyond all earthly power.

Sincerely your friend in a common affliction—
A. LINCOLN

"SUSPEND THE WRIT OF HABEAS CORPUS"

Letter to General Winfield Scott

JULY 2, 1861

Though some public officials, especially Democrats, believed that only Congress had the power to suspend the privileges of the writ of habeas corpus, Lincoln acted quickly, firmly, and some say, autocratically, to suspend civil liberties in Maryland. He argued that he must do so in order to safeguard the movement of troops from the North to the defense of Washington and also to prevent local secessionists from convening to take that state out of the Union. Whether or not the president acted legally is still in dispute—the Supreme Court, years later, ruled he had not—but Lincoln's actions almost certainly prevented Maryland from

*seceding and thereby isolating the national capital within hostile Con-
federate territory. A few years into the war, Congress ratified and broad-
ened the suspension of the writ.*

To the Commanding General of the Army of the United States.

You are engaged in repressing an insurrection against the laws of
the United States. If, at any point, on or in the vicinity of any military line which is now, or which shall be used, between the City of
New York and the City of Washington, you find resistance which
renders it necessary to suspend the writ of Habeas Corpus for the
Public Safety, you, personally, or through the Officer in command,
at the point where resistance occurs, are authorized to suspend that
writ.

> Given under my hand, and the Seal of the United States,
> at the City of Washington, this second day of July,
> A.D. 1861, and of the Independence of the United States
> the 85th.

By the President of the United States: ABRAHAM LINCOLN
WILLIAM H. SEWARD, Secretary of State

"THE FOLLY OF BEING THE BEGINNERS OF A WAR"

From a Message to a Special Session of Congress

JULY 4, 1861

*One of Lincoln's most important and impressive state papers, this mes-
sage to the long-awaited special session of the House and Senate skill-
fully defined the coming war as a historic struggle to save not just the
Union, but democracy itself—and defended the president's extraordinary use of executive power to suppress rebellion. Widely praised by
the Republican press, the message was not surprisingly criticized in the*

South. One Baltimore newspaper condemned its author as "the equal, in despotic wickedness, of Nero or any of the other tyrants who have polluted the earth." In keeping with mid-nineteenth-century tradition, Lincoln wrote this message but did not deliver it in person; it was sent to Capitol Hill and read aloud to both houses of Congress by a clerk. Yet its broad publication provided many Northerners with an eloquent rationale for fighting to preserve the nation.

At the beginning of the present Presidential term, four months ago, the functions of the Federal Government were found to be generally suspended within the several States of South Carolina, Georgia, Alabama, Mississippi, Louisiana, and Florida, excepting only those of the Post Office Department.

Within these States, all the Forts, Arsenals, Dock-yards, Custom-houses, and the like, including the movable and stationary property in, and about them, had been seized, and were held in open hostility to this Government, excepting only Forts Pickens, Taylor, and Jefferson, on, and near the Florida coast, and Fort Sumter, in Charleston harbor, South Carolina. The Forts thus seized had been put in improved condition; new ones had been built; and armed forces had been organized, and were organizing, all avowedly with the same hostile purpose.

The Forts remaining in the possession of the Federal government, in, and near, these States, were either besieged or menaced by warlike preparations; and especially Fort Sumter was nearly surrounded by well-protected hostile batteries, with guns equal in quality to the best of its own, and outnumbering the latter as perhaps ten to one. A disproportionate share, of the Federal muskets and rifles, had somehow found their way into these States, and had been seized, to be used against the government. Accumulations of the public revenue, lying within them, had been seized for the same object. The Navy was scattered in distant seas; leaving but a very small part of it within the immediate reach of the government. Officers of the Federal Army and Navy, had resigned in great numbers; and, of those resigning, a large proportion had taken up arms against the government. Simultaneously, and in connection, with all this, the purpose to sever the Federal Union, was openly avowed. In accordance with this purpose, an ordinance had been adopted in each of these States, declaring the States, respectively, to be separated from the National Union. A formula for instituting a combined government of these states had been promulgated; and this illegal organization, in the character of confederate States was already invoking recognition, aid, and intervention, from Foreign Powers.

Finding this condition of things, and believing it to be an imperative duty upon the incoming Executive, to prevent, if possible, the consummation of such attempt to destroy the Federal Union, a choice of means to that end became indispensable. This choice was made; and was declared in the Inaugural address. The policy chosen looked to the exhaustion of all peaceful measures, before a resort to any stronger ones. It sought only to hold the public places and property, not already wrested from the Government, and to collect the revenue; relying for the rest, on time, discussion, and the ballot-box. It promised a continuance of the mails, at government expense, to the very people who were resisting the government; and it gave repeated pledges against any disturbance to any of the people, or any of their rights. Of all that which a president might constitutionally, and justifiably, do in such a case, everything was foreborne, without which, it was believed possible to keep the government on foot.

On the 5th of March, (the present incumbent's first full day in office) a letter of Major [Robert] Anderson, commanding at Fort Sumter, written on the 28th of February, and received at the War Department on the 4th of March, was, by that Department, placed in his hands. This letter expressed the professional opinion of the writer, that re-inforcements could not be thrown into that Fort within the time for his relief, rendered necessary by the limited supply of provisions, and with a view of holding possession of the same, with a force of less than twenty thousand good, and well-disciplined men. This opinion was concurred in by all the officers of his command; and their *memoranda* on the subject, were made enclosures

of Major Anderson's letter. The whole was immediately laid before Lieutenant General Scott, who at once concurred with Major
Anderson in opinion. On reflection, however, he took full time, consulting with other officers, both of the Army and the Navy; and, at
the end of four days, came reluctantly, but decidedly, to the same
conclusion as before. He also stated at the same time that no such
sufficient force was then at the control of the Government, or could
be raised, and brought to the ground, within the time when the provisions in the Fort would be exhausted. In a purely military point of
view, this reduced the duty of the administration, in the case, to the
mere matter of getting the garrison safely out of the Fort.

It was believed, however, that to so abandon that position, under
the circumstances, would be utterly ruinous; that the *necessity* under
which it was to be done, would not be fully understood—that, by
many, it would be construed as a part of a *voluntary* policy—that,
at home, it would discourage the friends of the Union, embolden its
adversaries, and go far to insure to the latter, a recognition abroad—
that, in fact, it would be our national destruction consummated.
This could not be allowed. Starvation was not yet upon the garrison;
and ere it would be reached, *Fort Pickens* might be reinforced. This
last, would be a clear indication of *policy,* and would better enable
the country to accept the evacuation of Fort Sumter, as a military
necessity. An order was at once directed to be sent for the landing
of the troops from the Steamship Brooklyn, into Fort Pickens. This
order could not go by land, but must take the longer, and slower
route by sea. The first return news from the order was received just
one week before the fall of Fort Sumter. The news itself was, that the
officer commanding the Sabine, to which vessel the troops had been
transferred from the Brooklyn, acting upon some *quasi* armistice of
the late administration, (and of the existence of which, the present
administration, up to the time the order was despatched, had only
too vague and uncertain rumors, to fix attention) had refused to
land the troops. To now re-inforce Fort Pickens, before a crisis would
be reached at Fort Sumter was impossible—rendered so by the near

exhaustion of provisions in the latter-named Fort. In precaution against such a conjuncture, the government had, a few days before, commenced preparing an expedition, as well adapted as might be, to relieve Fort Sumter, which expedition was intended to be ultimately used, or not, according to circumstances. The strongest anticipated case, for using it, was now presented; and it was resolved to send it forward. As had been intended, in this contingency, it was also resolved to notify the Governor of South Carolina, that he might expect an attempt would be made to provision the Fort; and that, if the attempt should not be resisted, there would be no effort to throw in men, arms, or ammunition, without further notice, or in case of an attack upon the Fort. This notice was accordingly given; where-upon the Fort was attacked, and bombarded to its fall, without even awaiting the arrival of the provisioning expedition.

It is thus seen that the assault upon, and reduction of, Fort Sumter, was, in no sense, a matter of self defence on the part of the assailants. They well knew that the garrison in the Fort could, by no possibility, commit aggression upon them. They knew—they were expressly notified—that the giving of bread to the few brave and hungry men of the garrison, was all which would on that occasion be attempted, unless themselves, by resisting so much, should provoke more. They knew that this Government desired to keep the garrison in the Fort, not to assail them, but merely to maintain visible possession, and thus to preserve the Union from actual, and immediate dissolution— trusting, as herein-before stated, to time, discussion, and the ballot-box, for final adjustment; and they assailed, and reduced the Fort, for precisely the reverse object—to drive out the visible authority of the Federal Union, and thus force it to immediate dissolution.

That this was their object, the Executive well understood; and having said to them in the inaugural address, "You can have no conflict without being yourselves the aggressors," he took pains, not only to keep this declaration good, but also to keep the case so free from the power of ingenious sophistry, as that the world should not be able to misunderstand it. By the affair at Fort Sumter, with its surrounding circumstances, that point was reached. Then, and thereby, the assailants of the Government, began the conflict of arms, without a gun in sight, or in expectancy, to return their fire, save only the few in the Fort, sent to that harbor, years before, for their own protection, and still ready to give that protection, in whatever was lawful. In this act, discarding all else, they have forced upon the country, the distinct issue: "Immediate dissolution, or blood."

And this issue embraces more than the fate of these United States. It presents to the whole family of man, the question, whether a constitutional republic, or a democracy—a government of the people, by the same people—can, or cannot, maintain its territorial integrity, against its own domestic foes. It presents the question, whether discontented individuals, too few in numbers to control administration, according to organic law, in any case, can always, upon the pretences made in this case, or on any other pretences, or arbitrarily, without any pretence, break up their Government, and thus practically put an end to free government upon the earth. It forces us to ask: "Is there, in all republics, this inherent, and fatal weakness?" "Must a government, of necessity, be too *strong* for the liberties of its own people, or too *weak* to maintain its own existence?"

So viewing the issue, no choice was left but to call out the war power of the Government; and so to resist force, employed for its destruction, by force, for its preservation.

The call was made; and the response of the country was most gratifying; surpassing, in unanimity and spirit, the most sanguine expectation. Yet none of the States commonly called Slave states, except Delaware, gave a Regiment through regular State organization. A few regiments have been organized within some others of those states, by individual enterprise, and received into the government service. Of course the seceded States, so called, (and to which Texas had been joined about the time of the inauguration,) gave no troops to the cause of the Union. The border States, so called, were not uniform in their actions; some of them being almost *for* the Union, while in others—as Virginia, North Carolina, Tennessee, and Arkansas— the Union sentiment was nearly repressed, and silenced.

· · · · · · · · ·

It is now recommended that you give the legal means for making this contest a short, and a decisive one; that you place at the control of the government, for the work, at least four hundred thousand men, and four hundred millions of dollars. That number of men is about one tenth of those of proper ages within the regions where, apparently, *all* are willing to engage; and the sum is less than a twenty-third part of the money value owned by the men who seem ready to devote the whole. A debt of six hundred millions of dollars *now,* is a less sum per head, than was the debt of our revolution, when we came out of that struggle; and the money value in the country now, bears even a greater proportion to what it was *then,* than does the population. Surely each man has as strong a motive *now,* to *preserve* our liberties, as each had *then,* to *establish* them.

A right result, at this time, will be worth more to the world, than ten times the men, and ten times the money. The evidence reaching us from the country, leaves no doubt, that the material for the work is abundant; and that it needs only the hand of legislation to give it legal sanction, and the hand of the Executive to give it practical shape and efficiency. One of the greatest perplexities of the government, is to avoid receiving troops faster than it can provide for them. In a word, the people will save their government, if the government itself, will do its part, only indifferently well.

It might seem, at first thought, to be of little difference whether the present movement at the South be called "secession" or "rebellion." The movers, however, well understand the difference. At the beginning, they knew they could never raise their treason to any respectable magnitude, by any name which implies *violation* of law. They knew their people possessed as much of moral sense, as much of devotion to law and order, and as much pride in, and reverence for, the history, and government, of their common country, as any other civilized, and patriotic people. They knew they could make no advancement directly in the teeth of these strong and noble sentiments. Accordingly they commenced by an insidious debauching of the public mind. They invented an ingenious sophism, which, if conceded, was followed by perfectly logical steps, through all the incidents, to the complete destruction of the Union. The sophism itself is, that any state of the Union may, *consistently* with the national Constitution, and therefore *lawfully*, and *peacefully*, withdraw from the Union, without the consent of the Union, or of any other state. The little disguise that the supposed right is to be exercised only for just cause, themselves to be the sole judge of its justice, is too thin to merit any notice.

With rebellion thus sugar-coated, they have been drugging the public mind of their section for more than thirty years; and, until at length, they have brought many good men to a willingness to take up arms against the government the day *after* some assemblage of men have enacted the farcical pretence of taking their State out of the Union, who could have been brought to no such thing the day *before*.

This sophism derives much—perhaps the whole—of its currency, from the assumption, that there is some omnipotent, and sacred supremacy, pertaining to a *State*—to each State of our Federal Union. Our States have neither more, nor less power, than that reserved to them, in the Union, by the Constitution—no one of them ever having been a State *out* of the Union. The original ones passed into the Union even *before* they cast off their British colonial dependence; and the new ones each came into the Union directly from a condition of dependence, excepting Texas. And even Texas, in its temporary independence, was never designated a State. The new ones only took the designation of States, on coming into the Union, while that name was first adopted for the old ones, in, and by, the Declaration of Independence. Therein the "United Colonies" were declared to be "Free and Independent States"; but, even then, the object plainly was not to declare their independence of *one another*, or of the *Union;* but directly the contrary, as their mutual pledge, and their mutual action, before, at the time, and afterwards, abundantly show. The express plighting of faith, by each and all of the original thirteen, in the Articles of Confederation, two years later, that the Union shall be perpetual, is most conclusive. Having never been States, either in substance, or in name, *outside* of the Union, whence this magical omnipotence of "State rights," asserting a claim of power to lawfully destroy the Union itself? Much is said about the "sovereignty" of the States; but the word, even, is not in the national Constitution; nor, as is believed, in any of the State constitutions. What is a "sovereignty," in the political sense of the term? Would it be far wrong to define it "A political community, without a political superior"? Tested by this, no one of our States, except Texas, ever was a sovereignty. And even Texas gave up the character on coming into the Union; by which act, she acknowledged the Constitution of the United States, and the laws and treaties of the United States made in pursuance of the Constitution, to be, for her, the supreme law of the land. The States have their *status* IN the Union, and they have no other *legal status*. If they break from this, they can only do so against law, and by revolution. The Union, and not themselves separately, procured their independence, and their liberty. By conquest, or purchase, the Union gave each of them, whatever of independence, and liberty, it has. The Union is older than any of the States; and, in fact, it created them as States. Originally, some dependent colonies made the Union; and, in turn, the Union threw off their old dependence, for them, and made them States, such as they are. Not one of them ever had a State constitution, independent of the Union. Of course, it is not forgotten that all the new States framed their constitutions, before they entered the Union; nevertheless, dependent upon, and preparatory to, coming into the Union.

Unquestionably the States have the powers, and rights, reserved to them in, and by the National Constitution; but among these, surely, are not included all conceivable powers, however mischievous, or destructive; but, at most, such only, as were known in the world, at the time, as governmental powers; and certainly, a power to destroy the government itself, had never been known as a governmental— as a merely administrative power. This relative matter of National power, and State rights, as a principle, is no other than the principle of *generality*, and *locality*. Whatever concerns the whole, should be confided to the whole—to the general government; while, whatever concerns *only* the State, should be left exclusively, to the State. This is all there is of original principle about it. Whether the National Constitution, in defining boundaries between the two, has applied the principle with exact accuracy, is not to be questioned. We are all bound by that defining, without question.

What is now combatted, is the position that secession is *consistent* with the Constitution—is *lawful*, and *peaceful*. It is not contended that there is any express law for it; and nothing should ever be implied as law, which leads to unjust, or absurd consequences. The nation purchased, with money, the countries out of which several of these States were formed. Is it just that they shall go off without leave, and without refunding? The nation paid very large sums, (in the aggregate, I believe, nearly a hundred millions) to relieve Florida of the aboriginal tribes. Is it just that she shall now be off without consent, or without making any return? The nation is now in debt for money applied to the benefit of these so-called seceding States, in common with the rest. Is it just, either that creditors shall go unpaid, or the remaining States pay the whole? A part of the present national debt was contracted to pay the old debts of Texas. Is it just that she shall leave, and pay no part of this herself?

Again, if one State may secede, so may another; and when all shall have seceded, none is left to pay the debts. Is this quite just to creditors? Did we notify them of this sage view of ours, when we borrowed their money? If we now recognize this doctrine, by allowing the seceders to go in peace, it is difficult to see what we can do, if others choose to go, or to extort terms upon which they will promise to remain.

The seceders insist that our Constitution admits of secession. They have assumed to make a National Constitution of their own, in which, of necessity, they have either *discarded*, or *retained*, the right of secession, as they insist, it exists in ours. If they have discarded it, they thereby admit that, on principle, it ought not to be in ours.

If they have retained it, by their own construction of ours they show that to be consistent they must secede from one another, whenever they shall find it the easiest way of settling their debts, or effecting any other selfish, or unjust object. The principle itself is one of disintegration, and upon which no government can possibly endure.

If all the States, save one, should assert the power to *drive* that one out of the Union, it is presumed the whole class of seceder politicians would at once deny the power, and denounce the act as the greatest outrage upon State rights. But suppose that precisely the same act, instead of being called "driving the one out," should be called "the seceding of the others from that one," it would be exactly what the seceders claim to do; unless, indeed, they make the point, that the one, because it is a minority, may rightfully do, what the others, because they are a majority, may not rightfully do. These politicians are subtle, and profound, on the rights of minorities. They are not partial to that power which made the Constitution, and speaks from the preamble, calling itself "We, the People."

It may well be questioned whether there is, to-day, a majority of the legally qualified voters of any State, except perhaps South Carolina, in favor of disunion. There is much reason to believe that the Union men are the majority in many, if not in every other one, of the so-called seceded States. The contrary has not been demonstrated in any one of them. It is ventured to affirm this, even of Virginia and Tennessee; for the result of an election, held in military camps, where the bayonets are all on one side of the question voted upon, can scarcely be considered as demonstrating popular sentiment. At such an election, all that large class who are, at once, *for* the Union, and *against* coercion, would be coerced to vote against the Union.

It may be affirmed, without extravagance, that the free institutions we enjoy, have developed the powers, and improved the condition, of our whole people, beyond any example in the world. Of this we now have a striking, and an impressive illustration. So large an army as the government has now on foot, was never before known, without a soldier in it, but who had taken his place there, of his own free

choice. But more than this: there are many single Regiments whose
members, one and another, possess full practical knowledge of all
the arts, sciences, professions, and whatever else, whether useful or
elegant, is known in the world; and there is scarcely one, from which
there could not be selected, a President, a Cabinet, a Congress, and
perhaps a Court, abundantly competent to administer the government itself. Nor do I say this is not true, also, in the army of our late
friends, now adversaries, in this contest; but if it is, so much better
the reason why the government, which has conferred such benefits
on both them and us, should not be broken up. Whoever, in any section, proposes to abandon such a government, would do well to consider, in deference to what principle it is, that he does it—what better
he is likely to get in its stead—whether the substitute will give, or
be intended to give, so much of good to the people. There are some
foreshadowings on this subject. Our adversaries have adopted some
Declarations of Independence; in which, unlike the good old one,
penned by Jefferson, they omit the words "all men are created equal."
Why? They have adopted a temporary national constitution, in the
preamble of which, unlike our good old one, signed by Washington,
they omit "We, the People," and substitute "We, the deputies of the
sovereign and independent States." Why? Why this deliberate pressing out of view, the rights of men, and the authority of the people?

This is essentially a People's contest. On the side of the Union, it
is a struggle for maintaining in the world, that form, and substance
of government, whose leading object is, to elevate the condition of
men—to lift artificial weights from all shoulders—to clear the paths
of laudable pursuit for all—to afford all, an unfettered start, and a
fair chance, in the race of life. Yielding to partial, and temporary departures, from necessity, this is the leading object of the government
for whose existence we contend.

I am most happy to believe that the plain people understand, and
appreciate this. It is worthy of note, that while in this, the government's hour of trial, large numbers of those in the Army and Navy,
who have been favored with the offices, have resigned, and proved

false to the hand which had pampered them, not one common soldier, or common sailor is is [sic] known to have deserted his flag.

Great honor is due to those officers who remain true, despite the example of their treacherous associates; but the greatest honor, and most important fact of all, is the unanimous firmness of the common soldiers, and common sailors. To the last man, so far as known, they have successfully resisted the traitorous efforts of those, whose commands, but an hour before, they obeyed as absolute law. This is the patriotic instinct of the plain people. They understand, without an argument, that destroying the government, which was made by Washington, means no good to them.

Our popular government has often been called an experiment. Two points in it, our people have already settled—the successful *establishing*, and the successful *administering* of it. One still remains— its successful *maintenance* against a formidable internal attempt to overthrow it. It is now for them to demonstrate to the world, that those who can fairly carry an election, can also suppress a rebellion— that ballots are the rightful, and peaceful, successors of bullets; and that when ballots have fairly, and constitutionally, decided, there can be no successful appeal, back to bullets; that there can be no successful appeal, except to ballots themselves, at succeeding elections. Such will be a great lesson of peace; teaching men that what they cannot take by an election, neither can they take it by a war—teaching all, the folly of being the beginners of a war.

Lest there be some uneasiness in the minds of candid men, as to what is to be the course of the government, towards the Southern States, *after* the rebellion shall have been suppressed, the Executive deems it proper to say, it will be his purpose then, as ever, to be guided by the Constitution, and the laws; and that he probably will have no different understanding of the powers, and duties of the Federal government, relatively to the rights of the States, and the people, under the Constitution, than that expressed in the inaugural address.

He desires to preserve the government, that it may be administered for all, as it was administered by the men who made it. Loyal citizens everywhere, have the right to claim this of their government; and the government has no right to withhold, or neglect it. It is not perceived that, in giving it, there is any coercion, any conquest, or any subjugation, in any just sense of those terms.

The Constitution provides, and all the States have accepted the provision, that "The United States shall guarantee to every State in this Union a republican form of government." But, if a State may lawfully go out of the Union, having done so, it may also discard the republican form of government; so that to prevent its going out, is an indispensable *means*, to the *end*, of maintaining the guaranty mentioned; and when an end is lawful and obligatory, the indispensable means to it, are also lawful, and obligatory.

It was with the deepest regret that the Executive found the duty of employing the war-power, in defence of the government, forced upon him. He could but perform this duty, or surrender the existence of the government. No compromise, by public servants, could, in this case, be a cure; not that compromises are not often proper, but that no popular government can long survive a marked precedent, that those who carry an election, can only save the government from immediate destruction, by giving up the main point, upon which the people gave the election. The people themselves, and not their servants, can safely reverse their own deliberate decisions. As a private citizen, the Executive could not have consented that these institutions shall perish; much less could he, in betrayal of so vast, and so sacred a trust, as these free people had confided to him. He felt that he had no moral right to shrink; nor even to count the chances of his own life, in what might follow. In full view of his great responsibility, he has, so far, done what he has deemed his duty. You will now, according to your own judgment, perform yours. He sincerely hopes that your views, and your action, may so accord with his, as to assure all faithful citizens, who have been disturbed in their rights, of a certain, and speedy restoration to them, under the Constitution, and the laws.

And having thus chosen our course, without guile, and with pure purpose, let us renew our trust in God, and go forward without fear, and with manly hearts.

"A GENTLE, BUT FIRM, AND CERTAIN HAND"

Memoranda on Military Policy Suggested by the Bull Run Defeat

JULY 23 AND 27, 1861

The first real battle of the Civil War at Manassas, Virginia, in July, ended in a shocking and humiliating defeat for federal forces under General Irvin McDowell. With the army in disarray and public confidence in the administration understandably plummeting, Lincoln took up his pen to coolly analyze the desperate situation and plot the army's next moves. He showed confidence under pressure and a remarkably sophisticated view of strategy, particularly for a man who had never before held an executive position or major military command. Though he often took elaborate pains merely to suggest action to his commanders, rather than order it directly, his informal notes surely had much the same effect as outright commands.

JULY 23. 1861.

1 Let the plan for making the Blockade effective be pushed forward with all possible despatch.

2 Let the volunteer forces at Fort-Monroe & vicinity under Genl. Butler be constantly drilled, disciplined, and instructed without more for the present.

3 Let Baltimore be held, as now, with a gentle, but firm, and certain hand.

4 Let the force now under Patterson, or Banks, be strengthened, and made secure in it's possition.

5 Let the forces in Western Virginia act, till further orders, according to instructions, or orders from Gen. McClellan.

6 [Let] Gen. Fremont push forward his organization, and operations in the West as rapidly as possible, giving rather special attention to Missouri.

7 Let the forces late before Manassas, except the three months
men, be reorganized as rapidly as possible, in their camps here and
about Arlington

8 Let the three months forces, who decline to enter the longer
service, be discharged as rapidly as circumstances will permit.

9 Let the new volunteer forces be brought forward as fast as
possible; and especially into the camps on the two sides of the river
here.

July 27, 1861

When the foregoing shall have been substantially attended to—

1. Let Manassas junction, (or some point on one or other of the
railroads near it;); and Strasburg, be seized, and permanently held,
with an open line from Washington to Manassas; and and [sic]
open line from Harper's Ferry to Strasburg—the military men to
find the way of doing these.

2. This done, a joint movement from Cairo on Memphis; and
from Cincinnati on East Tennessee.

"To Preserve the Peace of My Own Native State"

Letter to Governor Beriah Magoffin

AUGUST 24, 1861

The governor of the border state of Kentucky—Lincoln's birthplace—had written to the president to protest "recruitment and establishment of camps" there "without the advice or consent of the Authorities of the State." Lincoln made this reply, again affirming the federal power over individual states.

Sir:

Your letter of the 19th. Inst. in which you "*urge the removal from the limits of Kentucky of the military force now organized, and in camp within said State*" is received.

I may not possess full and precisely accurate knowledge upon this subject; but I believe it is true that there is a military force in camp within Kentucky, acting by authority of the United States, which force is not very large, and is not now being augmented.

I also believe that some arms have been furnished to this force by the United States.

I also believe this force consists exclusively of Kentuckians, having their camp in the immediate vicinity of their own homes, and not assailing, or menacing, any of the good people of Kentucky.

In all I have done in the premises, I have acted upon the urgent solicitation of many Kentuckians, and in accordance with what I believed, and still believe, to be the wish of a majority of all the Union-loving people of Kentucky.

While I have conversed on this subject with many eminent men of Kentucky, including a large majority of her Members of Congress, I do not remember that any one of them, or any other person, except your Excellency and the bearers of your Excellency's letter, has urged me to remove the military force from Kentucky, or to disband it. One other very worthy citizen of Kentucky did solicit me to have the augmenting of the force suspended for a time.

Taking all the means within my reach to form a judgment, I do not believe it is the popular wish of Kentucky that this force shall be removed beyond her limits; and, with this impression, I must respectfully decline to so remove it.

I most cordially sympathize with your Excellency, in the wish to preserve the peace of my own native State, Kentucky; but it is with regret I search, and can not find, in your not very short letter, any declaration, or intimation, that you entertain any desire for the preservation of the Federal Union.

Your Obedient Servant,

A. LINCOLN

"SHOULD YOU SHOOT A MAN"

Letter to General John C. Frémont

SEPTEMBER 2, 1861

Without clearing it in advance with the president, General John C. Frémont had issued an order to confiscate Rebel property—including slaves—and to execute traitors. The general threatened that "[a]ll persons who shall be taken with arms in their hands within these lines, shall be tried by court-martial, and if found guilty will be shot." Though Lincoln suggested here that Frémont save face by rescinding his order himself, the general huffily replied that if Lincoln decided "I am wrong in the article respecting the liberation if slaves, I have to ask that you will openly direct me to make the correction." This Lincoln soon made explicitly clear. Such enormous power he reserved to himself.

Private and confidential.

My dear Sir:

Two points in your proclamation of August 30th give me some anxiety. First, should you shoot a man, according to the proclamation, the Confederates would very certainly shoot our best man in their hands in retaliation; and so, man for man, indefinitely. It is therefore my order that you allow no man to be shot, under the proc-lamation, without first having my approbation or consent.

Secondly, I think there is great danger that the closing paragraph, in relation to the confiscation of property, and the liberating slaves of traiterous owners, will alarm our Southern Union friends, and turn them against us perhaps ruin our rather fair prospect for Kentucky. Allow me therefore to ask, that you will as of your own motion, mod-ify that paragraph so as to conform to the *first* and *fourth* sections of the act of Congress, entitled, "An act to confiscate property used for insurrectionary purposes," approved August, 6th, 1861, and a copy of which act I herewith send you. This letter is written in a spirit of cau-tion and not of censure.

I send it by a special messenger, in order that it may certainly and speedily reach you.

Yours very truly

A. LINCOLN

"THERE IS SOMETHING IN IT"

Comment on the Plan for the USS Monitor

SEPTEMBER 10, 1861

There is little in the written record about Lincoln's role in spearhead-ing development of the Union's first ironclad warship: inventor John Ericsson's USS Monitor. Shipbuilder Cornelius Bushnell, however, heard Lincoln make these decisively encouraging, if homespun, com-ments when shown the initial plans at the naval board. The Monitor was commissioned and quickly built in Brooklyn, New York, and ar-rived in Newport News, Virginia, the following March, just in time to confront and turn back the fearsome Confederate ironclad CSS Vir-ginia. This is what Lincoln said when he first saw—and recognized the potential of—Ericsson's proposal.

All I have to say, is what the girl said when she stuck her foot into the stocking. "It strikes me there is something in it."

"ILLINOIS DOES NOT DISAPPOINT US"

Letter to General John A. McClernand

NOVEMBER 10, 1861

The president wrote this letter to one of his so-called political generals—a Democrat from Illinois—to soothe ruffled feathers after a modest Union success at the Battle of Belmont, Missouri. The officer who emerged from that fray with a growing reputation was not McClernand, but Ulysses S. Grant, destined to win national fame at Shiloh the following year. McClernand, who led three Illinois regiments at the engagement, replied to this letter by complaining about "a want of military unity" in the West. Lincoln always took pains to recognize troops from his home state. Reviewing the Thirty-ninth Illinois in May 1862, he called out: "You boys are a good ways from home, ain't you?"

My dear Sir

This is not an official but a social letter. You have had a battle, and without being able to judge as to the precise measure of its value, I think it is safe to say that you, and all with you have done honor to yourselves and the flag and service to the country. Most gratefully do I thank you and them. In my present position, I must care for the whole nation; but I hope it will be no injustice to any other state, for me to indulge a little home pride, that Illinois does not disappoint us.

I have just closed a long interview with Mr. [Elihu] Washburne [an Illinois Congressman and chief civilian advocate for Grant—ed.] in which he has detailed the many difficulties you, and those with you labor under. Be assured, we do not forget or neglect you. Much, very much, goes undone: but it is because we have not the power to do it faster than we do. Some of your forces are without arms, but the same is true here, and at every other place where we have considerable bodies of troops. The plain matter-of-fact is, our good people have rushed to the rescue of the Government, faster than the government can find arms to put into their hands.

It would be agreeable to each division of the army to know its own precise destination: but the Government cannot immediately, nor inflexibly at any time, determine as to all; nor if determined, can it tell its *friends* without at the same time telling its *enemies*.

We know you do all as wisely and well as you can; and you will not be deceived if you conclude the same is true of us. Please give my respects and thanks to all[.]

Yours very truly
A. LINCOLN.

"A WAR UPON THE FIRST PRINCIPLE OF POPULAR GOVERNMENT"

From the Annual Message to Congress

DECEMBER 3, 1861

Lincoln's first annual message to Congress—the equivalent of today's State of the Union addresses—included a stern warning to foreign powers that they resist interfering in the American Civil War. The commander in chief added a detailed and rather optimistic account of the progress of the effort to suppress the Rebellion. And he ended with a ringing defense of the Union cause.

A disloyal portion of the American people have, during the whole year, been engaged in an attempt to divide and destroy the Union. A nation which endures factious domestic division, is exposed to disrespect abroad; and one party, if not both, is sure, sooner or later, to invoke foreign intervention.

Nations, thus tempted to interfere, are not always able to resist the counsels of seeming expediency, and ungenerous ambition, although measures adopted under such influences seldom fail to be unfortunate and injurious to those adopting them.

. . . .

It continues to develop that the insurrection is largely, if not exclusively, a war upon the first principle of popular government—the rights of the people. Conclusive evidence of this is found in the most grave and maturely considered public documents, as well as in the general tone of the insurgents. In those documents we find the abridgement of the existing right of suffrage and the denial to the people of all right to participate in the selection of public officers, except the legislative boldly advocated, with labored arguments to prove that large control of the people in government, is the source of all political evil. Monarchy itself is sometimes hinted at as a possible refuge from the power of the people.

In my present position, I could scarcely be justified were I to omit raising a warning voice against this approach of returning despotism.

It is not needed, nor fitting here, that a general argument should be made in favor of popular institutions; but there is one point, with its connexions, not so hackneyed as most others, to which I ask a brief attention. It is the effort to place *capital* on an equal footing with, if not above *labor*, in the structure of government. It is assumed that labor is available only in connexion with capital; that nobody labors unless somebody else, owning capital, somehow by the use of it, induces him to labor. This assumed, it is next considered whether it is best that capital shall *hire* laborers, and thus induce them to work by their own consent, or *buy* them, and drive them to it without their consent. Having proceeded so far, it is naturally concluded that all laborers are either *hired* laborers, or what we call slaves. And further it is assumed that whoever is once a hired laborer, is fixed in that condition for life.

Now, there is no such relation between capital and labor as assumed; nor is there any such thing as a free man being fixed for life in the condition of a hired laborer. Both these assumptions are false, and all inferences from them are groundless.

Labor is prior to, and independent of, capital. Capital is only the fruit of labor, and could never have existed if labor had not first existed. Labor is the superior of capital, and deserves much the higher consideration. Capital has its rights, which are as worthy of protection as any other rights. Nor is it denied that there is, and probably always will be, a relation between labor and capital, producing mutual benefits. The error is in assuming that the whole labor of community exists within that relation. A few men own capital, and that few avoid labor themselves, and, with their capital, hire or buy another few to labor for them. A large majority belong to neither class—neither work for others, nor have others working for them. In most of the southern States, a majority of the whole people of all colors are neither slaves nor masters; while in the northern a large majority are neither hirers nor hired. Men with their families—wives, sons, and daughters—work for themselves, on their farms, in their houses, and in their shops, taking the whole product to themselves, and asking no favors of capital on the one hand, nor of hired laborers or slaves on the other. It is not forgotten that a considerable number of persons mingle their own labor with capital—that is, they labor with their own hands, and also buy or hire others to labor for them; but this is only a mixed, and not a distinct class. No principle stated is disturbed by the existence of this mixed class.

Again: as has already been said, there is not, of necessity, any such thing as the free hired laborer being fixed to that condition for life. Many independent men everywhere in these States, a few years back in their lives, were hired laborers. The prudent, penniless beginner in the world, labors for wages awhile, saves a surplus with which to buy tools or land for himself; then labors on his own account another while, and at length hires another new beginner to help him. This is the just, and generous, and prosperous system, which opens the way to all—gives hope to all, and consequent energy, and progress, and improvement of condition to all. No men living are more worthy to be trusted than those who toil up from poverty—none less inclined to take, or touch, aught which they have not honestly earned. Let them beware of surrendering a political power which they already possess, and which, if surrendered, will surely be used to close the door of advancement against such as they, and to fix new disabilities and burdens upon them, till all of liberty shall be lost.

From the first taking of our national census to the last are seventy years; and we find our population at the end of the period eight times as great as it was at the beginning. The increase of those other things which men deem desirable has been even greater. We thus have at one view, what the popular principle applied to government, through the machinery of the States and the Union, has produced in a given time; and also what, if firmly maintained, it promises for the future. There are already among us those, who, if the Union be preserved, will live to see it contain two hundred and fifty millions. The struggle of today, is not altogether for today—it is for a vast future also. With a reliance on Providence, all the more firm and earnest, let us proceed in the great task which events have devolved upon us.

"He Who Does Something at the Head of One Regiment"

Letter to General David Hunter

DECEMBER 31, 1861

David Hunter, an increasingly hapless general whose high rank testified to Lincoln's loyalty to friends and early inability to choose commanders wisely had written the president to complain that he was "very deeply mortified, humiliated, insulted and disgraced" to be reassigned to Fort Leavenworth. He likened it to being sent "into banishment" for "the sin" of "carrying out your views." The usually patient commander in chief responded with one of the sharpest messages he ever sent to any general. Even Lincoln could lose his temper—but, typically, he tabled this letter for a month, then sent it on to the General with instructions that it be delivered only when he "was in a good humor!!!!" Recalling this, a somewhat chastened Hunter filed it with the notation: "The President in reply to my 'ugly letter.'"

Dear Sir:

Yours of the 23rd. is received; and I am constrained to say it is difficult to answer so ugly a letter in good temper. I am, as you intimate, losing much of the great confidence I placed in you, not from any act or omission of yours touching the public service, up to the time you were sent to Leavenworth, but from the flood of grumbling despatches and letters I have seen from you since. I knew you were being ordered to Leavenworth at the time it was done; and I aver that with as tender a regard for your honor and your sensibilities as I had for my own, it never occurred to me that you were being "humiliated, insulted and disgraced"; nor have I, up to this day, heard an intimation that you have been wronged, coming from any one but yourself. No one has blamed you for the retrograde movement from Springfield, nor for the information you gave Gen. Cameron [a reference to the secretary of war—ed.]; and this you could readily understand, if it were not for your unwarranted assumption that the ordering you to Leavenworth must necessarily have been done as a *punishment* for some *fault.* I thought then, and think yet, the position assigned to you is as respo[n]sible, and as honorable, as that assigned to [General Don Carlos] Buell [then planning a campaign into Tennessee—ed.]. I know that Gen. McClellan expected more important results from it. My impression is that at the time you were assigned to the new Western Department, it had not been determined to re-place Gen. Sherman in Kentucky; but of this I am not certain, because the idea that a command in Kentucky was very desireable, and one in the farther West, very undesireable, had never occurred to me. You constantly speak of being placed in command of only 3000. Now tell me, is not this mere impatience? Have you not known all the while that you are to command four or five times that many?

I have been, and am sincerely your friend; and if, as such, I dare to make a suggestion, I would say you are adopting the best possible way to ruin yourself. "Act well your part, there all the honor lies." He who does *something* at the head of one Regiment, will eclipse him who does *nothing* at the head of a hundred.

Your friend as ever,
A. LINCOLN

"THE BOTTOM IS OUT OF THE TUB"

*Comments to Quartermaster-General Montgomery Meigs
and General Irvin McDowell*

JANUARY 10, 1862

Lincoln offered these desperate assessments of the Union military situation to Montgomery Meigs and Irvin McDowell, respectively, after General McClellan fell ill, promising to prolong his army's frustrating inactivity.

General, what shall I do? The people are impatient; [Secretary of the Treasury Salmon P.] Chase has no money, and he tells me he can raise no more; the General of the Army has typhoid fever. The bottom is out of the tub. What shall I do?

. . . .

If something was not done soon, the bottom would be out of the whole affair, and if General McClellan did not want to use the army, he would like to borrow it, provided he could see how it could be made to do something.

"THE DAY FOR A GENERAL MOVEMENT"

General War Order Number 1

JANUARY 27, 1862

Determined to set the army on the march, Lincoln decided to issue orders of his own for a major offensive to commence—as a means of inspiring the troops, he hoped—on Washington's Birthday. He was seldom more directly engaged. Though in this case somewhat naïve, for February was not an easy time to move armies. McClellan replied by stressing his heroic work training his army and insisting "many weeks may elapse before it is possible to commence the march."

President's General War Order No. 1

Ordered that the 22nd. day of February 1862, be the day for a general movement of the Land and Naval forces of the United States against the insurgent forces.

That especially—

The Army at & about, Fortress Monroe.

The Army of the Potomac.

The Army of Western Virginia[.]

The Army near Munfordsville [*sic*], Ky.

The Army and Flotilla at Cairo [Illinois—ed.]

And a Naval force in the Gulf of Mexico, be ready for a
movement on that day.

That all other forces, both on Land and Naval, with their respective commanders, obey existing orders, for the time, and be ready to obey additional orders when duly given.

That the Heads of Departments, and especially the Secretaries of War and of the Navy, with all their subordinates; and the General-in-Chief, with all other commanders and subordinates, of Land and Naval forces, will severally be held to their strict and full responsibilities, for the prompt execution of this order.

ABRAHAM LINCOLN

[Lincoln added the following extra notation to the copy he sent his new secretary of war, Edwin M. Stanton, who had recently replaced Simon Cameron in that post.—ed.]

The Secretary of War will enter this Order in his Department, and execute it to the best of his ability.

A. LINCOLN

"YOU AND I HAVE DISTINCT, AND DIFFERENT PLANS"

Letter and Memorandum to General George B. McClellan

FEBRUARY 3, 1862

General McClellan succeeded brilliantly in reorganizing and retraining the demoralized Army of the Potomac—what the vain general regarded as "a mere collection of regiments cowering on the banks of the Potomac"—after its humiliating defeat at Bull Run. But Lincoln was rapidly losing patience with the general's elaborate and delayed plans for attack, as the following letter and memorandum suggest.

My dear Sir:

You and I have distinct, and different plans for a movement of the Army of the Potomac—yours to be down the Chesapeake, up the Rappahannock to Urbana, and across land to the terminus of the Railroad on the York River—, mine to move directly to a point on the Railroad South West of Manassas.

If you will give me satisfactory answers to the following questions, I shall gladly yield my plan to yours.

1st. Does not your plan involve a greatly larger expenditure of *time*, and *money* than mine?

2nd. Wherein is a victory *more certain* by your plan than mine?

3rd. Wherein is a victory *more valuable* by your plan than mine?

4th. In fact, would it not be *less* valuable, in this, that it would break no great line of the enemie's communications, while mine would?

5th. In case of disaster, would not a safe retreat be more difficult by your plan than by mine?

Yours truly
A. LINCOLN

[Memorandum accompanying Letter to McClellan]

1. Suppose the enemy should attack us in force *before* we reach the Ocoquan [River—ed.], what? In view of the possibility of this, might it not be safest to have our entire force to move together from above the Ocoquan.

2. Suppose the enemy, in force, shall dispute the crossing of the Ocoquan, what? In view of this, might it not be safest for us to cross the Ocoquan at Colchester rather than at the village of Ocoquan? This would cost the enemy two miles more of travel to meet us, but would, on the contrary, leave us two miles further from our ultimate destination.

3. Suppose we reach Maple valley without an attack, will we not be attacked there, in force, by the enemy marching by the several roads from Manassas? and if so, what?

"ENGAGED, AS I AM, IN A GREAT WAR"

Letter to Reverend Samuel Boyd Tobey

MARCH 19, 1862

Reverend Samuel Boyd Tobey, one of the leading ministers of the Society of Friends in New England, had given a recent speech expressing support for the Lincoln administration's peaceful handling of the Trent affair. That Christmastime diplomatic crisis with England had begun when a Union ship seized two Confederate emissaries bound for diplomatic posts from international waters. After some very tense days—it was, in a way, the Cuban missile crisis of the nineteenth century—Lincoln relented and ordered the diplomats freed. The president could fight, he said, only "one war at a time." He was eager for the support from the Friends (Quakers), who hated slavery but opposed war.

My dear Sir:

A domestic affliction, of which doubtless you are informed [the recent death of Lincoln's son, Willie—ed.], has delayed me so long in making acknowledgment for the very kind and appropriate letter, signed, on behalf, and by direction of a Meeting of the Representatives of the Society of Friends for New-England, held at Providence, Rhode Island the 8th. of second month 1862, by Samuel Boyce, clerk, and presented to me by yourself and associates.

Engaged, as I am, in a great war, I fear it will be difficult for the world to understand how fully I appreciate the principles of peace, inculcated in this letter, and everywhere, by the Society of Friends. Grateful to the good people you represent for their prayers in behalf of our common country, I look forward hopefully to an early end of war, and return of peace.

Your obliged friend
A. LINCOLN

"TIME FOR YOU TO STRIKE A BLOW"

Letter to General George B. McClellan

APRIL 9, 1862

Increasingly impatient with General McClellan's chronic hesitancy, and his frequent requests for reenforcements, Lincoln wrote this acerbic note again to urge "Little Mac" to fight. The day before, bristling under Lincoln's pressure, McClellan wrote his wife to tell her that if the commander-in-chief wanted to "break the enemy's lines at once . . . he had better come & do it himself."

My dear Sir.

Your despatches complaining that you are not properly sustained, while they do not offend me, do pain me very much.

[Ludwig] Blencker's [sic] Division [Lincoln had ordered Blenker's troops detoured to safeguard Washington—ed.] was withdrawn from you before you left here; and you knew the pressure under which I did it, and, as I thought, acquiesced in it—certainly not without reluctance.

After you left, I ascertained that less than twenty thousand unorganized men, without a single field battery, were all you designed to be left for the defence of Washington, and Manassas Junction; and part of this even, was to go to Gen. Hooker's old position. Gen. Banks' corps, once designed for Manassas Junction, was diverted, and tied up on the line of Winchester and Strausburg, and could not leave it without again exposing the upper Potomac, and the Baltimore and Ohio Railroad. This presented, (or would present, when McDowell and Sumner should be gone) a great temptation to the enemy to turn back from the Rappahanock, and sack Washington. My explicit order that Washington should, by the judgment of *all* the commanders of Army corps, be left entirely secure, had been neglected. It was precisely this that drove me to detain McDowell.

I do not forget that I was satisfied with your arrangement to leave Banks at Mannassas Junction; but when that arrangement was broken up, and *nothing* was substituted for it, of course I was not satisfied. I was constrained to substitute something for it myself. And now allow me to ask "Do you really think I should permit the line from Richmond, *via* Mannassas Junction, to this city to be entirely open, except what resistance could be presented by less than twenty thousand unorganized troops?" This is a question which the country will not allow me to evade.

There is a curious mystery about the *number* of the troops now with you. When I telegraphed you on the 6th. saying you had over a hundred thousand with you, I had just obtained from the Secretary of War, a statement, taken as he said, from your own returns, making 108,000 then with you, and *en route* to you. You now say you will have but 85,000, when all *en route* to you shall have reached you. How can the discrepancy of 23,000 be accounted for?

As to Gen. [John] Wool's command, I understand it is doing for you precisely what a like number of your own would have to do, if that command was away.

I suppose the whole force which has gone forward for you, is with you by this time; and if so, I think it is the precise time for you to strike a blow. By delay the enemy will relatively gain upon you—that is, he will gain faster, by *fortifications* and *re-inforcements,* than you can by re-inforcements alone.

And, once more let me tell you, it is indispensable to *you* that you strike a blow. *I* am powerless to help this. You will do me the justice to remember I always insisted, that going down the Bay in search of a field, instead of fighting at or near Mannassas, was only shifting, and not surmounting, a difficulty—that we would find the same enemy, and the same, or equal, intrenchments, at either place. The country will not fail to note—is now noting—that the present hesitation to move upon an intrenched enemy, is but the story of Manassas repeated.

I beg to assure you that I have never written you, or spoken to you, in greater kindness of feeling than now, nor with a fuller purpose to sustain you, so far as in my most anxious judgment, I consistently can. *But you must act.*

Yours very truly
A. LINCOLN

"THE CASUALTIES AND CALAMITIES OF SEDITION"

Proclamation of Thanksgiving for Victories

APRIL 10, 1862

Lincoln often issued thanksgiving proclamations after military suc-cesses—even modest ones—indicating not only his growing reliance on divine guidance but also his canny gift for linking the Union cause with God's will. This typical example followed Ulysses S. Grant's costly but confidence-building victory at the Battle of Shiloh. This same day, Lincoln approved a milestone congressional resolution calling for gradual emancipation in slaveholding Union states like Maryland and Delaware.

By the President of the United States of America. A Proclamation.

It has pleased Almighty God to vouchsafe signal victories to the land and naval forces engaged in suppressing an internal rebellion, and at the same time to avert from our country the dangers of for-eign intervention and invasion.

It is therefore recommended to the People of the United States that, at their next weekly assemblages in their accustomed places of public worship which shall occur after notice of this proclama-tion shall have been received, they especially acknowledge and ren-der thanks to our Heavenly Father for these inestimable blessings; that they then and there implore spiritual consolations in behalf of all who have been brought into affliction by the casualties and ca-lamities of sedition and civil war, and that they reverently invoke the Divine Guidance for our national counsels, to the end that they may speedily result in the restoration of peace, harmony, and unity throughout our borders, and hasten the establishment of fraternal relations among all the countries of the earth.

In witness whereof, I have hereunto set my hand and caused the seal of the United States to be affixed.

Done at the City of Washington, this tenth day of April, in the year of our Lord one thousand eight hundred and sixty-two, and of the Independence of the United States the eighty-sixth.

By the President: ABRAHAM LINCOLN

WILLIAM H. SEWARD, Secretary of State.

"IS ANYTHING TO BE DONE"

Telegram to General George B. McClellan

MAY 1, 1862

A few days earlier, General McClellan had told Secretary of War Edwin M. Stanton he would "soon be ready to open" his long-planned campaign on the Virginia Peninsula but wanted first to have at his disposal more troops as well as the transfer of thirty-pound Parrott guns currently protecting Washington. After receiving this, the president's irritable reply, McClellan tried explaining: "I asked for the parrott guns from Washington for the reason that some expected had been two weeks nearly on the way and could not be heard from. . . . My object was to hasten not procrastinate." Privately, the general told his wife, "I feel that I have not one single friend at the seat of Govt." McClellan finally launched his offensive, but his sluggish effort to capture the Confederate capital of Richmond failed.

Major Gen. McClellan

Your call for Parrott guns from Washington alarms me—chiefly because it argues indefinite procrastination. Is anything to be done?

A. LINCOLN

"BRILLIANT OPERATIONS OF THE SQUADRON"

Message to Congress on the Capture of New Orleans

MAY 14, 1862

Always generous with praise, Lincoln submitted this request for congressional thanks for the heroes of the New Orleans campaign. The president listed thirty-one names in all for commendation. The House and Senate passed such a resolution on July 11.

To the Senate and House of Representatives:

I submit, herewith, a list of naval officers who commanded vessels engaged in the recent brilliant operations of the squadron commanded by Flag-Officer [David G.] Farragut, which led to the capture of Forts Jackson and St. Philip [on the Mississippi—ed.], city of New Orleans, and the destruction of rebel gunboats, rams, &c., in April, 1862. For their services and gallantry on those occasions I cordially recommend that they should by name, receive a vote of thanks of Congress.

"SUCH SUPPOSED POWER . . . I RESERVE TO MYSELF"

Proclamation Revoking General David Hunter's Emancipation Order

MAY 19, 1862

On May 9, General David Hunter declared martial law and abolished slavery throughout his Department of the South (South Carolina, Georgia, and Florida). Ten days later, the president rebuked and revoked the precipitant order. As he explained to Secretary of the Treasury Salmon P. Chase, "No commanding general shall do such a thing, on my responsibility, without consulting me." But Lincoln also used what he called this "counter-proclamation" in part to offer another eloquent plea for compensated emancipation everywhere—a last-ditch effort to move liberation forward before he resorted to an emancipation proclamation of his own.

By the President of the United States of America.
A Proclamation.

Whereas there appears in the public prints, what purports to be a proclamation, of Major General Hunter, in the words and figures following, towit:

Headquarters Department of the South,
Hilton Head, S.C., May 9, 1862.

General Orders No. 11.—The three States of Georgia, Florida, and South Carolina, comprising the military department of the South, having deliberately declared themselves no longer under the protection of the United States of America, and having taken up arms against the said United States, it becomes a military necessity to declare them under martial law. This was accordingly done on the 25th day of April, 1862. Slavery and martial law in a free country are altogether incompatible; the persons in these three States—Georgia, Florida and South Carolina—heretofore held as slaves, are therefore declared forever free.

(Official)   David Hunter . . .

And whereas the same is producing some excitement, and misunderstanding: therefore

I, Abraham Lincoln, president of the United States, proclaim and declare, that the government of the United States, had no knowledge, information, or belief, of an intention on the part of General Hunter to issue such a proclamation; nor has it yet, any authentic information that the document is genuine. And further, that neither General Hunter, nor any other commander, or person, has been authorized by the Government of the United States, to make proclamations declaring the slaves of any State free; and that the supposed proclamation, now in question, whether genuine or false, is altogether void, so far as respects such declaration.

I further make known that whether it be competent for me, as Commander-in-Chief of the Army and Navy, to declare the Slaves of any state or states, free, and whether at any time, in any case, it shall have become a necessity indispensable to the maintenance of the government, to exercise such supposed power, are questions which, under my responsibility, I reserve to myself, and which I can not feel justified in leaving to the decision of commanders in the field. These are totally different questions from those of police regulations in armies and camps.

On the sixth day of March last, by a special message, I recommended to Congress the adoption of a joint resolution to be substantially as follows:

Resolved. That the United States ought to co-operate with any State which may adopt a gradual abolishment of slavery, giving to such State pecuniary aid, to be used by such State in its discretion to compensate for the inconveniences, public and private, produced by such change of system.

The resolution, in the language above quoted, was adopted by large majorities in both branches of Congress, and now stands [as] an authentic, definite, and solemn proposal of the nation to the States and people most immediately interested in the subject matter. To the people of those states I now earnestly appeal. I do not argue. I beseech you to make the arguments for yourselves. You can not if you would, be blind to the signs of the times. I beg of you a calm and enlarged consideration of them, ranging, if it may be, far above personal and partizan politics. This proposal makes common cause for a common object, casting no reproaches upon any. It acts not the pharisee. The change it contemplates would come gently as the dews of heaven, not rending or wrecking anything. Will you not embrace it? So much good has not been done, by one effort, in all past time, as, in the providence of God, it is now your high previlege to do. May the vast future not have to lament that you have neglected it.

In witness whereof, I have hereunto set my hand, and caused the seal of the United States to be affixed.

> Done at the City of Washington this nineteenth day of May, in the year of our Lord, one thousand eight hundred and sixty-two, and of the Independence of the United States the eighty-sixth.

By the President: ABRAHAM LINCOLN.
WILLIAM H. SEWARD, Secretary of State.

"STAND ON THE DEFENSIVE"

Letter to Secretary of War Edwin M. Stanton

JUNE 8, 1862

With the Army of the Potomac advancing ever so slowly westward along the Virginia Peninsula toward Richmond, facing endless diversionary thrusts from Confederate defenders, Lincoln took up his pen to remind his new secretary of war (Stanton had replaced Simon Cameron in January) that the Rebel capital remained the main objective of the campaign. Lincoln's grasp of details had become quite impressive, even if the poorly executed union offensive was destined for failure.

My dear Sir:

Richmond is the principal point for active operation. Accordingly it is the object of the enemy to create alarms everywhere else and thereby to divert as much of our force from that point as possible. On the contrary, as a general rule, we should stand on the defensive everywhere else, and direct as much force as possible to Richmond. You will therefore please make orders substantially as follows. Let the Western line of the Mountain Department be moved Eastward so as to throw all or nearly all of Kentucky and Tennessee into Gen. Halleck's Department. Let the Eastern boundary of the

Mountain Department and the Eastern boundary of the Department of the Shenandoah be changed substantially as suggested by Gen. McDowell in his despatch upon that subject. Let Gen. Fremont, with his main force, take position, at or near Harrisonburg, with the double object of guarding against raids down the valley of the Shenandoah, and also, in conjunction with his force under Gen. [Jacob D.] Cox, against raids into Western Virginia. Let Gen [Nathaniel] Banks occupy Front-Royal, with an advance at Luray or other point in supporting distance of Gen. Fremont, and also with detachments in the old positions of Gen. [John W.] Geary and Gen. [Abram] Duryea on the Railroads. And let Gen. McDowell move upon Richmond.

Yours truly
A. LINCOLN

"My Visit to West Point"

Impromptu Remarks at Jersey City, New Jersey

JUNE 24, 1862

As president, Lincoln was a reluctant and often surprisingly ineffective extemporaneous speaker. These rather lame remarks came at a railroad station in New Jersey in response to crowds who unexpectedly gathered to see him when he paused there en route home to Washington from what was supposed to be a top-secret visit to retired general Winfield Scott at West Point. Scott had advised Lincoln that "the defeat of the Rebels, at Richmond, or their forced retreat, thence, combined without previous victories, would be a virtual end of the rebellion, & soon restore entire Virginia to the Union." But it was not to be—not yet. And Lincoln's amusing, rather evasive remarks at Jersey City probably did little to build public confidence in the administration.

When birds and animals are looked at through a fog they are seen to disadvantage, and so it might be with you if I were to attempt to tell you why I went to see Gen. Scott. I can only say that my visit to West Point did not have the importance which has been attached to it; but it conceived [concerned—ed.] matters that you understand quite as well as if I were to tell you all about them. Now, I can only remark that it had nothing whatever to do with making or unmaking any General in the country. [Laughter and applause.] The Secretary of War, you know, holds a pretty tight rein on the Press, so that they shall not tell more than they ought to, and I'm afraid that if I blab too much he might draw a tight rein on me.

"THE PRESENT CONDITION OF THE WAR"

Letter to Secretary of State William H. Seward

JUNE 28, 1862

Lincoln prepared this report for William Seward's use in urging Union governors to supply the army with fresh troops. The personal touch failed to work, so on July 1 the president issued a formal call for three hundred thousand more volunteers, chiefly infantry, with specific enrollment quotas for each state. This letter is interesting, though, for its valuable update from the commander in chief on the progress of the war after a year of fighting. Five days later, Lincoln told the governors: "The quicker you send [troops], the fewer you will have to send. Time is everything."

My dear Sir

My view of the present condition of the War is about as follows:

The evacuation of Corinth, and our delay by the flood in the Chicahominy, has enabled the enemy to concentrate too much force in Richmond for McClellan to successfully attack. In fact there soon will be no substantial rebel force any where else. But if we send all the force from here to McClellan, the enemy will, before we can know of it, send a force from Richmond and take Washington. Or, if a large part of the Western Army be brought here to McClellan, they will let us have Richmond, and retake Tennessee, Kentucky, Missouri &c. What should be done is to hold what we have in the West, open the Mississippi, and, take Chatanooga & East Tennessee, without more—a reasonable force should, in every event, be kept about Washington for it's protection. Then let the country give us a hundred thousand new troops in the shortest possible time, which added to McClellan, directly or indirectly, will take Richmond, without endangering any other place which we now hold—and will substantially end the war. I expect to maintain this contest until successful, or till I die, or am conquered, or my term expires, or Congress or the country forsakes me; and I would publicly appeal to the country for this new force, were it not that I fear a general panic and stampede would follow—so hard is it to have a thing understood as it really is. I think the new force should be all, or nearly all infantry, principally because such can be raised most cheaply and quickly.

Yours very truly
A. LINCOLN

"SAVE YOUR ARMY AT ALL EVENTS"

Letter to General George B. McClellan

JUNE 28, 1862

Following his defeat at the Battle of Gaines's Mill, Virginia, on June 27, McClellan sent a blistering report to Secretary of War Edwin M. Stanton blaming the loss on the administration's reluctance to send reinforcements from Washington. Calling this second of the so-called Seven Days' Battles "a terrible fight against vastly superior numbers"— an exaggeration, as usual—McClellan's account was so insubordinate ("If I save this Army now I tell you plainly that I owe no thanks to you or any other persons in Washington," he told Stanton), the telegraph operator deleted this section before delivering it to the War Department. This is Lincoln's reply.

Major Gen. McClellan

Save your Army at all events. Will send re-inforcements as fast as we can. Of course they can not reach you to-today, to-morrow, or next day. I have not said you were ungenerous for saying you needed re-inforcement. I thought you were ungenerous in assuming that I did not send them as fast as I could. I feel any misfortune to you and your Army quite as keenly as you feel it yourself. If you have had a drawn battle, or a repulse, it is the price we pay for the enemy not being in Washington. We protected Washington, and the enemy concentrated on you; had we stripped Washington, he would have been upon us before the troops sent could have got to you. Less than a week ago you notified us that re-inforcements were leaving Richmond to come in front of us. It is the nature of the case, and neither you or the government that is to blame. Please tell at once the present condition and aspect of things.

A. LINCOLN

P.S. Gen. Pope thinks if you fall back, it would be much better towards York River, than towards the James. As Pope now has charge of the Capital, please confer with him through the telegraph.

A.L.

"IS THE ARMY SECURE?"

Notes from Lincoln's Visit to the Front

HARRISON'S LANDING, VIRGINIA, JULY 8–9, 1862

Following McClellan's Peninsula Campaign disaster, Lincoln spent more than two days visiting army headquarters at Fortress Monroe and Harrison's Landing, Virginia, interviewing several generals and taking these meticulous notes on the state of the army. The president was rousingly cheered by the troops—but hardly consoled by the inertia of his high command. The nature and repetition of the questions he carefully recorded below suggest Lincoln had much concern about the

soldiers' well-being and little faith in the reliability of McClellan's analy-
sis. Perhaps reeling from the contrary data, Lincoln moved two days
later to promote Henry W. Halleck to general in chief "to command the
whole land forces of the United States," including McClellan's Army of
the Potomac.

GEN. McCLELLAN JULY 8. 1862

What amount of force have you now?

About 80-000—cant vary much—certainly 75-000.

What is likely to be your condition as to health in this camp?

Better than in any encampment since landing at Fort Monroe.

Where is the enemy now?

From four to 5. miles from us on all the roads—I think nearly
the whole Army. Both Hills—Longstreet, Jackson, Magruder,
Huger.

If you desired, could you remove your army safely?

It would be a delicate & very difficult matter.

Cavalry about 5000—

GEN. [EDWIN VOSE "BULL HEAD"] SUMNER—JULY 9. 1862

What is the whole amount of your corps with you now?

About 16,000

What is the aggregate of your killed, wounded, and missing from
the attack on the 26th. ult [the beginning of the Seven Days'
Battles—ed.] till now?

1175

In your present encampment what is the present and prospective
condition as to health?

As good as any part of Eastern Va.

Where, & in what condition do you believe the enemy to now be

I think they have retired from our front, were much damaged,
especially in their best troops in the late actions from superiority
of our arms

If it were desired to get the Army away, could it be safely effected?

    I think we could, but I think we give up the cause if we do it. [Withdrawal, of course, would have conceded the impossibility of capturing Richmond.—ed.]

Is the Army secure in its present position?

    Perfectly so, in my judgment.

GEN. [CHARLES] HEINZELMAN—JULY 9, 1862

What is the whole amount of your corps now with you?

    15-000 for duty

What is the aggregate of your killed, wounded, and missing from the attack on the 16. ult. Till now?

    Not large. 745.

In your present encampment, what is the present and prospective condition as to health?

    Excellent for health & present health improving.

Where, and in what condition do you believe the enemy to now be?

    Dont think they are in force in our vicinity.

If it were desired to get the Army away from here could it be safely effected?

    Perhaps we could, but think it would be ruinous to the country.

Is the Army secure in its present position? [Not in Lincoln's handwriting—ed.]

    I think it is safe.

GEN. [ERASMUS D.] KEYES—JULY 9. 1862

What is the whole amount of your corps with you now?

    About 12-500

What is the aggregate of your killed, wounded, and missing, from the attack on the 26th till now?

    Less than 500.

In your present encampment, what is the present & prospective condition as to health?

    A little improved, but think camp is getting worse

Where, and in what condition, do you believe the enemy to now be?
   Think he has withdrawn & think preparing to go to
   Washington.
If it were desired to get the Army away, could it be safely effected?
   With help of Gen. B[urnisde]. can hold position.

GEN [FITZ JOHN] PORTER

What is the amount of your corps now with you? [This and all
questions to Porter in another handwriting; all answers in
Lincoln's hand—ed.]
   About 23,000
   Fully 20-000 fit, for duty.
What is the aggregate of your killed wounded and missing from
the attack on the 26th. ult. until now?
   Over 5000.
In your present encampment, what is the present and prospective
condition as to health?
   Very good.
Where and in what condition do you believe the enemy now to be?
   Believe he is mainly near Richmond. He feels he dare not attack
   us here.
If it were desired to get the army away from here, could it be safely
effected?
   Perfectly so. Not only but, we are ready to begin moving
   forward.

"A FIT AND NECESSARY MILITARY MEASURE"

First Draft of an Emancipation Proclamation

[JULY 22, 1862]

Lincoln read this roughly drafted decree—which he later described as the "Emancipation Proclamation as first sketched and shown to the Cabinet in July 1862"—at a Cabinet meeting on the twenty-second. But Lincoln received scant support for its issuance from his ministers. Secretary of State William H. Seward, who thought the North would react as if it were the administration's "last shriek, on the retreat," urged the president to postpone his order until the Union army could win a military victory. Lincoln agreed to do so. The proclamation (which he ultimately rewrote) remained unissued for two more months.

In pursuance of the sixth section of the act of congress entitled "An act to suppress insurrection and to punish treason and rebellion, to seize and confiscate property of rebels, and for other purposes" [this section gave Rebels sixty days to cease their insurrection or face seizure of their property—ed.] Approved July 17, 1862, and which act, and the Joint Resolution explanatory thereof, are herewith published, I, Abraham Lincoln, President of the United States, do hereby proclaim to, and warn all persons within the contemplation of said sixth section to cease participating in, aiding, countenancing, or abetting the existing rebellion, or any rebellion against the government of the United States, and to return to their proper allegiance to the United States, on pain of the forfeitures and seizures, as within and by said sixth section provided.

And I hereby make known that it is my purpose, upon the next meeting of congress, to again recommend the adoption of a practical measure for tendering pecuniary aid to the free choice or rejection, of any and all States which may then be recognizing and practically sustaining the authority of the United States, and which may then have voluntarily adopted, or thereafter may voluntarily adopt, gradual abolishment of slavery within such State or States—that the object is to practically restore, thenceforward to be maintain[ed], the constitutional relation between the general government, and each, and all the states, wherein that relation is now suspended, or disturbed; and that, for this object, the war, as it has been, will be, prossecuted. And, as a fit and necessary military measure for effecting this object, I, as Commander-in-Chief of the Army and Navy of the United States, do order and declare that on the first day of January in the year of Our Lord one thousand, eight hundred and sixty-three, all persons held as slaves within any state or states, wherein the constitutional authority of the United States shall not then be practically recognized, submitted to, and maintained, shall then, thenceforward, and forever, be free.

"RECRUITING SLAVES"

Memorandum on Black Recruitment

CA. JULY 22, 1862

As Lincoln pondered his next steps on emancipation, he began formulating new government policy on black recruitment—another precedent-shattering decision initiated by the recent congressional Confiscation Act, which called for freedom for slaves in rebellious states, but left enforcement to federal courts, which basically no longer functioned in the South. Lincoln likely wrote down these thoughts at the same time he drafted his initial proclamation.

To recruiting free negroes, no objection.

To recruiting slaves of *disloyal* owners, no objection.

To recruiting slaves of loyal owners, *with their consent*, no objection.

To recruiting slaves of loyal owners *without* consent, objection, *unless the necessity is urgent.*

To conducting offensively, while recruiting, and to carrying away slaves not suitable for recruits, objection.

"SEIZE AND USE ANY PROPERTY"

Instructions to Secretary of War Edwin M. Stanton

CA. JULY 22, 1862

These instructions became, officially, General Order No. 109 in mid-August, further revolutionizing government policy on slavery.

1.

Ordered that Military commanders, within the States of Virginia, South Carolina, Georgia, Florida, Alabama, Mississippi, Louisiana, Texas and Arkansas, in an orderly manner, seize and use any property, real or personal, which may be necessary or convenient for their several commands, as supplies, or for other military purposes; and that, while property may be destroyed for proper military objects, none shall be destroyed, in wantonness or malice.

2.

That military, and Naval commanders shall employ, as laborers, within, and from said States, so many persons of African descent, as can be advantageously used, for Military or Naval purposes, giving them reasonable wages for their labor [Lincoln deleted the following addition: "and subsistence for themselves, and the helpless members of their families with them, if any"—ed.].

[3.]

That as to both property, and persons of African descent, accounts shall be kept, sufficiently accurate, and in detail to show quantities and amounts and from whom, both property, and such persons shall have come, as a basis upon which compensation can be made in proper cases. And the several Departments of this government shall attend to, and perform their appropriate parts towards the execution of these orders.

"ELDER-STALK SQUIRTS, CHARGED WITH ROSE WATER"

Letter to Cuthbert Bullitt

JULY 28, 1862

Lincoln wrote this frustrated letter to the acting collector of customs at New Orleans who, with a local pro-Union ally, Thomas Durant, had exchanged letters to protest what they considered the harsh occupation of the city by the Union army. By prearrangement, this letter was also made public—despite the president's strong language promising a harsh war.

Private

Sir:

The copy of a letter addressed to yourself by Mr. Thomas J. Durant, has been shown to me. The writer appears to be an able, a dispassionate, and an entirely sincere man. The first part of the letter is devoted to an effort to show that the Secession Ordinance of Louisiana was adopted against the will of a majority of the people. This is probably true; and in that fact may be found some instruction. Why did they allow the Ordinance to go into effect? Why did they not assert themselves? Why stand passive and allow themselves to be trodden down by a minority? Why did they not hold popular meetings, and have a convention of their own, to express and enforce the true sentiment of the state? If preorganization was against them *then,* why not do this *now,* that the United States Army is present to protect them? The paralysis—the dead palsy—of the government in this whole struggle is, that this class of men will do nothing for the government, nothing for themselves, except demanding that the government shall not strike its open enemies, lest they be struck by accident!

Mr. Durant complains that in various ways the relation of master and slave is disturbed by the presence of our Army; and he considers it particularly vexatious that this, in part, is done under cover of an act of Congress, while constitutional guaranties are suspended on the plea of military necessity. The truth is, that what is done, and omitted, about slaves, is done and omitted on the same military necessity. It is a military necessity to have men and money; and we can get neither, in sufficient numbers, or amounts, if we keep from, or drive from, our lines, slaves coming to them. Mr. Durant cannot be ignorant of the pressure in this direction; nor of my efforts to hold it within bounds till he, and such as he shall have time to help themselves.

I am not posted to speak understandingly on all the police regulations of which Mr. Durant complains. If experience shows any one of them to be wrong, let them be set right. I think I can perceive, in the freedom of trade, which Mr. Durant urges, that he would relieve both friends and enemies from the pressure of the blockade. By this he would serve the enemy more effectively than the enemy is able to serve himself. I do not say or believe that to serve the enemy is the purpose of Mr. Durant; or that he is conscious of any purpose, other than national and patriotic ones. Still, if there were a class of men who, having no choice of sides in the contest, were anxious only to have quiet and comfort for themselves while it rages, and to fall in with the victorious side at the end of it, without loss to themselves, their advice as to the mode of conducting the contest would be precisely such as his is. He speaks of no duty—apparently thinks of none—resting upon Union men. He even thinks it injurious to the Union cause that they should be restrained in trade and passage without taking sides. They are to touch neither a sail nor a pump, but to be merely passengers,—dead-heads at that—to be carried snug and dry, throughout the storm, and safely landed right side up. Nay, more; even a mutineer is to go untouched lest these sacred passengers receive an accidental wound.

Of course the rebellion will never be suppressed in Louisiana, if the professed Union men there will neither help to do it, nor permit the government to do it without their help.

Now, I think the true remedy is very different from what is suggested by Mr. Durant. It does not lie in rounding the rough angles of the war, but in removing the necessity for the war. The people of Louisiana who wish protection to person and property, have but to reach forth their hands and take it. Let them, in good faith, re-inaugurate the national authority, and set up a State Government conforming thereto under the constitution. They know how to do it, and can have the protection of the Army while doing it. The Army will be withdrawn so soon as such State government can dispense with its presence; and the people of the State can then upon the old Constitutional terms, govern themselves to their own liking. This is very simple and easy.

If they will not do this, if they prefer to hazard all for the sake of destroying the government, it is for them to consider whether it is probable I will surrender the government to save them from losing all. If they decline what I suggest, you scarcely need to ask what I will do. What would you do in my position? Would you drop the war where it is? Or, would you prosecute it in future, with elder-stalk squirts, charged with rose water? Would you deal lighter blows rather than heavier ones? Would you give up the contest, leaving any available means unapplied.

I am in no boastful mood. I shall not do *more* than I can, and I shall do *all* I can to save the government, which is my sworn duty as well as my personal inclination. I shall do nothing in malice. What I deal with is too vast for malicious dealing.

Yours truly

A. LINCOLN

"I WILL MAKE QUICK WORK WITH THEM"

Letter to Governor John A. Andrew

AUGUST 12, 1862

Massachusetts governor John A. Andrew had wired the president to alert him that bureaucratic complications within the military in his home state were causing delays in sending troops south. Lincoln fired off this explosive reply the following day.

Gov. Andrew,
Boston, Mass.

Your dispatch saying "I cant get those regts. off because I cant get quick work out of the U. S. disbursing officer & the Paymaster" is received.

Please say to these gentlemen that if they do not work quickly I will make quick work with them. In the name of all that is reasonable, how long does it take to pay a couple of Regts.?

We were never more in need of the arrival of Regts. than now— even to-day.

A. LINCOLN.

"MY PARAMOUNT OBJECT IN THIS STRUGGLE"

Letter to Horace Greeley

AUGUST 22, 1862

On August 20, Horace Greeley's New York Tribune *published "The Prayer of Twenty Millions," a scathing editorial characterizing Lincoln as "strangely and disastrously remiss . . . with regard to the emancipating provisions of the new Confiscation Act" (a flawed new law authorizing the liberation of slaves to punish Rebels, but lacking a reliable means of enforcement). Lincoln seized the opportunity to write this widely published reply, which has often been quoted oversimplistically to suggest he cared more about Union than freedom. But Lincoln composed it knowing he had already met the* Tribune's *demands by drafting an emancipation proclamation, whose announcement awaited only a military victory. Greeley did not realize it, but he had given Lincoln a perfect opportunity to couch his forthcoming order as a matter of military necessity, rather than a humanitarian gesture, which would have elicited far more opposition. Notwithstanding all these political and public relations complications, the letter still stands as one of Lincoln's most brilliant expressions of Union-preserving ideology and strategy.*

Dear Sir

I have just read yours of the 19th. addressed to myself through the New-York Tribune. If there be in it any statements, or assumptions of fact, which I may know to be erroneous, I do not, now and here, controvert them. If there be in it any inferences which I may believe to be falsely drawn, I do not now and here, argue against them. If there be perceptible in it an impatient and dictatorial tone, I waive it in deference to an old friend, whose heart I have always supposed to be right.

As to the policy I "seem to be pursuing" as you say, I have not meant to leave any one in doubt.

I would save the Union. I would save it the shortest way under the Constitution. The sooner the national authority can be restored; the nearer the Union will be "the Union as it was." [Lincoln crossed out the following sentence: "Broken eggs can never be mended, and the longer the breaking proceeds the more will be broken."—ed.] If there be those who would not save the Union unless they could at the same time *destroy* slavery, I do not agree with them. My paramount object in this struggle *is* to save the Union, and is *not* either to save or destroy slavery. If I could save the Union without freeing *any* slave I would do it, and if I could save it by freeing *all* the slaves I would do it; and if I could save it by freeing some and leaving others alone I would also do that. What I do about slavery, and the colored race, I do because I believe it helps to save the Union; and what I forbear, I forbear because I do *not* believe it would help to save the Union. I shall do *less* whenever I shall believe what I am doing hurts the cause, and I shall do *more* whenever I shall believe doing more will help the cause. I shall try to correct errors when shown to be errors; and I shall adopt new views so fast as they shall appear to be true views.

I have here stated my purpose according to my view of *official* duty; and I intend no modification of my oft-expressed *personal* wish that all men every where could be free.

Yours,
A. LINCOLN

"WE MAY AS WELL STOP FIGHTING"

Comments to Assistant Private Secretary John Hay

AUGUST 31, SEPTEMBER 1, 1862

Lincoln had dismissed George McClellan in August, giving command to General John Pope. The president made these anguished comments in the wake of the Army of the Potomac's loss under the hapless Pope at the Second Battle of Bull Run. Days later, with few options left, Lincoln reinstated McClellan.

Well, John, we are whipped again, I am afraid. The enemy reinforced on Pope and drove back his left wing, and he has retired to Centreville [Virginia—ed.], where he says he will be able to hold his men. I don't like that expression. I don't like to hear him admit that his men need "holding."

. . . .

Mr. Hay, we must rip these people now. Pope must fight them. If they are too strong for him, he can gradually retire to these fortifications. If this be not so, if we are really whipped and to be whipped, we may as well stop fighting.

"THESE ARE NOT ... THE DAYS OF MIRACLES"

From a Reply to Chicago Christians

SEPTEMBER 13, 1862

A public meeting of Chicago Christians of all denominations had adopted a call for immediate emancipation on September 7, and two ministers then traveled to Washington to give the president its so-called memorial, or petition to the government. Still struggling to find a rationale—and opportunity—to pursue the very policy his visitors proposed, Lincoln replied with the following remarks, which ironically were reported in the Chicago papers in the same editions that carried the news of his Emancipation Proclamation.

What *good* would a proclamation of emancipation from me do, especially as we are now situated? I do not want to issue a document that the whole world will see must necessarily be inoperative, like the Pope's bull against the comet! Would *my word* free the slaves, when I cannot even enforce the Constitution in the rebel States? Is there a single court, or magistrate, or individual that would be influenced by it there? And what reason is there to think it would have any greater effect upon the slaves than the late law of Congress, which I approved, and which offers protection and freedom to the slaves of rebel masters who come within our lines? Yet I cannot learn that that law has caused a single slave to come over to us. And suppose they could be induced by a proclamation of freedom from me to throw themselves upon us, *what should we do with them?* How can we feed and care for such a multitude? Gen. Butler wrote me a few days since that he was issuing more rations to the slaves who have rushed to him than to all the white troops under his command. They *eat,* and that is all, though it is true Gen. Butler is feeding the whites also by the thousand; for it nearly amounts to a famine there. If, now, the pressure of the war should call off our forces from New Orleans to defend some other point, what is to prevent the masters from reducing the blacks to slavery again; for I am told that whenever the rebels take any black prisoners, free or slave, they immediately auction them off! They did so with those they took from a boat that was aground in the Tennessee river a few days ago. And then *I am very ungenerously arracked for it*! For instance, when, after the late battles at and near Bull Run, an expedition went out from Washington under a flag of truce to bury the dead and bring in the wounded, and the rebels seized the blacks who went along to help and sent them into slavery, Horace Greely said in his paper that the Government would probably do nothing about it. What *could* I do? [Here your delegation suggested that this was a gross outrage on a flag of truce, which covers and protects all over which it waves, and that whatever he could do if *white* men had been similarly detained he *could* do in this case.]

Now, then, tell me, if you please, what possible result of good would follow the issuing of such a proclamation as you desire? Understand, I raise no objections against it on legal or constitutional grounds; for, as commander-in-chief of the army and navy, in time of war, I suppose I have a right to take any measure which may best subdue the enemy. Nor do I urge objections of a moral nature, in view of possible consequences of insurrection and massacre at the South. I view the matter as a practical war measure, to be decided upon according to the advantages or disadvantages it may offer to the suppression of the rebellion.

I admit that slavery is the root of the rebellion, or at least its *sine qua non*. The ambition of politicians may have instigated them to act, but they would have been impotent without slavery as their instrument. I will also concede that emancipation would help us in Europe, and convince them that we are incited by something more than ambition. I grant further that it would help *somewhat* at the North, though not so much, I fear, as you and those you represent imagine. Still, some additional strength would be added in that way to the war. And then unquestionably it would weaken the rebels by drawing off their laborers, which is of great importance. But I am not so sure we could do much with the blacks. If we were to arm them, I fear that in a few weeks the arms would be in the hands of the rebels; and indeed thus far we have not had arms enough to equip our white troops. I will mention another thing, though it meet only your scorn and contempt: There are fifty thousand bayonets in the Union armies from the Border Slave States. It would be a serious matter if, in consequence of a proclamation such as you desire, they should go over to the rebels. I do not think they all would—not so many indeed as a year ago, or as six months ago—not so many to-day as yesterday. Every day increases their Union feeling. They are also getting their pride enlisted, and want to beat the rebels. Let me say one thing more: I think you should admit that we already have an important principle to rally and unite the people in the fact that constitutional government is at stake. This is a fundamental idea, going down about as deep as any thing.

"THENCEFORWARD AND FOREVER FREE"

The Preliminary Emancipation Proclamation

SEPTEMBER 22, 1862

General McClellan finally won a major victory at the Battle of Antietam on September 17. Five days later, keeping a promise he had made—he told his cabinet—to God, Lincoln issued this "preliminary" proclamation, which gave Confederate slave owners one hundred days to return to the Union and lay down their arms, or else lose their "property" forever.

By the President of the United States of America
A Proclamation.

I, Abraham Lincoln, President of the United States of America, and Commander-in-chief of the Army and Navy thereof, do hereby proclaim and declare that hereafter, as heretofore, the war will be prossecuted for the object of practically restoring the constitutional relation between the United States, and each of the states, and the people thereof, in which states that relation is, or may be suspended, or disturbed.

That it is my purpose, upon the next meeting of Congress to again recommend the adoption of a practical measure tendering pecuniary aid to the free acceptance or rejection of all slave-states, so called, the people whereof may not then be in rebellion against the United States, and which states, may then have voluntarily adopted, or thereafter may voluntarily adopt, immediate, or gradual abolishment of slavery within their respective limits; and that the effort to colonize persons of African descent, with their consent, upon this continent, or elsewhere, with the previously obtained consent of the Governments existing there, will be continued.

That on the first day of January in the year of our Lord, one thousand eight hundred and sixty-three, all persons held as slaves within any state, or designated part of a state, the people whereof shall then be in rebellion against the United States shall be then, thenceforward, and forever free; and the executive government of the United States, including the military and naval authority thereof, will recognize and maintain the freedom of such persons, and will do no act or acts to repress such persons, or any of them, in any efforts they may make for their actual freedom.

That the executive will, on the first day of January aforesaid, by proclamation, designate the States, and parts of states, if any, in which the people thereof respectively, shall then be in rebellion against the United States; and the fact that any state, or the people thereof shall, on that day be, in good faith represented in the Congress of the United States, by members chosen thereto, at elections wherein a majority of the qualified voters of such state shall have participated, shall, in the absence of strong countervailing testimony, be deemed conclusive evidence that such state and the people thereof, are not then in rebellion against the United States.

That attention is hereby called to an act of Congress entitled "An act to make an additional Article of War" approved March 13, 1862, and which act is in the words and figure following:

[Here Lincoln pasted in clipped sections of the published bill. —ed.]

Be it enacted by the Senate and House of Representatives of the United States of America in Congress assembled, That hereafter the following shall be promulgated as an additional article of war for the government of the army of the United States, and shall be obeyed and observed as such:

Article—. All officers or persons in the military or naval service of the United States are prohibited from employing any of the forces under their respective commands for the purpose of returning fugitives from service or labor, who may have escaped from any persons to whom such service or labor is claimed to be due, and any officer who shall be found guilty by a court-martial of violating this article shall be dismissed from the service.

SEC. 2. *And be it further enacted,* That this act shall take effect from and after its passage.

Also to the ninth and tenth sections of an act entitled "An Act to suppress Insurrection, to punish Treason and Rebellion, to seize and confiscate property of rebels, and for other purposes," approved July 17, 1862, and which sections are in the words and figures following:

SEC. 9. *And be it further enacted,* That all slaves of persons who shall hereafter be engaged in rebellion against the government of the United States, or who shall in any way give aid or comfort thereto, escaping from such persons and taking refuge within the lines of the army; and all slaves captured from such persons or deserted by them and coming under the control of the government of the United States; and all slaves of such persons found *on* (or) being within any place occupied by rebel forces and afterwards occupied by the forces of the United States, shall be deemed captives of war, and shall be forever free of their servitude and not again held as slaves.

SEC. 10. *And be it further enacted,* That no slave escaping into any State, Territory, or the District of Columbia, from any other State, shall be delivered up, or in any way impeded or hindered of his liberty, except for crime, or some offence against the laws, unless the person claiming said fugitive shall first make oath that the person to whom the labor or service of such fugitive is alleged to be due is his lawful owner, and has not borne arms against the United States in the present rebellion, nor in any way given aid and comfort thereto; and no person engaged in the military or naval service of the United States shall, under any pretence whatever, assume to decide on the validity of the claim of any person to the service or labor of any other person, or surrender up any such person to the claimant, on pain of being dismissed from the service.

And I do hereby enjoin upon and order all persons engaged in the military and naval service of the United States to observe, obey, and enforce, within their respective spheres of service, the act, and sections above recited.

And the executive will in due time recommend that all citizens of the United States who shall have remained loyal thereto throughout the rebellion, shall (upon the restoration of the constitutional relation between the United States, and their respective states, and people, if that relation shall have been suspended or disturbed) be compensated for all losses by acts of the United States, including the loss of slaves.

In witness whereof, I have hereunto set my hand, and caused the seal of the United States to be affixed.

> Done at the City of Washington, this twenty second day of September, in the year of our Lord, one thousand eight hundred and sixty two, and of the Independence of the United States, the eighty seventh.

By the President: ABRAHAM LINCOLN
WILLIAM H. SEWARD, Secretary of State.

"A NECESSARY MEASURE"

Proclamation Suspending the Writ of Habeas Corpus

SEPTEMBER 24, 1862

Issued just two days after the Emancipation Proclamation—to nearly as large a public uproar—this order greatly widened the government's authority to arrest civilians for undermining the war effort. Thus, in the space of just two days, the commander in chief had issued executive orders both expanding freedom (emancipation) and reducing it. If the boldness of a signature can constitute evidence, the president believed as heartily in this order as he did in the emancipation. He signed it with a large, firm "Abraham Lincoln." It remains Lincoln's most controversial policy decision to this day.

**By the President of the United States of America:
A Proclamation.**

Whereas, it has become necessary to call into service not only volunteers but also portions of the militia of the States by draft in order to suppress the insurrection existing in the United States, and disloyal persons are not adequately restrained by the ordinary processes of law from hindering this measure and from giving aid and comfort in various ways to the insurrection;

Now, therefore, be it ordered, first, that during the existing insurrection and as a necessary measure for suppressing the same, all Rebels and Insurgents, their aiders and abettors within the United States, and all persons discouraging volunteer enlistments, resisting militia drafts, or guilty of any disloyal practice, affording aid and comfort to Rebels against the authority of the United States, shall be subject to martial law and liable to trial and punishment by Courts Martial or Military Commissions.

Second. That the Writ of Habeas Corpus is suspended in respect to all persons arrested, or who are now, or hereafter during the rebellion shall be, imprisoned in any fort, camp, arsenal, military prison, or other place of confinement by any military authority or by the sentence of any Court Martial or Military Commission.

In witness whereof, I have hereunto set my hand, and caused the seal of the United States could be affixed.

> Done at the City of Washington this twenty fourth day of September, in the year of our Lord one thousand eight hundred and sixty-two, and of the Independence of the United States the 87th.

By the President: ABRAHAM LINCOLN.
WILLIAM H. SEWARD, Secretary of State.

"BREATH ALONE KILLS NO REBELS"

Letter to Vice President Hannibal Hamlin

SEPTEMBER 28, 1862

Vice President Hannibal Hamlin, back in his home state of Maine for the congressional recess, had written admiringly to Lincoln after hearing news of the preliminary Emancipation Proclamation. "It will stand as the great act of the age," predicted the vice president. "It will be enthusiastically approved and sustained." But Lincoln was finding the initial public response, including that of troops in the field, to be quite different—and quite negative. He so confided gloomily in this reply.

My Dear Sir:

Your kind letter of the 25th is just received. It is known to some that while I hope something from the proclamation, my expectations are not as sanguine as are those of some friends. The time for its effect southward has not come; but northward the effect should be instantaneous.

It is six days old, and while commendation in newspapers and by distinguished individuals is all that a vain man could wish, the stocks have declined, and troops come forward more slowly than ever. This, looked soberly in the face, is not very satisfactory. We have fewer troops in the field at the end of six days than we had at the beginning—the attrition among the old outnumbering the addition by the new. The North responds to the proclamation sufficiently in breath; but breath alone kills no rebels.

I wish I could write more cheerfully; nor do I thank you the less for the kindness of your letter.

Yours very truly,
A. LINCOLN.

"McClellan's Bodyguard"

Remark to Ozias M. Hatch

HEADQUARTERS OF THE ARMY OF THE POTOMAC,
NEAR HARPERS FERRY, VIRGINIA, OCTOBER 3, 1862

The president made this caustic comment to his old friend, Illinois' secretary of state Ozias M. Hatch, after spending the night with him at Army of the Potomac headquarters near Harpers Ferry, Virginia. According to Hatch's recollections, the two men left their tent before sunrise, scaled a nearby hilltop, then gazed down at the vast array of campfires in the distance, prompting Lincoln to ask his friend: "Do you know what that is?" To Hatch's reply, "That is the Army of the Potomac," Lincoln answered as follows:

No, you are mistaken; that is General McClellan's bodyguard.

"Your Over-Cautiousness"

Letter to General George B. McClellan

OCTOBER 13, 1862

After his defeat at Antietam, General Robert E. Lee had marched his battered army back to Virginia unmolested—and Lincoln resumed his pressure on the victorious McClellan to pursue him. But following Lincoln's recent visit, the ever-suspicious general believed more than ever that the president "does feel very kindly toward me personally." He seemed unconcerned that his commander in chief remained disappointed only in his lack of aggressiveness. Lincoln followed up with this brutally frank critique, accompanied by a series of detailed orders, which ended with the caveat, out of respect for the military chain of command, that they were only suggestions.

My dear Sir.

You remember my speaking to you of what I called your over-cautiousness. Are you not over-cautious when you assume that you can not do what the enemy is constantly doing? Should you not claim to be at least his equal in prowess, and act upon the claim?

As I understand, you telegraph[ed] Gen. Halleck ["the most stupid idiot I ever heard of," McClellan had complained—ed.] that you can not subsist your army at Winchester unless the Railroad from Harper's Ferry to that point be put in working order. But the enemy does now subsist his army at Winchester at a distance nearly twice as great from railroad transportation as you would have to do without the railroad last named. He now wagons from Culpepper C[ourt].H[ouse]. which is just about twice as far as you would have to do from Harper's Ferry. He is certainly not more than half as well provided with wagons as you are. I certainly should be pleased for you to have the advantage of the Railroad from Harper's Ferry to Winchester, but it wastes all the remainder of autumn to give it to you; and, in fact ignores the question of *time,* which can not, and must not be ignored.

Again, one of the standard maxims of war, as you know, is "to operate upon the enemy's communications as much as possible without
exposing your own." You seem to act as if this applies *against* you,
but can not apply in your *favor.* Change positions with the enemy,
and think you not he would break your communication with Richmond within the next twentyfour hours? You dread his going into
Pennsylvania. But if he does so in full force, he gives up his communications to you absolutely [by abandoning home territory to the
South—ed.], and you have nothing to do but to follow, and ruin him;
if he does so with less than full force, fall upon, and beat what is left
behind all the easier.

Exclusive of the water line, you are now nearer Richmond than the
enemy is by the route that you *can,* and he *must* take. Why can you
not reach there before him, unless you admit that he is more than
your equal on a march. His route is the arc of a circle, while yours is
the chord. The roads are as good on yours as on his.

You know I desired, but did not order, you to cross the Potomac
below, instead of above the Shenandoah and Blue Ridge. My idea
was that this would at once menace the enemies' communications,
which I would seize if he would permit. If he should move Northward I would follow him closely, holding his communications. If he
should prevent our seizing his communications, and move towards
Richmond, I would press closely to him, fight him if a favorable opportunity should present, and, at least, try to beat him to Richmond
on the inside track. I say "try"; if we never try, we shall never succeed.
If he makes a stand at Winchester, moving neither North or South, I
would fight him there, on the idea that if we can not beat him when
he bears the wastage of coming to us, we never can when we bear
the wastage of going to him. This proposition is a simple truth, and
is too important to be lost sight of for a moment. In coming to us, he
tenders us an advantage which we should not waive. We should not
so operate as to merely drive him away. As we must beat him some-
where, or fail finally, we can do it, if at all, easier near to us, than far

President Abraham Lincoln and General George B. McClellan
confer inside a tent at the headquarters of the Army of the Potomac,
near Harpers Ferry, Virginia, on October 3, 1862. Two weeks before
Alexander Gardner took this—the first photograph of an American
president on a battlefield—the Union won a victory at Antietam.
(Library of Congress)

away. If we can not beat the enemy where he now is, we never can, he
again being within the entrenchments of Richmond.

Recurring to the idea of going to Richmond on the inside track, the
facility of supplying from the side away from the enemy is remarkable—as it were, by the different spokes of a wheel extending from

the hub towards the rim—and this whether you move directly by the chord, or on the inside arc, hugging the Blue Ridge more closely. The chord-line, as you see, carries you by Aldie, Hay-Market, and Fredericksburg; and you see how turn-pikes, railroads, and finally, the Potomac by Acquia Creek, meet you at all points from Washington. The same, only the lines lengthened a little, if you press closer to the Blue Ridge part of the way. The gaps through the Blue Ridge I understand to be about the following distances from Harper's Ferry, towit: Vestal's five miles; Gregorie's, thirteen, Snicker's eighteen, Ashby's, twenty-eight, Mannassas, thirty-eight, Chester fortyfive, and Thornton's fiftythree. I should think it preferable to take the route nearest the enemy, disabling him to make an important move without your knowledge, and compelling him to keep his forces together, for dread of you. The gaps would enable you to attack if you should wish. For a great part of the way, you would be practically between the enemy and both Washington and Richmond, enabling us to spare you the greatest number of troops from here. When at length, running for Richmond ahead of him enables him to move this way; if he does so, turn and attack him in rear. But I think he should be engaged long before such point is reached. It is all easy if our troops march as well as the enemy; and it is unmanly to say they can not do it.

This letter is in no sense an order.

Yours truly
A. LINCOLN.

"MAKE A VERY DESTRUCTIVE MISSILE"

Letter to George D. Ramsay

OCTOBER 15, 1862

Lincoln's fascination with newfangled weaponry—understandable for the only American president to hold a patent for an invention—grew exponentially during the war. He allocated money for the development of new technologies, and encouraged the development of everything from repeating guns to reconnaissance balloons—and in this letter to the commander of the Washington Arsenal, a new kind of artillery shell.

My dear Sir:

The bearer of this, well recommended to me, wishes you to furnish him a few shells, and give him some assistance in filling them according to his direction. He thinks he can make a very destructive missile, and, if not too much trouble to you, I shall be obliged, if you can accommodate him.

Yours very truly
A. LINCOLN

"WHAT THE HORSES OF YOUR ARMY HAVE DONE"

Telegram to General George B. McClellan

OCTOBER 25, 1862

Earlier this day, ever procrastinating, General McClellan had defended his reluctance to resume the offensive against General Lee, explaining, "We have in camp 267 horses . . . of these, 128 are positively and absolutely unable to leave the camp, from the following causes, viz, sore-tongue, grease, and consequent lameness, and sore backs. . . . The horses, which are still sound, are absolutely broken down from fatigue and want of flesh." This was Lincoln's acerbic reply. Privately, an infuriated McClellan angrily confided: "There never was a truer epithet applied to a certain individual [meaning Lincoln] than of the 'Gorilla.'" Lincoln subsequently relieved McClellan for a second and final time, and named Ambrose E. Burnside to replace him as commander of the Army of the Potomac. He was still a commander in chief in desperate search for a winning general.

Majr. Genl. McClellan

I have just read your despatch about sore tongued and fatiegued horses. Will you pardon me for asking what the horses of your army have done since the battle of Antietam that fatigue anything?

A. LINCOLN

"A FIERY TRIAL"

Remarks after a Quaker Prayer Service

OCTOBER 26, 1862

Lincoln made this well-known statement, transcribed by an eyewitness, after participating in a White House prayer service and meeting with Eliza P. Gurney, wife of English Quaker leader Joseph J. Gurney. This is what the president said to his visitor.

I am glad of this interview, and glad to know that I have your sympathy and prayers. We are indeed going through a great trial—a fiery trial. In the very responsible position in which I happen to be placed, being a humble instrument in the hands of our Heavenly Father, as I am, and as we all are, to work out his great purposes, I have desired that all my works and acts may be according to his will, and that it might be so, I have sought his aid—but if after endeavoring to do my best in the light which he affords me, I find my efforts fail, I must believe that for some purpose unknown to me, He wills it otherwise. If I had had my way, this war would never have been commenced; If I had been allowed my way this war would have been ended before this, but we find it still continues; and we must believe that He permits it for some wise purpose of his own, mysterious and unknown to us; and though with our limited understandings we may not be able to comprehend it, yet we cannot but believe, that he who made the world still governs it.

"GOD WILLS THIS CONTEST"

Meditation on the Divine Will

CA. OCTOBER 26, 1862

Though dated September 2 in the official version of Lincoln's Collected Works, many historians now believe this rumination was inspired by— and immediately followed—his visit with Quaker Eliza Gurney.

The will of God prevails. In great contests each party claims to act in accordance with the will of God. Both *may* be, and one *must* be wrong. God can not be *for*, and *against* the same thing at the same time. In the present civil war it is quite possible that God's purpose is something different from the purpose of either party—and yet the human instrumentalities, working just as they do, are of the best adaptation to effect His purpose. I am almost ready to say this is probably true—that God wills this contest, and wills that it shall not end yet. By his mere quiet power, on the minds of the now contestants, He could have either *saved* or *destroyed* the Union without a human contest. Yet the contest began. And having begun He could give the final victory to either side any day. Yet the contest proceeds.

"ALMOST AS BAD AS DESERTION"

Memorandum on Army Furloughs

NOVEMBER [?] 1862

By this time, Lincoln was fully engaged in every aspect of military policy—tactics as well strategy. Here he considers the indiscriminate granting of furloughs, which he felt depleted troop strength at crucial moments.

The Army is constantly depleted by company officers who give their men leave of absence in the very face of the enemy, and on the eve of an engagement, which is almost as bad as desertion. At this very moment there are between seventy and one hundred thousand men absent on furlough from the Army of the Potomac. The army, like the nation, has become demoralized by the idea that the war is to be ended, the nation united, and peace restored, by *strategy,* and not by hard desperate fighting. Why, then, should not the soldiers have furloughs?

"THE WAR IS UNSUCCESSFUL"

Letter to General Carl Schurz

NOVEMBER 24, 1862

With Northerners understandably impatient about the slow progress and huge cost of the war, and with the Emancipation Proclamation infuriating moderates and conservatives alike, Lincoln here tells his longtime German-American ally, General Carl Schurz, that his own confidence is ebbing, and that he almost envies Union martyrs like E. D. Baker who died in battle.

My dear Sir

I have just received, and read, your letter of the 20th. The purport of it is that we lost the late elections, and the administration is failing, because the war is unsuccessful; and that I must not flatter myself that I am not justly to blame for it. I certainly know that if the war fails, the administration fails, and that I *will* be blamed for it, whether I deserve it or not. And I ought to be blamed, if I could do better. You think I could do better; therefore you blame me already. I think I could not do better; therefore I blame you for blaming me. I understand you *now* to be willing to accept the help of men, who are not republicans, provided they have "heart in it." Agreed. I want no others. But who is to be the judge of hearts, or of "heart in it"? If I must discard my own judgment, and take yours, I must also take that of others; and by the time I should reject all I should be advised to reject, I should have none left, republicans, or others—not even yourself. For, be assured, my dear sir, there are men who have "heart in it" that think you are performing your part as poorly as you think I am performing mine. I certainly have been dissatisfied with the slowness of Buell and McClellan; but before I relieved them I had great fears I should not find successors to them, who would do better; and I am sorry to add, that I have seen little since to relieve those fears. I do not clearly see the prospect of any more rapid movements. I fear we shall at last find out that the difficulty is in our case, rather than in particular generals. I wish to disparage no one—certainly not those who sympathize with me; but I must say I need success more than I need sympathy, and that I have not seen the so much greater evidence of getting success from my sympathizers, than from those who are denounced as the contrary. It does seem to me that in the field the two classes have been very much alike, in what they have done, and what they have failed to do. In sealing their faith with their blood, Baker, an[d] Lyon, and Bohlen, and Richardson, republicans, did all that men could do; but did they any more than Kearney, and Stevens, and Reno, and Mansfield, none of whom were republicans, and some, at least of whom, have been bitterly, and repeatedly, denounced to me as secession sympathizers? I will not perform the ungrateful task of comparing cases of failure.

In answer to your question "Has it not been publicly stated in the newspapers, and apparantly proved as a fact, that from the commencement of the war, the enemy was continually supplied with information by some of the confidential subordinates of as important an officer as Adjutant General Thomas?" I must say "no" so far as my knowledge extends. And I add that if you can give any tangible evidence upon that subject, I will thank you to come to the City and do so.

Very truly Your friend
A. LINCOLN

"WE CANNOT ESCAPE HISTORY"

From the Annual Message to Congress

DECEMBER 1, 1862

Often recalled chiefly for its progressive-sounding conclusion, Lincoln's second and most famous annual message actually began with an extremely conservative blueprint for ending slavery in the states not affected by the Emancipation Proclamation. The president proposed a plan to compensate slave owners in the loyal slave states, delay universal freedom for nearly forty years, and offer ex-slaves colonization in Africa or the Caribbean. Yet the speech ended with one of the president's most ringing rallying cries for freedom.

Our national strife springs not from our permanent part; not from the land we inhabit; not from our national homestead. There is no possible severing of this, but would multiply, and not mitigate, evils among us. In all its adaptations and aptitudes, it demands union, and abhors separation. In fact, it would, ere long, force re-union, however much of blood and treasure the separation might have cost.

Our strife pertains to ourselves—to the passing generations of men; and it can, without convulsion, be hushed forever with the passing of one generation.

In this view, I recommend the adoption of the following resolution and articles amendatory to the Constitution of the United States:

"*Resolved by the Senate and House of Representatives of the United States of America in Congress assembled,* (two thirds of both houses concurring,) That the following articles be proposed to the legislatures (or conventions) of the several States as amendments to the Constitution of the United States, all or any of which articles when ratified by three-fourths of the said legislatures (or conventions) to be valid as part or parts of the said Constitution, viz:

"Article—.

"Every State, wherein slavery now exists, which shall abolish the same therein, at any time, or times, before the first day of January, in the year of our Lord one thousand and nine hundred, shall receive compensation from the United States as follows, to wit:

"The President of the United States shall deliver to every such State, bonds of the United States, bearing interest at the rate of   per cent, per annum, to an amount equal to the aggregate sum of for each slave shown to have been therein, by the eig[h]th census of the United States, said bonds to be delivered to such State by instalments, or in one parcel, at the completion of the abolishment, accordingly as the same shall have been gradual, or at one time, within such State; and interest shall begin to run upon any such bond, only from the proper time of its delivery as aforesaid. Any State having received bonds as aforesaid, and afterwards reintroducing or tolerating slavery therein, shall refund to the United States the bonds so received, or the value thereof, and all interest paid thereon.

"Article—.

"All slaves who shall have enjoyed actual freedom by the chances of the war, at any time before the end of the rebellion, shall be forever free; but all owners of such, who shall not have been disloyal, shall be compensated for them, at the same rates as is provided for States adopting abolishment of slavery, but in such way, that no slave shall be twice accounted for.

"Article—.

"Congress may appropriate money, and otherwise provide, for colonizing free colored persons, with their own consent, at any place or places without the United States."

I beg indulgence to discuss these proposed articles at some length. Without slavery the rebellion could never have existed; without slavery it could not continue.

. . . .

This plan is recommended as a means, not in exclusion of, but additional to, all others for restoring and preserving the national authority throughout the Union. The subject is presented exclusively in its economical aspect. The plan would, I am confident, secure peace more speedily, and maintain it more permanently, than can be done by force alone; while all it would cost, considering amounts, and manner of payment, and times of payment, would be easier paid than will be the additional cost of the war, if we rely solely upon force. It is much—very much—that it would cost no blood at all.

The plan is proposed as permanent constitutional law. It cannot become such without the concurrence of, first, two-thirds of Congress, and, afterwards, three-fourths of the States. The requisite three-fourths of the States will necessarily include seven of the Slave states. Their concurrence, if obtained, will give assurance of their severally adopting emancipation, at no very distant day, upon the new constitutional terms. This assurance would end the struggle now, and save the Union forever.

I do not forget the gravity which should characterize a paper addressed to the Congress of the nation by the Chief Magistrate of the nation. Nor do I forget that some of you are my seniors, nor that many of you have more experience than I, in the conduct of public affairs. Yet I trust that in view of the great responsibility resting upon me, you will perceive no want of respect to yourselves, in any undue earnestness I may seem to display.

Is it doubted, then, that the plan I propose, if adopted, would shorten the war, and thus lessen its expenditure of money and of blood? Is it doubted that it would restore the national authority and national prosperity, and perpetuate both indefinitely? Is it doubted that we here—Congress and Executive—can secure its adoption? Will not the good people respond to a united, and earnest appeal from us? Can we, can they, by any other means, so certainly, or so speedily, assure these vital objects? We can succeed only by concert. It is not "can *any* of us *imagine* better?" but "can we *all* do better?'" Object whatsoever is possible, still the question recurs "can we do better?" The dogmas of the quiet past, are inadequate to the stormy present. The occasion is piled high with difficulty, and we must rise with the occasion. As our case is new, so we must think anew, and act anew. We must disenthrall our selves, and then we shall save our country.

Fellow-citizens, *we* cannot escape history. We of this Congress and this administration, will be remembered in spite of ourselves. No personal significance, or insignificance, can spare one or another of us. The fiery trial through which we pass, will light us down, in honor or dishonor, to the latest generation. We *say* we are for the Union. The world will not forget that we say this. We know how to save the Union. The world knows we do know how to save it. We— even *we here*—hold the power, and bear the responsibility. In *giving* freedom to the *slave,* we *assure* freedom to the *free*—honorable alike in what we give, and what we preserve. We shall nobly save, or meanly lose, the last best, hope of earth. Other means may succeed; this could not fail. The way is plain, peaceful, generous, just—a way which, if followed, the world will forever applaud, and God must forever bless.

"THERE WOULD SOON BE NO ARMY"

Memorandum on Sick Soldiers

DECEMBER 20, 1862

Involving himself in minutiae as well as strategy, policy, and public re-lations, Lincoln wrote this memo after being asked to discharge a sol-dier on account of illness. To Orville H. Browning, Lincoln complained, "There was never an army in the world, so far as he could learn, of which so small a per centage could be got into battle as ours."

If this boy is sick in this case he must be dealt with as other sick are dealt with by the rules. Of course I can not discharge a soldier merely because a mother asks it. There would soon be no army.

COLUMBIA DEMANDS HER CHILDREN !

Joseph E. Baker's harsh wartime cartoon criticized Lincoln's call for additional troops—and demanded an accounting for the five hundred thousand soldiers already in the field or dead and wounded. *(Library of Congress)*

"ALTHOUGH YOU WERE NOT SUCCESSFUL"

Message to the Army of the Potomac after Fredericksburg

DECEMBER 22, 1862

Under General Ambrose E. Burnside's command, the Army of the Potomac suffered a catastrophic defeat at Fredericksburg, Virginia, on December 13, 1862, with more than twelve thousand killed, wounded, and missing. This is the bereft commander in chief's message of thanks to his crushed troops. It was distributed in the form of a leaflet.

I have just read your Commanding General's preliminary report of the battle of Fredericksburg. Although you were not successful, the attempt was not an error, nor the failure other than an accident.

The courage with which you, in an open field, maintained the contest against an entrenched foe, and the consummate skill and success with which you crossed and re-crossed the river, in face of the enemy, show that you possess all the qualities of a great army, which will yet give victory to the cause of the country and of popular government. Condoling with the mourners for the dead, and sympathizing with the severely wounded, I congratulate you that the number of both is comparatively so small.

I tender to you, officers and soldiers, the thanks of the nation.

ABRAHAM LINCOLN.

Abraham Lincoln a week before his fifty-sixth and final birthday,
February 5, 1865—some two months before the end of the Civil War—in a
photograph by Alexander Gardner, Washington. *(Library of Congress)*

III

A NEW BIRTH OF FREEDOM
1863–1865

On the first day of the third year of the Civil War, Abraham Lincoln kept the promise—some viewed it as the threat—that he had made to the nation a hundred days earlier: he wrote and signed the final Emancipation Proclamation. Though it applied only to those states in rebellion, and therefore outside Lincoln's immediate control, it signaled the transformation of the war from a fight merely to restore the imperfect Union as it was, to a struggle to forge what he would call, in his Gettysburg Address ten months later, "a new birth of freedom"—a Union without slavery. Eventually, federal troops on the march began enforcing the proclamation, freeing hundreds of thousands of slaves under its terms. By 1864, Lincoln was ready to support a constitutional amendment ending slavery everywhere. (The amendment would not be ratified until after his death.) The war—and the country—changed dramatically and permanently.

But if the commander in chief thought that this expansion of the national mission would shorten the Rebellion, he soon learned otherwise. At the beginning of 1863, the Civil War was not even halfway over; in fact, more soldiers on both sides would die in the second half of the war than the first. And before Robert E. Lee finally surrendered to Ulysses S. Grant in April 1865, millions of acres of Southern territory were laid to ruin. This was the era of hard war—and, some later asserted, almost total war.

Throughout this period, Lincoln remained a tireless, active, deeply involved commander in chief, supervising his field commanders, lifting public morale with his speeches and public letters, and participating avidly in all the details of military leadership: weapon development, the raising of troops (now including black recruitment), pardons, and the endless massaging of fragile military egos.

Though he could claim no real military leadership experience when the war began, most historians agree that by war's end, Lincoln had become perhaps the nation's most skillful commander in chief ever. He triumphed not on the battlefield (where at one point he confided he would like to lead personally) but with the most powerful weapon at his disposal: his pen.

"SINCERELY BELIEVED TO BE AN ACT OF JUSTICE"

Final Emancipation Proclamation

JANUARY 1, 1863

Aware that he often complained about sluggish field commanders, modern historians often point out Lincoln's own slowness on emancipation. But even as late as New Year's Day 1863, many Americans believed the president would not sign this final version of the Emancipation Proclamation—it was still considered so radical by so many. Sign it he did, after attending a long White House holiday reception, then telling a small group of witnesses: "If my name ever goes into history it will be for this act, and my whole soul is in it." The text was not written to inspire—Lincoln wanted a legal document that could survive court challenges if necessary—but he was surely right that it enshrined his place in history and certainly redefined the war as well.

By the President of the United States of America: A Proclamation.

Whereas, on the twentysecond day of September, in the year of our Lord one thousand eight hundred and sixty two, a proclamation was issued by the President of the United States, containing, among other things, the following, towit:

"That on the first day of January, in the year of our Lord one thousand eight hundred and sixty-three, all persons held as slaves within any State or designated part of a State, the people whereof shall then be in rebellion against the United States, shall be then, thenceforward, and forever free; and the Executive Government of the United States, including the military and naval authority thereof, will recognize and maintain the freedom of such persons, and will do no act or acts to repress such persons, or any of them, in any efforts they may make for their actual freedom.

"That the Executive will, on the first day of January aforesaid, by proclamation, designate the States and parts of States, if any, in which the people thereof, respectively, shall then be in rebellion against the United States; and the fact that any State, or the people thereof, shall on that day be, in good faith, represented in the Congress of the United States by members chosen thereto at elections wherein a majority of the qualified voters of such State shall have participated, shall, in the absence of strong countervailing testimony, be deemed conclusive evidence that such State, and the people thereof, are not then in rebellion against the United States."

Now, therefore I, Abraham Lincoln, President of the United States, by virtue of the power in me vested as Commander-in-Chief, of the Army and Navy of the United States in time of actual armed rebellion against authority and government of the United States, and as a fit and necessary war measure for suppressing said rebellion, do, on this first day of January, in the year of our Lord one thousand eight hundred and sixty three, and in accordance with my purpose so to do publicly proclaimed for the full period of one hundred days, from the day first above mentioned, order and designate as the States and parts of States wherein the people thereof respectively, are this day in rebellion against the United States, the following, towit:

Arkansas, Texas, Louisiana, (except the Parishes of St. Bernard, Plaquemines, Jefferson, St. Johns, St. Charles, St. James[,] Ascension, Assumption, Terrebonne, Lafourche, St. Mary, St. Martin, and Orleans, including the City of New-Orleans) Mississippi, Alabama, Florida, Georgia, South-Carolina, North-Carolina, and Virginia, (except the fortyeight counties designated as West Virginia, and also the counties of Berkley, Accomac, Northampton, Elizabeth-City, York, Princess Ann, and Norfolk, including the cities of Norfolk & Portsmouth[ )]; and which excepted parts are, for the present, left precisely as if this proclamation were not issued [having fallen under Union control—ed.].

And by virtue of the power, and for the purpose aforesaid, I do order and declare that all persons held as slaves within said designated States, and parts of States, are, and henceforward shall be free; and that the Executive government of the United States, including

The legalistic words of the Emancipation Proclamation inspired this 1865 so-called allegorical tribute by Philadelphia printmaker P. S. Duval. Its "before" and "after" scenes suggest that the text not only changed the rationale and outcome of the war but dramatically changed the lives of enslaved African Americans. Lincoln's portrait was rendered in calligraphy, with some words highlighted in bold to form an outline likeness. *(Library of Congress)*

the military and naval authorities thereof, will recognize and maintain the freedom of said persons.

And I hereby enjoin upon the people so declared to be free to abstain from all violence, unless in necessary self-defence; and I recommend to them that, in all cases when allowed, they labor faithfully for reasonable wages.

And I further declare and make known, that such persons of suitable condition, will be received into the armed service of the United States to garrison forts, positions, stations, and other places, and to man vessels of all sorts in said service.

And upon this act, sincerely believed to be an act of justice, warranted by the Constitution, upon military necessity, I invoke the considerate judgment of mankind, and the gracious favor of Almighty God.

In witness whereof, I have hereunto set my hand and caused the seal of the United States to be affixed.

> Done at the City of Washington, this first day of
> January, in the year of our Lord one thousand eight
> hundred and sixty three, and of the Independence of the
> United States of America the eighty-seventh.

By the President: ABRAHAM LINCOLN
WILLIAM H. SEWARD, Secretary of State.

"GO FORTH AND GIVE US VICTORIES"

Letter to General Joseph Hooker

JANUARY 26, 1863

After the horror of the Battle of Fredericksburg in December, and the groteque, aptly named "mud march" in January, Ambrose Burnside lost the support of his army. Lincoln dismissed him and replaced him with "Fighting Joe" Hooker on January 25. The following day, the commander in chief sent him this, one of his most famous letters, warning him against his tendency to bravado. "It is a beautiful letter," Hooker remembered, "and, although I think he was harder on me than I deserved, I will say that I love the man who wrote it." He carried it with him for the rest of the war, but it apparently had little effect. After visiting Hooker at his headquarters in May, Lincoln still noticed: "That is the most depressing thing about Hooker. It seems to me that he is overconfident." The next month, Lee defeated Hooker at Chancellorsville.

General.

I have placed you at the head of the Army of the Potomac. Of course I have done this upon what appear to me to be sufficient reasons. And yet I think it best for you to know that there are some things in regard to which, I am not quite satisfied with you. I believe you to be a brave and skilful soldier, which, of course, I like. I also believe you do not mix politics with your profession, in which you are right. You have confidence in yourself, which is a valuable, if not an indispensable quality. You are ambitious, which, within reasonable bounds, does good rather than harm. But I think that during Gen. Burnside's command of the Army [which some critics believed Hooker had undermined—ed.], you have taken counsel of your ambition, and thwarted him as much as you could, in which you did a great wrong to the country, and to a most meritorious and honorable brother officer. I have heard, in such a way as to believe it, of your recently saying that both the Army and the Government needed a Dictator. Of course it was not *for* this, but in spite of it, that I have given you the command. Only those generals who gain successes, can set up dictators. What I now ask of you is military success, and I will risk the dictatorship. The government will support you to the utmost of it's ability, which is neither more nor less than it has done and will do for all commanders. I much fear that the spirit which you have aided to infuse into the Army, of criticising their Commander, and withholding confidence from him, will now turn upon you. I shall assist you as far as I can, to put it down. Neither you, nor

Napoleon, if he were alive again, could get any good out of an army, while such a spirit prevails in it.

And now, beware of rashness. Beware of rashness, but with energy, and sleepless vigilance, go forward, and give us victories.

Yours very truly

A. LINCOLN

"WE ARE NOT, AS A RACE, SO MUCH DISPOSED TO FIGHT"

Speech to a Delegation of Indian Chiefs

MARCH 27, 1863

Lincoln made these remarks to a delegation of American Indian chiefs, representing the Cheyenne, Apache, and other nations, who called on him in the East Room of the White House—his words frequently interrupted by assenting shouts of "ugh," as they were translated, according to one newspaper account. Lincoln wanted no war with Native Americans while preoccupied with a fight with fellow white men. Cordial replies followed from Arapaho chief Spotted Wolf and Cheyenne chief Lean Bear. When the rebellion ended, and with Lincoln dead, the federal armies resumed their wars against native peoples.

You have all spoken of the strange sights you see here, among your pale-faced brethren; the very great number of people that you see; the big wigwams; the difference between our people and your own. But you have seen but a very small part of the pale-faced people. You may wonder when I tell you that there are people here in this wigwam, now looking at you, who have come from other countries a great deal farther off than you have come.

We pale-faced people think that this world is a great, round ball, and we have people here of the pale-faced family who have come almost from the other side of it to represent their nations here and conduct their friendly intercourse with us, as you now come from your part of the round ball.

One of our learned men will now explain to you our notions about this great ball, and show you where you live . . .

. . . .

We have people now present from all parts of the globe—[pointing:] here, and here, and here. There is a great difference between this pale-faced people and their red brethren, both as to numbers and the way in which they live. We know not whether your own situation is best for your race, but this is what has made the difference in our way of living.

The pale-faced people are numerous and prosperous because they cultivate the earth, produce bread, and depend upon the products of the earth rather than wild game for a subsistence.

This is the chief reason of the difference; but there is another. Although we are now engaged in a great war between one another, we are not, as a race, so much disposed to fight and kill one another as our red brethren.

You have asked for my advice. I really am not capable of advising you whether, in the providence of the Great Spirit, who is the great Father of us all, it is best for you to maintain the habits and customs of your race, or adopt a new mode of life.

I can only say that I can see no way in which your race is to become as numerous and prosperous as the white race except by living as they do, by the cultivation of the earth.

It is the object of this Government to be on terms of peace with you, and with all our red brethren. We constantly endeavor to be so. We make treaties with you, and will try to observe them; and if our children should sometimes behave badly, and violate these treaties, it is against our wish.

You know it is not always possible for any father to have his children do precisely as he wishes them to do.

In regard to being sent back to your own country, we have an officer, the Commissioner of Indian Affairs, who will take charge of that matter, and make the necessary arrangements.

"THE ENEMY WILL MAKE EXTRA EFFORTS"

Letter to General David Hunter

APRIL 1, 1863

With black regiments now occupying Jacksonville, Florida, and with the Union ready to use black troops to help launch an attack on the birthplace of secession—Charleston—Lincoln remained eager to see so-called colored troops deployed but worried about their fate should they be attacked or captured.

My dear Sir:

I am glad to see the accounts of your colored force at Jacksonville, Florida. I see the enemy are driving at them fiercely, as is to be expected. It is important to the enemy that such a force shall *not* take shape, and grow, and thrive, in the South; and in precisely the same proportion, it is important to us that it *shall*. Hence the utmost caution and vigilance is necessary on our part. The enemy will make extra efforts to destroy them; and we should do the same to preserve and increase them.

Yours truly
A. LINCOLN

"WHAT NEXT?"

From Letters to General Joseph Hooker

MAY 7, MAY 14, JUNE 5, 1863

George McClellan had yielded to Ambrose Burnside, and Burnside to the confident Joseph Hooker, but still the Army of the Potomac could not win a major battle. Hooker's disastrous defeat at Chancellorsville in the first week of May 1863 provoked an anguished Lincoln to cry out: "My God! What will the country say?" But in his subsequent messages to Hooker, the commander in chief remained calm and encouraging. Just before the Battle of Gettysburg on July 1, though, Lincoln replaced Hooker with General George G. Meade. The following excerpts come from those successive letters.

The recent movement of your army is ended without effecting it's object, except perhaps some important breakings of the enemies communications. What next? If possible I would be very glad of another movement early enough to give us some benefit . . . but neither for this reason or any other, do I wish anything done in desperation or rashness. . . . Have you already in your mind a plan wholly, or partially formed? If you have, prossecute it without interference from me. If you have not, please inform me so that I, incompetent as I may be, can try [to] assist in the formation of some plan for the army.

It does not now appear probable to me that you can gain anything by an early renewal of the attempt to cross the Rappahannock. I therefore shall not complain, if you do no more, for a time, than to keep the enemy at bay, and out of other mischief, by menaces and occasional cavalry raids, if practicable; and to put your army in good condition again. . . . I must tell you I have some painful intimation that some of your corps and Division Commanders are not giving you their entire confidence. This would be ruinous, if true. . . .

In one word, I would not take any risk of being entangled upon the river, like an ox jumped half over a fence, and liable to be torn by dogs, front and rear, without a fair chance to gore one way or kick the other. If Lee would come to my side of the river, I would keep on the same side & fight him, or act on the defence, according as might be my estimate of his strength relative to my own. But these are mere suggestions which I desire to be controlled by the judgment of yourself and Gen. Halleck.

"Essential Service in Finishing the War"

Remarks to New York Committee on "Colored" Enlistment

MAY 30, 1863

Urgently serious about enlisting a "sable arm"—black troops—to swell the ranks of the Union army while denying home-front labor to the Confederacy, Lincoln made these imperfectly transcribed but unmistakably strong remarks to a delegation of New Yorkers who wanted the president to assign ten thousand "colored troops" to General John C. Frémont.

The President declared that he would gladly receive into the service not ten thousand but ten times ten thousand colored troops; expressed his determination to protect all who enlisted, and said that he looked to them for essential service in finishing the war. He believed that the command of them afforded scope for the highest ambition, and he would with all his heart offer it to Gen. Fremont.

"THE QUOTA OF TROOPS TO BE FURNISHED"

Draft Order for Military Conscription

[JUNE 1863]

One of the most controversial orders of the Lincoln administration was the nation's first military draft law. In the preliminary quota form below, the president attempted to create a uniform system for meeting conscription expectations. A month later, in response to the draft, New Yorkers erupted in a violent riot.

I, Abraham Lincoln, President of the United States of America and Commander-in-Chief of the Army and Navy thereof, having taken into consideration the number of volunteers and militia furnished by and from the several States, including the State of _____, and the period of service of said volunteers and militia since the commencement of the present rebellion, in order to equalize the numbers among the districts of the said States, and having considered and allowed for the number already furnished as aforesaid, and the time of their services aforesaid, do hereby assign _____ as the first proportional part of the quota of troops to be furnished by the district of the State of _____, under this, the first call made by me on the State of _____, under the act approved March 3, 1863, entitled, "An act for enrolling and calling out the national forces, and for other purposes," and, in pursuance of the act aforesaid, I order that a draft be made in the said _____ district of the State of _____, for the number of men herein assigned to said district, and 50 per cent. in addition.

In witness whereof I have hereunto set my hand and caused the seal of the United States to be affixed. Done at the city of Washington this _____ day of _____, in the year of our Lord one thousand eight hundred and sixty-three, and of the Independence of the United States the eighty-eighth.

"PUBLIC SAFETY DOES REQUIRE THE SUSPENSION"

From a Reply to Erastus Corning and Others on Civil Liberties in Wartime

[JUNE 12] 1863

Following the military arrest, trial, and conviction of a "Copperhead" ex-congressman from Ohio, Clement L. Vallandigham, for speaking out against Lincoln and the war, his fellow Democrats throughout the country criticized the administration's policy on so-called arbitrary arrests, suspension of habeas corpus, and the use of military tribunals for civilians. One of the angriest protests came from a meeting of Albany, New York, Democrats chaired by Erastus Corning. Lincoln sent this long, careful reply, making sure, as he did so often, that it was also published widely in the press. Most historians consider it the president's most skillful defense of his policy on military justice. Vallandigham, whose two-year prison sentence was commuted, was banished to the Confederacy, but later made his way to Canada, where he mounted a campaign-in-exile for Ohio governor in October—losing by an overwhelming one hundred thousand votes.

Prior to my instalation here it had been inculcated that any State had a lawful right to secede from the national Union; and that it would be expedient to exercise the right, whenever the devotees of the doctrine should fail to elect a President to their own liking. I was elected contrary to their liking; and accordingly, so far as it was legally possible, they had taken seven states out of the Union, had seized many of the United States Forts, and had fired upon the United States' Flag, all before I was inaugerated; and, of course, before I had done any official act whatever. The rebellion, thus began soon ran into the present civil war; and, in certain respects, it began on very unequal terms between the parties. The insurgents had been preparing for it more than thirty years, while the government had taken no steps to resist them. The former had carefully considered all the means which could be turned to their account. It undoubtedly was a well pondered reliance with them that in their own unrestricted effort to destroy Union, constitution, and law, all together, the government would, in great degree, be restrained by the same constitution and law, from arresting their progress. Their sympathizers pervaded all departments of the government, and nearly all communities of the people. From this material, under cover of "Liberty of speech" "Liberty of the press" and "*Habeas corpus*" they hoped to keep on foot amongst us a most efficient corps of spies, informers, suppliers, and aiders and abettors of their cause in a thousand ways. They knew that in times such as they were inaugerating, by the constitution itself, the "Habeas corpus" might be suspended; but they also knew they had friends who would make a question as to *who* was to suspend it; meanwhile their spies and others might remain at large to help on their cause. Or if, as has happened, the executive should suspend the writ, without ruinous waste of time, instances of arresting innocent persons might occur, as are always likely to occur in such cases; and then a clamor could be raised in regard to this, which might be, at least, of some service to the insurgent cause. It needed no very keen perception to discover this part of the enemies' programme, so soon as by open hostilities their machinery was fairly put in motion. Yet, thoroughly imbued with a reverence for the guarranteed rights of individuals, I was slow to adopt the strong measures, which by degrees I have been forced to regard as being within the exceptions of the constitution, and as indispensable to the public Safety. Nothing is better known to history than that courts of justice are utterly incompetent to such cases. Civil courts are organized chiefly for trials of individuals, or, at most, a few individuals acting in concert; and this in quiet times, and on charges of crimes well defined in the law. Even in times of peace, bands of horse-thieves and robbers frequently grow too numerous and powerful for the ordinary courts of justice. But what comparison, in numbers, have such bands ever borne to the insurgent sympathizers even in many of the loyal states? Again, a jury too frequently have at least one member, more ready to hang the panel than to hang the traitor. And yet again, he who dissuades one man from volunteering, or induces one soldier to desert, weakens the Union cause as much as he who kills a union soldier in battle. Yet this dissuasion, or inducement, may be so conducted as to be no defined crime of which any civil court would take cognizance.

Ours is a case of Rebellion—so called by the resolutions before me—in fact, a clear, flagrant, and gigantic case of Rebellion; and the provision of the constitution that "The previlege of the writ of Habeas Corpus shall not be suspended, unless when in cases of Rebellion or Invasion, the public Safety may require it" is *the* provision which specially applies to our present case. This provision plainly attests the understanding of those who made the constitution that ordinary courts of justice are inadequate to "cases of Rebellion"— attests their purpose that in such cases, men may be held in custody whom the courts acting on ordinary rules, would discharge. Habeas Corpus, does not discharge men who are proved to be guilty of defined crime; and its suspension is allowed by the constitution on purpose that, men may be arrested and held, who can not be proved to be guilty of defined crime, "when, in cases of Rebellion or Invasion the public Safety may require it." This is precisely our present case—a case of Rebellion, wherein the public Safety does require the suspension. Indeed, arrests by process of courts, and arrests in cases of rebellion, do not proceed altogether upon the same basis. The former is directed at the small per centage of ordinary and continuous perpetration of crime; while the latter is directed at sudden and extensive uprisings against the government, which, at most, will succeed or fail, in no great length of time. In the latter case, arrests are made, not so much for what has been done, as for what probably would be done. The latter is more for the preventive, and less for the vindictive, than the former. In such cases the purposes of men are much more easily understood, than in cases of ordinary crime. The man who stands by and says nothing, when the peril of his government is discussed, can not be misunderstood. If not hindered, he is sure to help the enemy. Much more, if he talks ambiguously—talks for his country with "buts" and "ifs" and "ands." Of how little value the constitutional provision I have quoted will be rendered, if arrests shall never be made until defined crimes shall have been committed, may be illustrated by a few notable examples. Gen. John C. Breckienridge [sic], Gen. Robert E. Lee, Gen. Joseph E. Johnston, Gen. John B. Magruder, Gen. William B. Preston, Gen. Simon B. Buckner, and Comodore [Franklin] Buchanan, now occupying the very highest places in the rebel war service, were all within the power of the government since the rebellion began, and were nearly as well known to be traitors then as now. Unquestionably if we had seized and held them, the insurgent cause would be much weaker. But no one of them had then committed any crime defined in the law. Every one of them if arrested would have been discharged on Habeas Corpus, were the writ allowed to operate. In view of these and similar cases, I think the time not unlikely to come when I shall be blamed for having made too few arrests rather than too many.

.   .   .   .

I understand the meeting, whose resolutions I am considering, to be in favor of suppressing the rebellion by military force—by armies. Long experience has shown that armies can not be maintained unless desertion shall be punished by the severe penalty of death. The case requires, and the law and the constitution, sanction this punishment. Must I shoot a simple-minded soldier boy who deserts, while I must not touch a hair of a wiley agitator who induces him to desert? This is none the less injurious when effected by getting a father, or brother, or friend, into a public meeting, and there working upon his feelings, till he is persuaded to write the soldier boy, that he is fighting in a bad cause, for a wicked administration of a contemptable government, too weak to arrest and punish him if he shall desert. I think that in such a case, to silence the agitator, and save the boy, is not only constitutional, but, withal, a great mercy.

If I be wrong on this question of constitutional power, my error lies in believing that certain proceedings are constitutional when, in cases of rebellion or Invasion, the public Safety requires them, which would not be constitutional when, in absence of rebellion or invasion, the public Safety does not require them—in other words, that the constitution is not in it's application in all respects the same, in cases of Rebellion or invasion, involving the public Safety, as it is in times of profound peace and public security. The constitution itself makes the distinction; and I can no more be persuaded that the government can constitutionally take no strong measure in time of rebellion, because it can be shown that the same could not be lawfully taken in time of peace, than I can be persuaded that a particular drug is not good medicine for a sick man, because it can be shown to not be good food for a well one. Nor am I able to appreciate the danger, apprehended by the meeting, that the American people will, by means of military arrests during the rebellion, lose the right of public discussion, the liberty of speech and the press, the law of evidence, trial by jury, and Habeas corpus, throughout the indefinite peaceful future which I trust lies before them, any more than I am able to believe that a man could contract so strong an appetite for emetics during temporary illness, as to persist in feeding upon them through the remainder of his healthful life.

. . . .

A. LINCOLN

"A GREAT SUCCESS TO THE CAUSE OF THE UNION"

Statement to the Nation on Recent Union Victories

JULY 4, 1863

Lincoln issued this public statement as soon as he was certain that the Army of the Potomac had indeed defeated the Army of Northern Virginia at Gettysburg after three days of bloody fighting. Many Americans at the time believed Lee's defeat would end the war; in fact, the conflict was only halfway over.

The President announces to the country that news from the Army of the Potomac, up to 10 P.M. of the 3rd. is such as to cover that Army with the highest honor, to promise a great success to the cause of the Union, and to claim the condolence of all for the many gallant fallen. And that for this, he especially desires that on this day, He whose will, not ours, should ever be done, be everywhere remembered and reverenced with profoundest gratitude.

ABRAHAM LINCOLN

"NOTHING ELSE, WILL BE RECEIVED BY THE PRESIDENT"

Order to Rear Admiral Samuel P. Lee

JULY [4], 1863

Lincoln learned that Confederate vice president Alexander H. Stephens—his Whig colleague in Congress decades earlier—had arrived at Union military headquarters at Fortress Monroe, Virginia, under a flag of truce, in a quest to negotiate an end to hostilities. But the president was not ready to begin peace talks on terms that he believed Stephens would require: recognition of the Confederacy and revocation of the Emancipation Proclamation. Lincoln issued this order all but banning Stephens from alighting at the Union stronghold.

Your despatch transmitting a note from Mr. Alexander H. Stephens has been received. You will not permit Mr. Stephens to proceed to Washington, or to pass the blockade. He does not make known the subjects to which the communication in writing from Mr. Davis relates, which he bears, and seeks to deliver in person to the President, and upon which he desires to confer. Those subjects can only be Military, or not Military, or partly both. Whatever may be military will be readily received, if offered through the well understood Military channel. Of course nothing else, will be received by the President, when offered, as in this case, in terms assuming the independence of the so-called Confederate States; and anything will be received and carefully considered by him, when offered by any influential person or persons, in terms not assuming the independence of the so-called Confederate States.

"This Is a Glorious Theme"

Response to a Victory Serenade

JULY 7, 1863

On the morning he delivered these extemporaneous remarks to a crowd that gathered on the White House lawn with a band of musicians to serenade him, Lincoln—and the entire North—learned that federal forces under Ulysses S. Grant had captured Vicksburg, and those under George G. Meade had won a major triumph at Gettysburg. In this brief talk to the throng of well-wishers that evening, Lincoln introduced a theme—that of a war to preserve the promise of the Declaration of Independence— he would later refine into the masterpiece that became known as the Gettysburg Address.

Fellow-citizens:

I am very glad indeed to see you to-night, and yet I will not say I thank you for this call, but I do most sincerely thank Almighty God for the occasion on which you have called. [Cheers.] How long ago is it?—eighty odd years—since on the Fourth of July for the first time in the history of the world a nation by its representatives, assembled and declared as a self-evident truth that "all men are created equal." [Cheers.] That was the birthday of the United States of America. Since then the Fourth of July has had several peculiar recognitions. The two most distinguished men in the framing and support of the Declaration were Thomas Jefferson and John Adams—the one having penned it and the other sustained it the most forcibly in debate— the only two of the fifty-five who sustained it being elected President of the United States. Precisely fifty years after they put their hands to the paper it pleased Almighty God to take both from the stage of action. This was indeed an extraordinary and remarkable event in our history. Another President, five years after, was called from this stage of existence on the same day and month of the year; and now, on this last Fourth of July just passed, when we have a gigantic Rebellion, at the bottom of which is an effort to overthrow the principle that all men were created equal, we have the surrender of a most powerful position and army on that very day, [cheers] and not only so, but in a succession of battles in Pennsylvania, near to us, through three days, so rapidly fought that they might be called one great battle on the 1st, 2d and 3d of the month of July; and on the 4th the cohorts of those who opposed the declaration that all men are created equal, "turned tail" and run. [Long and continued cheers.] Gentlemen, this is a glorious theme, and the occasion for a speech, but I am not prepared to make one worthy of the occasion. I would like to speak in terms of praise due to the many brave officers and soldiers who have fought in the cause of the Union and liberties of the country from the beginning of the war. These are trying occasions, not only in success, but for the want of success. I dislike to mention the name of one single officer lest I might do wrong to those I might forget. Recent events bring up glorious names, and particularly prominent ones, but these I will not mention. Having said this much, I will now take the music.

"YOU WERE RIGHT, AND I WAS WRONG"

Letter to General Ulysses S. Grant

JULY 13, 1863

While public attention was largely focused on the Eastern Theater of the war, Ulysses S. Grant lay siege to the vital Confederate stronghold of Vicksburg, Mississippi, finally triumphing on Independence Day. Lincoln had been skeptical of Grant's siege strategy, but when the city fell to the Union, he sent this extraordinarily gracious note to his victorious general.

My dear General

I do not remember that you and I ever met personally. I write this now as a grateful acknowledgment for the almost inestimable service you have done the country. I wish to say a word further. When you first reached the vicinity of Vicksburg, I thought you should do, what you finally did—march the troops across the neck, run the batteries with the transports, and thus go below; and I never had any faith, except a general hope that you knew better than I, that the Yazoo Pass expedition, and the like, could succeed. When you got below, and took Port-Gibson, Grand Gulf, and vicinity, I thought you should go down the river and join Gen. Banks; and when you turned Northward East of the Big Black, I feared it was a mistake. I now wish to make the personal acknowledgment that you were right, and I was wrong.

Yours very truly
A. LINCOLN

"THE MISFORTUNE INVOLVED IN LEE'S ESCAPE"

*Unsent Letter to General George G. Meade and Comments
to Robert Lincoln, John Hay, and Gideon Welles*

JULY 14, 1863

---

*The president had quite a different reaction to General George M.
Meade's Gettysburg success—after learning that he had failed to pursue
Lee's defeated forces and destroy them before they could cross the river
back into Confederate territory. Lincoln let off steam by composing this
highly critical letter, but in the end he decided not to mail it. Instead
he filed it away, marking it: "To Gen. Meade, never sent, or signed."
Lincoln's private thoughts to his nearly twenty-year-old son, to his secretary, and to his navy secretary follow in that order.*

Major General Meade

I have just seen your despatch to Gen. Halleck, asking to be relieved of your command, because of a supposed censure of mine. I
am very—*very*—grateful to you for the magnificient success you gave
the cause of the country at Gettysburg; and I am sorry now to be the
author of the slightest pain to you. But I was in such deep distress
myself that I could not restrain some expression of it. I had been op-
pressed nearly ever since the battles at Gettysburg, by what appeared
to be evidences that yourself, and Gen. [Darius] Couch, and Gen.
[William F.] Smith, were not seeking a collision with the enemy, but
were trying to get him across the river without another battle. What
these evidences were, if you please, I hope to tell you at some time,
when we shall both feel better. The case, summarily stated is this.
You fought and beat the enemy at Gettysburg; and, of course, to say
the least, his loss was as great as yours. He retreated; and you did not,
as it seemed to me, pressingly pursue him; but a flood in the river
detained him, till, by slow degrees, you were again upon him. You
had at least twenty thousand veteran troops directly with you, and as
many more raw ones within supporting distance, all in addition to
those who fought with you at Gettysburg; while it was not possible

that he had received a single recruit; and yet you stood and let the flood run down, bridges be built, and the enemy move away at his leisure, without attacking him. And Couch and Smith! The latter left Carlisle in time, upon all ordinary calculation, to have aided you in the last battle at Gettysburg; but he did not arrive. At the end of more than ten days, I believe twelve, under constant urging, he reached Hagerstown from Carlisle, which is not an inch over fiftyfive miles, if so much. And Couch's movement was very little different.

Again, my dear general, I do not believe you appreciate the magnitude of the misfortune involved in Lee's escape. He was within your easy grasp, and to have closed upon him would, in connection with our other late successes, have ended the war. As it is, the war will be prolonged indefinitely. If you could not safely attack Lee last monday, how can you possibly do so South of the river, when you can take with you very few more than two thirds of the force you then had in hand? It would be unreasonable to expect, and I do not expect you can now effect much. Your golden opportunity is gone, and I am distressed immeasureably because of it.

I beg you will not consider this a prossecution, or persecution of yourself. As you had learned that I was dissatisfied, I have thought it best to kindly tell you why.

If I had gone up there, I could have whipped them myself.

Our army held the war in the hollow in their hand, and they would not close it.

Well, to be candid, I have no faith that Meade will attack Lee; nothing looks like it to me. I believe he can never have another as good opportunity as that which he trifled away. Everything since has dragged with him. No, I don't believe he is going to fight.

"SENTENCE COMMUTED"

Orders to Judge Advocate General Joseph Holt

JULY 18, 1863

Evidently in a forgiving mood, Lincoln issued this succession of pardons two weeks after the Union triumph at Gettysburg. These are all endorsements scribbled on case files the president had personally reviewed. In one case, not printed here, he allowed a death sentence to stand. Inclined to be forgiving, and remembered by history as a softhearted pardoner, Lincoln also authorized large numbers of military executions. On one occasion, he told General George Stoneman: "Tomorrow night I shall have a terrible headache. Tomorrow is hangman's day and I shall have to act upon death sentences."

Let him [Private Michael Delany, Company K, First Colorado Cavalry, sentenced to be executed for desertion—ed.] fight instead of being shot[.]

Sentence commuted [for sixteen-year-old Private Francis Dew, Company G, Second Massachusetts Cavalry, sentenced to be executed for mutiny—ed.] according to the recommendation.

Sentence commuted [for Lieutenant Jacob Garcy, Company A, 82nd Pennsylvania Volunteers, sentenced to dismissal for disobeying orders—ed.] to forfeiture of pay for three months[.]

Sentence commuted [for Lieutenant Charles B. Leathe, 4th Massachusetts Volunteers, sentenced to dismissal for being absent without leave—ed.] to forfeiture of pay for one month[.]

"With Pomp, and Mighty Swell"

Doggerel on Lee's Repulse at Gettysburg

JULY 19, 1863

Lincoln merrily scribbled these verses two weeks after the Union victory at Gettysburg. They remained unknown and unpublished for more than a hundred years.

Gen. Lees invasion of the North written by himself—

In eighteen sixty three, with pomp,
and mighty swell,
Me and Jeff's Confederacy, went
forth to sack Phil-del,
The Yankees they got arter us, and
giv us particular hell,
And we skedaddled back again,
and didn't sack Phil-del.

"General Instructions . . . to Our Naval Commanders"

Orders to Secretary of the Navy Gideon Welles

JULY 25, 1863

Welles believed that Secretary of State William H. Seward—his bitter cabinet enemy—was behind Lincoln's August 12 request that Welles specify department policy on the navy's conduct at neutral ports. Welles firmly believed: "We injure neither ourselves nor Great Britain by an honest and firm maintenance of our rights." But Lincoln wanted no further quarrels with the British.

Sir:

Certain matters have come to my notice, and considered by me, which induce me to believe, that it will conduce to the public interest for you to add to the general instructions given to our Naval Commanders, in relation to contraband trade, propositions substantially as follows, to wit:

"1st. You will avoid the reality, and as far as possible, the appearance, of using any neutral port, to watch neutral vessels, and then to dart out and seize them on their departure.

"Note—Complaint is made that this has been practiced at the Port of St. Thomas, which practice, if it exist, is disapproved, and must cease.

"2nd. You will not, in any case, detain the crew of a captured neutral vessel, or any other subject, of a neutral power on board such vessel, as prisoners of war, or otherwise, except the small number necessary as witnesses in the prize court.

"Note—The practice here forbidden is also charged to exist, which, if true, is disapproved, and must cease."

My dear Sir, it is not intended to be insinuated that you have been remiss in the performance of the arduous and responsible duties of your Department, which I take pleasure in affirming has, in your hands, been conducted with admirable success. Yet while your subordinates are, almost of necessity, brought into angry collision with the subjects of foreign States, the representatives of those States and yourself do not come into immediate contact, for the purpose of keeping the peace, in spite of such collisions. At that point there is an ultimate, and heavy responsibility upon me.

What I propose is in strict accordance with international law, and is therefore unobjectionable; while if it do no other good, it will contribute to sustain a considerable portion of the present British Ministry in their places, who, if displaced, are sure to be replaced by others more unfavorable to us.

Your Obt. Servt.
ABRAHAM LINCOLN

"The Same Protection to All Its Soldiers"
Retaliation Order
JULY 30, 1863

Around the time this order was issued, Lincoln had heard from the mother of one of the black soldiers who participated in (and survived) the bloody assault by the Fifty-fourth Massachusetts against Fort Wagner in South Carolina, made famous in the film Glory. *Grateful that her son had not been taken prisoner (because captured African Americans, even free men, were often sent into slavery), she had urged Lincoln to make certain that all prisoners were treated equally: "I know that a colored man ought to run no greater risques than a white. . . . Will you see that the colored men fighting now, are fairly treated. You ought to do this at once." Indeed, Lincoln had just done precisely that by signing the following order.*

It is the duty of every government to give protection to its citizens, of whatever class, color, or condition, and especially to those who are duly organized as soldiers in the public service. The law of nations and the usages and customs of war as carried on by civilized powers, permit no distinction as to color in the treatment of prisoners of war as public enemies. To sell or enslave any captured person, on account of his color, and for no offense against the laws of war, is a relapse into barbarism and a crime against the civilization of the age.

The government of the United States will give the same protection to all its soldiers, and if the enemy shall sell or enslave anyone because of his color, the offense shall be punished by retaliation upon the enemy's prisoners in our possession.

It is therefore ordered that for every soldier of the United States killed in violation of the laws of war, a rebel soldier shall be executed; and for every one enslaved by the enemy or sold into slavery, a rebel soldier shall be placed at hard labor on the public works and continued at such labor until the other shall be released and receive the treatment due to a prisoner of war.

ABRAHAM LINCOLN

"PEACE DOES NOT APPEAR SO DISTANT AS IT DID"

Speech Prepared for Delivery to His Old Springfield Neighbors (Letter to James C. Conkling)

AUGUST 26, 1863

African American soldiers were by now flooding into the ranks of the Union army to fight for their own freedom, impressing many once-skeptical Northerners with their bravery, but alarming, even outraging, others. Invited to speak at a Union rally in his old Illinois hometown, where resentment over black enlistment reigned, Lincoln prepared this ringing defense of his recruitment policy. In the end the beleaguered president did not travel west after all but, determined to make his views known, asked his onetime neighbor James C. Conkling, whom he considered an able public reader, to deliver it to the crowd "very slowly." Harriet Beecher Stowe called the result—which was promptly published in many newspapers—"a masterly" product of "a mind both strong and generous."

My Dear Sir.

Your letter inviting me to attend a mass-meeting of unconditional Union-men, to be held at the Capital of Illinois, on the 3d day of September, has been received.

It would be very agreeable to me, to thus meet my old friends, at my own home; but I can not, just now, be absent from here, so long as a visit there, would require.

The meeting is to be of all those who maintain unconditional devotion to the Union; and I am sure my old political friends will thank me for tendering, as I do, the nation's gratitude to those other noble men, whom no partizan malice, or partizan hope, can make false to the nation's life.

There are those who are dissatisfied with me. To such I would say: You desire peace; and you blame me that we do not have it. But how can we attain it? There are but three conceivable ways. First, to suppress the rebellion by force of arms. This, I am trying to do. Are you for it? If you are, so far we are agreed. If you are not for it, a second way is, to give up the Union. I am against this. Are you for it? If you are, you should say so plainly. If you are not for *force*, nor yet for *dissolution*, there only remains some imaginable *compromise*. I do not believe any compromise, embracing the maintenance of the Union, is now possible. All I learn, leads to a directly opposite belief. The strength of the rebellion, is its military—its army. That army dominates all the country, and all the people, within its range. Any offer of terms made by any man or men within that range, in opposition to that army, is simply nothing for the present; because such man or men, have no power whatever to enforce their side of a compromise, if one were made with them. To illustrate—Suppose refugees from the South, and peace men of the North, get together in convention, and frame and proclaim a compromise embracing a restoration of the Union; in what way can that compromise be used to keep Lee's army out of Pennsylvania? Meade's army can keep Lee's army out of Pennsylvania; and, I think, can ultimately drive it out of existence. But no paper compromise, to which the controllers of Lee's army are not agreed, can, at all, affect that army. In an effort at such compromise we should waste time, which the enemy would improve to our disadvantage; and that would be all. A compromise, to be effective, must be made either with those who control the rebel army, or with the people first liberated from the domination of that army, by the success of our own army. Now allow me to assure you, that no word or intimation, from that rebel army, or from any of the men controlling it, in relation to any peace compromise, has ever come to my knowledge or belief. All charges and insinuations to the contrary, are deceptive and groundless. And I promise you, that if any such proposition shall hereafter come, it shall not be rejected, and kept a secret from you. I freely acknowledge myself the servant of the people, according to the bond of service—the United States constitution; and that, as such, I am responsible to them.

But, to be plain, you are dissatisfied with me about the negro.

Quite likely there is a difference of opinion between you and myself upon that subject. I certainly wish that all men could be free, while I suppose you do not. Yet I have neither adopted, nor proposed any measure, which is not consistent with even your view, provided you are for the Union. I suggested compensated emancipation; to which you replied you wished not to be taxed to buy negroes. But I had not asked you to be taxed to buy negroes, except in such way, as to save you from greater taxation to save the Union exclusively by other means.

You dislike the emancipation proclamation; and, perhaps, would have it retracted. You say it is unconstitutional—I think differently. I think the constitution invests its commander-in-chief, with the law of war, in time of war. The most that can be said, if so much, is, that slaves are property. Is there—has there ever been—any question that by the law of war, property, both of enemies and friends, may be taken when needed? And is it not needed whenever taking it, helps us, or hurts the enemy? Armies, the world over, destroy enemies' property when they can not use it; and even destroy their own to keep it from the enemy. Civilized belligerents do all in their power to help themselves, or hurt the enemy, except a few things regarded as barbarous or cruel. Among the exceptions are the massacre of vanquished foes, and non-combatants, male and female.

But the proclamation, as law, either is valid, or is not valid. If it is not valid, it needs no retraction. If it is valid, it can not be retracted, any more than the dead can be brought to life. Some of you profess to think its retraction would operate favorably for the Union. Why better *after* the retraction, than *before* the issue? There was more than a year and a half of trial to suppress the rebellion before the proclamation issued, the last one hundred days of which passed under an explicit notice that it was coming, unless averted by those in revolt, returning to their allegiance. The war has certainly progressed as favorably for us, since the issue of the proclamation as before. I know as fully as one can know the opinions of others, that some of the commanders of our armies in the field who have given us our most important successes, believe the emancipation policy, and the use of colored troops, constitute the heaviest blow yet dealt to the rebellion; and that, at least one of those important successes, could not have been achieved when it was, but for the aid of black soldiers. Among the commanders holding these views are some who have never had any affinity with what is called abolitionism, or with republican party politics; but who hold them purely as military opinions. I submit these opinions as being entitled to some weight against the objections, often urged, that emancipation, and arming the blacks, are unwise as military measures, and were not adopted, as such, in good faith.

You say you will not fight to free negroes. Some of them seem willing to fight for you; but, no matter. Fight you, then, exclusively to save the Union. I issued the proclamation on purpose to aid you in saving the Union. Whenever you shall have conquered all resistance to the Union, if I shall urge you to continue fighting, it will be an apt time, then, for you to declare you will not fight to free negroes.

I thought that in your struggle for the Union, to whatever extent the negroes should cease helping the enemy, to that extent it weakened the enemy in his resistance to you. Do you think differently? I thought that whatever negroes can be got to do as soldiers, leaves just so much less for white soldiers to do, in saving the Union. Does it appear otherwise to you? But negroes, like other people, act upon motives. Why should they do any thing for us, if we will do nothing for them? If they stake their lives for us, they must be prompted by the strongest motive—even the promise of freedom. And the promise being made, must be kept.

The signs look better. The Father of Waters [the Mississippi—ed.] again goes unvexed to the sea. Thanks to the great North-West for it. Nor yet wholly to them. Three hundred miles up, they met New-England, Empire, Key-Stone, and Jersey, hewing their way right and left. The Sunny South too, in more colors than one, also lent a hand. On the spot, their part of the history was jotted down in black and white. The job was a great national one; and let none be banned who bore an honorable part in it. And while those who have cleared the great river may well be proud, even that is not all. It is hard to say that anything has been more bravely, and well done, than at Antietam, Murfreesboro, Gettysburg, and on many fields of lesser note. Nor must Uncle Sam's Web-feet be forgotten. At all the watery margins they have been present. Not only on the deep sea, the broad bay, and the rapid river, but also up the narrow muddy bayou, and wherever the ground was a little damp, they have been, and made their tracks. Thanks to all. For the great republic—for the principle it lives by, and keeps alive—for man's vast future,—thanks to all.

Peace does not appear so distant as it did. I hope it will come soon, and come to stay; and so come as to be worth the keeping in all future time. It will then have been proved that, among free men, there can be no successful appeal from the ballot to the bullet; and that they who take such appeal are sure to lose their case, and pay the cost. And then, there will be some black men who can remember that, with silent tongue, and clenched teeth, and steady eye, and well-poised bayonet, they have helped mankind on to this great consummation; while, I fear, there will be some white ones, unable to forget that, with malignant heart, and deceitful speech, they have strove to hinder it.

Still let us not be over-sanguine of a speedy final triumph. Let us be quite sober. Let us diligently apply the means, never doubting that a just God, in his own good time, will give us the rightful result.

Yours very truly
A. LINCOLN.

"You Began the War, and You Can End It"

Fragment on the Rebellion

[CA. AUGUST 26, 1863]

*Lincoln may have crafted this fragment as part of his Conkling letter—
he often wrote out ideas for speeches in advance on small scraps of
paper. If so, he ultimately decided to exclude it. Nonetheless, it merits
attention from history as an honest summary of the state of the Union
war effort at midconflict.*

Suppose those now in rebellion should say: "We cease fighting: re-
establish the national authority amongst us—customs, courts, mails,
land-offices,—all as before the rebellion—we claiming to send members to both branches of Congress, as of yore, and to hold our slaves
according to our State laws, notwithstanding anything or all things
which has occurred during the rebellion." I probably should answer:
"It will be difficult to justify in reason, or to maintain in fact, a war
on one side, which shall have ceased on the other. You began the
war, and you can end it. If questions remain, let them be solved by
peaceful means—by courts, and votes. This war is an appeal, by you,
from the ballot to the sword; and a great object with me has been to
teach the futility of such appeal—to teach that what is decided by
the ballot, can not be reversed by the sword—to teach that there can
be no successful appeal from a fair election, but to the next election.
Whether persons sent to congress, will be admitted to seats is, by the
constitution, left to each House to decide, the President having nothing to do with it. Yet the question can not be one of indifference to
me. I shall dread, and I think we all should dread, to see the [*sic*] 'the
disturbing element' so brought back into the government, as to make
probable a renewal of the terrible scenes through which we are now
passing. During my continuance here, the government will return
no person to slavery who is free according to the proclamation, or
to any of the acts of congress, unless such return shall be held to be
a legal duty, by the proper court of final resort, in which case I will
promptly act as may then appear to be my personal duty.["]

Congress has left to me very large powers to remit forfeitures and personal penalties; and I should exercise these to the greatest extent which might seem consistent with the future public safety. I have thus told you, once more, so far as it is for me to say, what you are fighting for. The prospects of the Union have greatly improved recently; still, let us not be over-sanguine of a speedy final triumph. Let us diligently apply the means, never doubting that a just God, in his own good time, will give us the rightful result.

"Sumpter Is *Certainly* Battered Down"

Telegram to Mary Lincoln

August 29, 1863

Seeking to escape Washington's torrid summer heat, Mary Lincoln, with sons Robert and Tad in tow, left town for a vacation in the mountains of Vermont. Alone at his summer cottage at the Soldiers' Home outside Washington, the lonely president kept his wife posted on important news from the front, in this case the Union attack on the very South Carolina fort that Confederates had shelled more than two years earlier to begin the war.

Mrs. A. Lincoln.

All quite well. Fort-Sumpter [*sic*] is *certainly* battered down, and utterly useless to the enemy, and it is *believed* here, but not entirely certain, that both Sumpter and Fort-Wagner [where black troops of the Fifty-fourth Massachusetts had died in such great numbers the month before—ed.], are occupied by our forces. It is also certain that Gen. [Quincy Adams] Gil[l]more has thrown some shot into Charleston [using the new long-range, eight-inch Parrot rifles nicknamed "Swamp Angels"—ed.]

A. Lincoln

"TENNESSEE IS NOW CLEAR"

Letter to Governor Andrew Johnson

SEPTEMBER 11, 1863

Andrew Johnson—Lincoln's future vice president and successor—was then serving as military governor of Tennessee. He replied to this letter just as the president hoped: "I have taken decided ground for . . . immediate emancipation from gradual emancipation. Now is the time for settlement of this question. Hence I am for immediate emancipation." This is the letter that inspired the crucial policy shift, which Lincoln had advocated for nearly a year.

My dear Sir:

All Tennessee is now clear of armed insurrectionists. You need not to be reminded that it is the nick of time for re-inaugurating a loyal State government. Not a moment should be lost. You, and the co-operating friends there, can better judge of the ways and means, than can be judged by any here. I only offer a few suggestions. The re-inauguration must not be such as to give control of the State, and it's representation in Congress, to the enemies of the Union, driving it's friends there into political exile. The whole struggle for Tennessee will have been profitless to both State and Nation, if it so ends that Gov. Johnson is put down, and Gov. [Isham Green] Harris [a secessionist-minded Democrat—ed.] is put up. It must not be so. You must have it otherwise. Let the reconstruction be the work of such men only as can be trusted for the Union. Exclude all others, and trust that your government, so organized, will be recognized here, as being the one of republican form, to be guarranteed to the state, and to be protected against invasion and domestic violence.

It is something on the question of *time,* to remember that it can not be known who is next to occupy the position I now hold, nor what he will do.

I see that you have declared in favor of emancipation in Tennessee, for which, may God bless you. Get emancipation into your new State government—Constitution—and there will be no such word as fail for your case.

The raising of colored troops I think will greatly help every way.

Yours very truly

A. LINCOLN

"HAS THE MANHOOD OF OUR RACE RUN OUT?"

From an Opinion on the Legality of the Draft

[SEPTEMBER 14? 1863]

On September 14, 1863, a worried Lincoln told his cabinet he feared that local judges—intent on pardoning reluctant draftees—would undermine the conscription law already under violent challenge by rioters in several Northern cities. Announcing that he was "determined to put a stop to these factious and mischievous proceeding," he prepared the following public statement, which he ultimately, inexplicably, decided not to issue. The president had not yet accepted the fact that public resistance to the draft arose in part over its original provision allowing wealthier men to buy substitutes.

At the beginning of the war, and ever since, a variety of motives pressing, some in one direction and some in the other, would be presented to the mind of each man physically fit for a soldier, upon the combined effect of which motives, he would, or would not, voluntarily enter the service. Among these motives would be patriotism, political bias, ambition, personal courage, love of adventure, want of employment, and convenience, or the opposites of some of these. We already have, and have had in the service, as appears, substantially all that can be obtained upon this voluntary weighing of motives. And yet we must somehow obtain more, or relinquish the original object of the contest, together with all the blood and treasure already expended in the effort to secure it. To meet this necessity the law for the draft has been enacted. You who do not wish to be soldiers, do not like this law. This is natural; nor does it imply want of patriotism. Nothing can be so just, and necessary, as to make us like it, if it is disagreeable to us. We are prone, too, to find false arguments with which to excuse ourselves for opposing such disagreeable things. In this case those who desire the rebellion to succeed, and others who seek reward in a different way, are very active in accomodating us with this class of arguments. They tell us the law is unconstitutional. It is the first instance, I believe, in which the power of congress to do a thing has ever been questioned, in a case when the power is given by the constitution in express terms. Whether a power can be implied, when it is not expressed, has often been the subject of controversy; but this is the first case in which the degree of effrontery has been ventured upon, of denying a power which is plainly and distinctly written down in the constitution. The constitution declares that "The congress shall have power . . . To raise and support armies; but no appropriation of money to that use shall be for a longer term than two years." The whole scope of the conscription act is "to raise and support armies." There is nothing else in it. It makes no appropriation of money; and hence the money clause just quoted, is not touched by it. The case simply is the constitution provides that the congress shall have power to raise and support armies; and, by this act, the congress has exercised the power to raise and support armies. This is the whole of it. It is a law made in litteral pursuance of this part of the United States Constitution; and another part of the same constitution declares that "This constitution, and the laws made in pursuance thereof . . . shall be the supreme law of the land, and the judges in every state shall be bound thereby, anything in the constitution or laws of any state to the contrary notwithstanding."

Do you admit that the power is given to raise and support armies, and yet insist that by this act congress has not exercised the power in a constitutional mode?—has not done the thing, in the right way? Who is to judge of this? The constitution gives congress the power, but it does not prescribe the mode, or expressly declare who shall prescribe it. In such case congress must prescribe the mode, or relinquish the power. There is no alternative. Congress could not exercise the power to do the thing, if it had not the power of providing a way to do it, when no way is provided by the constitution for doing it. In fact congress would not have the power to raise and support armies, if even by the constitution, it were left to the option of any other, or others, to give or withhold the only mode of doing it. If the constitution had prescribed a mode, congress could and must follow that mode; but as it is, the mode necessarily goes to congress, with the power expressly given. The power is given fully, completely, unconditionally. It is not a power to raise armies *if* State authorities consent; nor *if* the men to compose the armies are entirely willing; but it is a power to raise and support armies given to congress by the constitution, without an if.

. . . .

The principle of the draft, which simply is involuntary, or enforced service, is not new. It has been practiced in all ages of the world. It was well known to the framers of our constitution as one of the modes of raising armies, at the time they placed in that instrument the provision that "the congress shall have power to raise and support armies." It has been used, just before, in establishing our independence; and it was also used under the constitution in 1812. Wherein is the peculiar hardship now? Shall we shrink from the necessary means to maintain our free government, which our grand-fathers employed to establish it, and our own fathers have already employed once to maintain it? Are we degenerate? Has the manhood of our race run out?

Again, a law may be both constitutional and expedient, and yet may be administered in an unjust and unfair way. This law belongs to a class, which class is composed of those laws whose object is to distribute burthens or benefits on the principle of equality. No one of these laws can ever be practically administered with that exactness which can be conceived of in the mind. A tax law, the principle of which is that each owner shall pay in proproportion [*sic*] to the value of his property, will be a dead letter, if no one can be compelled to pay until it can be shown that every other one will pay in precisely the same proportion according to value; nay even, it will be a dead letter, if no one can be compelled to pay until it is certain that every other one will pay at all—even in unequal proportion. Again the United States House of representatives is constituted on the principle that each member is sent by the same number of people that each other one is sent by; and yet in practice no two of the whole number, much less the whole number, are ever sent by precisely the same number of constituents. The Districts can not be made precisely equal in population at first, and if they could, they would become unequal in a single day, and much more so in the ten years, which the Districts, once made, are to continue. They can not be re-modelled every day; nor, without too much expence and labor, even every year.

This sort of difficulty applies in full force, to the practical administration of the draft law. In fact the difficulty is greater in the case of the draft law. First, it starts with all the inequality of the congressional Districts; but these are based on entire population, while the draft is based upon those only who are fit for soldiers, and such may not bear the same proportion to the whole in one District, that they do in another. Again, the facts must be ascertained, and credit given, for the unequal numbers of soldiers which have already gone from the several Districts. In all these points errors will occur in spite of the utmost fidelity. The government is bound to administer the law with such an approach to exactness as is usual in analagous cases, and as entire good faith and fidelity will reach. If so great departures as to be inconsistent with such good faith and fidelity, or great departures occurring in any way, be pointed out, they shall be corrected; and any agent shown to have caused such departures intentionally, shall be dismissed.

With these views, and on these principles, I feel bound to tell you it is my purpose to see the draft law faithfully executed.

"You Steadily Move the Contrary Way"

Unsent Letter to General Ambrose E. Burnside

SEPTEMBER 25, 1863

Lincoln had ordered Ambrose E. Burnside, now assigned to the Department of the Ohio, to join forces with General William Rosecrans on September 21. Two days later, Burnside wired his assent, and commended "the wisdom of the order," and yet indicated he was still busy with minor military actions of his own. In response, Lincoln vented in another of those angry letters he decided not to send. But it does reflect the control he insisted upon maintaining over all movements of Union forces. In the end, Burnside acquitted himself well by successfully defending Knoxville.

Major General Burnside

Yours of the 23rd. is just received, and it makes me doubt whether I am awake or dreaming. I have been struggling for ten days, first through Gen. Halleck, and then directly, to get you to go to assist Gen. Rosecrans in an extremity, and you have repeatedly declared you would do it, and yet you steadily move the contrary way. On the 19th. you telegraph once from Knoxville, and twice from Greenville, acknowledging receipt of order, and saying you will hurry support to Rosecrans. On the 20th. you telegraph again from Knoxville, saying you will do all you can, and are hurrying troops to Rosecrans. On the 21st. you telegraph from Morristown, saying you will hurry support to Rosecrans; and now your despatch of the 23rd. comes in from Carter's Station, still farther away from Rosecrans, still saying you will assist him, but giving no account of any progress made towards assisting him.

You came in upon the Tennessee River at Kingston, Loudon, and Knoxville; and what bridges or the want of them upon the Holston, can have to do in getting the troops towards Rosecrans at Chattanooga is incomprehensible. They were already many miles nearer Chattanooga than any part of the Holston river is, and on the right side of it. If they are now on the wrong side of it, they can only have got so by going from the direction of Chattanooga, and that too, since you have assured us you would move to Chattanooga; while it would seem too, that they could re-cross the Holston, by whatever means they crossed it going East.

"FROM THESE HONORED DEAD"

The Gettysburg Address

GETTYSBURG, PENNSYLVANIA, NOVEMBER 19, 1863

Lincoln was not invited to give the principal address at the dedication of the soldiers' cemetery at Gettysburg. That honor went to famed public speaker Edward Everett, who had run for vice president (against the Lincoln ticket) three years earlier. Everett declaimed grandiloquently for two hours, offering a detailed history of the battle. Lincoln chose to devote his "few appropriate remarks" to the greater meaning of the conflict. The next day, Everett graciously wrote the president: "I should be glad, if I could flatter myself that I came as near to the central idea of the occasion, in two hours, as you did in two minutes." Indeed, no one remembers what Everett said at Gettysburg, while Lincoln's elegy is widely considered the greatest presidential speech in history. This is the last of the five drafts of the speech that survive in Lincoln's hand. He wrote it in February 1864 as a donation to the Baltimore Sanitary Fair, an event organized to raise funds for the benefit of Union Soldiers. Today, the original handwritten copy sits in the Lincoln Bedroom (then Lincoln's office) in the White House.

Address delivered at the dedication of the Cemetery at Gettysburg.

Four score and seven years ago our fathers brought forth on this continent, a new nation, conceived in Liberty, and dedicated to the proposition that all men are created equal.

Now we are engaged in a great civil war, testing whether that

Lincoln (bare-headed, looking down, center) on the speakers' platform at the Gettysburg National Cemetery on November 19, 1863. On this day he would deliver his most famous speech, dedicating the Civil War to "the great task remaining before us." *(Library of Congress)*

nation, or any nation so conceived and so dedicated, can long endure. We are met on a great battle-field of that war. We have come to dedicate a portion of that field, as a final resting place for those who here gave their lives that that nation might live. It is altogether fitting and proper that we should do this.

But, in a larger sense, we can not dedicate—we can not consecrate—we can not hallow—this ground. The brave men, living and dead, who struggled here, have consecrated it, far above our poor power to add or detract. The world will little note, nor long remember what we say here, but it can never forget what they did here. It is for us the living, rather, to be dedicated here to the unfinished work which they who fought here have thus far so nobly advanced. It is rather for us to be here dedicated to the great task remaining before us—that from these honored dead we take increased devotion to that cause for which they gave the last full measure of devotion—that we here highly resolve that these dead shall not have died in vain—that this nation, under God, shall have a new birth of freedom—and that government of the people, by the people, for the people, shall not perish from the earth.

"OUR CHIEFEST CARE . . . TO THE ARMY AND NAVY"

From the Annual Message to Congress

DECEMBER 8, 1863

President Lincoln's third such message offered the requisite, numbing details about the federal budget, foreign relations, and other matters, but it also focused uniquely on the growth and future of the U.S. Navy and the perceived improvement in Northern morale, which, as it turned out, was only temporary.

Fellow citizens of the Senate and House of Representatives:

Another year of health, and of sufficiently abundant harvests has passed. For these, and especially for the improved condition of our national affairs, our renewed, and profoundest gratitude to God is due.

We remain in peace and friendship with foreign powers.

The efforts of disloyal citizens of the United States to involve us in foreign wars, to aid an inexcusable insurrection, have been unavailing. Her Britannic Majesty's government, as was justly expected, have exercised their authority to prevent the departure of new hostile expeditions from British ports. The Emperor of France has, by a like proceeding, promptly vindicated the neutrality which he proclaimed at the beginning of the contest. Questions of great intricacy and importance have arisen out of the blockade, and other belligerent operations, between the government and several of the maritime powers, but they have been discussed, and, as far as was possible, accommodated in a spirit of frankness, justice, and mutual good will. It is especially gratifying that our prize courts, by the impartiality of their adjudications, have commanded the respect and confidence of maritime powers.

The supplemental treaty between the United States and Great Britain for the suppression of the African slave trade, made on the 17th. day of February last, has been duly ratified, and carried into execution. It is believed that, so far as American ports and American citizens are concerned, that inhuman and odious traffic has been brought to an end.

.   .   .   .

The duties devolving on the naval branch of the service during the year, and throughout the whole of this unhappy contest, have been discharged with fidelity and eminent success. The extensive blockade has been constantly increasing in efficiency, as the navy has expanded; yet on so long a line it has so far been impossible to entirely suppress illicit trade. From returns received at the Navy Department, it appears that more than one thousand vessels have been captured since the blockade was instituted, and that the value of prizes already sent in for adjudication amounts to over thirteen millions of dollars.

The naval force of the United States consists at this time of five hundred and eighty-eight vessels, completed and in the course of completion, and of these seventy-five are iron-clad or armored steamers. The events of the war give an increased interest and importance to the navy which will probably extend beyond the war itself.

The armored vessels in our navy completed and in service, or which are under contract and approaching completion, are believed to exceed in number those of any other power. But while these may be relied upon for harbor defence and coast service, others of greater strength and capacity will be necessary for cruising purposes, and to maintain our rightful position on the ocean.

The change that has taken place in naval vessels and naval warfare, since the introduction of steam as a motive-power for ships-of-war, demands either a corresponding change in some of our existing navy yards, or the establishment of new ones, for the construction and necessary repair of modern naval vessels. No inconsiderable embarrassment, delay, and public injury have been experienced from the want of such governmental establishments. The necessity of such a navy yard, so furnished, at some suitable place upon the Atlantic seaboard, has on repeated occasions been brought to the attention of Congress by the Navy Department, and is again presented in the report of the Secretary which accompanies this communication. I think it my duty to invite your special attention to this subject, and also to that of establishing a yard and depot for naval purposes upon one of the western rivers. A naval force has been created on those interior waters, and under many disadvantages, within little more than two years, exceeding in numbers the whole naval force of the country at the commencement of the present administration. Satisfactory and important as have been the performances of the heroic men of the navy at this interesting period, they are scarcely more wonderful than the success of our mechanics and artisans in the production of war vessels which has created a new form of naval power.

. . . .

The increase of the number of seamen in the public service, from seven thousand five hundred men, in the spring of 1861, to about thirty four thousand at the present time has been accomplished without special legislation, or extraordinary bounties to promote that increase. It has been found, however, that the operation of the draft, with the high bounties paid for army recruits, is beginning to affect injuriously the naval service, and will, if not corrected, be likely to impair its efficiency, by detaching seamen from their proper vocation and inducing them to enter the Army. I therefore respectfully suggest that Congress might aid both the army and naval services by a definite provision on this subject, which would at the same time be equitable to the communities more especially interested.

I commend to your consideration the suggestions of the Secretary of the Navy in regard to the policy of fostering and training seamen, and also the education of officers and engineers for the naval service. The Naval Academy is rendering signal service in preparing midshipmen for the highly responsible duties which in after life they will be required to perform. In order that the country should not be deprived of the proper quota of educated officers, for which legal provision has been made at the naval school, the vacancies caused by the neglect or omission to make nominations from the States in insurrection have been filled by the Secretary of the Navy.

The school is now more full and complete than at any former period, and in every respect to the favorable consideration of Congress.

· · · · · · · · · ·

When Congress assembled a year ago the war had already lasted nearly twenty months, and there had been many conflicts on both land and sea, with varying results.

The rebellion had been pressed back into reduced limits; yet the tone of public feeling and opinion, at home and abroad, was not satisfactory. With other signs, the popular elections, then just past, indicated uneasiness among ourselves, while amid much that was cold and menacing the kindest words coming from Europe were uttered in accents of pity, that we were too blind to surrender a hopeless cause. Our commerce was suffering greatly by a few armed vessels built upon and furnished from foreign shores, and we were threatened with such additions from the same quarter as would sweep our trade from the sea and raise our blockade. We had failed to elicit from European governments anything hopeful upon this subject. The preliminary emancipation proclamation, issued in September, was running its assigned period to the beginning of the new year. A month later the final proclamation came, including the announcement that colored men of suitable condition would be received into the war service. The policy of emancipation, and of employing black soldiers, gave to the future a new aspect, about which hope, and fear, and doubt contended in uncertain conflict. According to our political system, as a matter of civil administration, the general government had no lawful power to effect emancipation in any State, and for a long time it had been hoped that the rebellion could be suppressed without resorting to it as a military measure. It was all the while deemed possible that the necessity for it might come, and that if it should, the crisis of the contest would then be presented. It came, and as was anticipated, it was followed by dark and doubtful days. Eleven months having now passed, we are permitted to take another review. The rebel borders are pressed still further back, and by the complete opening of the Mississippi the country dominated by the rebellion is divided into distinct parts, with no practical communication between them. Tennessee and Arkansas have been substantially cleared of insurgent control, and influential citizens in each, owners of slaves and advocates of slavery at the beginning of the rebellion, now declare openly for emancipation in their respective States. Of those States not included in the emancipation proclamation, Maryland, and Missouri, neither of which three years ago would tolerate any restraint upon the extension of slavery into new territories, only dispute now as to the best mode of removing it within their own limits.

Of those who were slaves at the beginning of the rebellion, full one hundred thousand are now in the United States military service, about one-half of which number actually bear arms in the ranks; thus giving the double advantage of taking so much labor from the insurgent cause, and supplying the places which otherwise must be filled with so many white men. So far as tested, it is difficult to say they are not as good soldiers as any. No servile insurrection, or tendency to violence or cruelty, has marked the measures of emancipation and arming the blacks. These measures have been much discussed in foreign countries, and contemporary with such discussion the tone of public sentiment there is much improved. At home the same measures have been fully discussed, supported, criticised, and denounced, and the annual elections following are highly encouraging to those whose official duty it is to bear the country through this great trial. Thus we have the new reckoning. The crisis which threatened to divide the friends of the Union is past.

. . . .

In the midst of other cares, however important, we must not lose sight of the fact that the war power is still our main reliance. To that power alone can we look, yet for a time, to give confidence to the people in the contested regions, that the insurgent power will not again overrun them. Until that confidence shall be established, little can be done anywhere for what is called reconstruction. Hence our chiefest care must still be directed to the army and navy, who have thus far borne their harder part so nobly and well. And it may be esteemed fortunate that in giving the greatest efficiency to these indispensable arms, we do also honorably recognize the gallant men, from commander to sentinel, who compose them, and to whom, more than to others, the world must stand indebted for the home of freedom disenthralled, regenerated, enlarged, and perpetuated.

"TO REINAUGURATE LOYAL STATE GOVERNMENTS"

Proclamation of Amnesty and Reconstruction

DECEMBER 8, 1863

Included in his annual message was this handwritten proclamation, offering a framework for reestablishing civilian governments once seceded states returned to the Union. The Richmond Examiner *promptly denounced the offer, declaring: "In proposing these utterly infamous terms, this Yankee monster of inhumanity and falsehood, has the audacity to declare that in some of the Confederate States the elements of reconstruction were ready for action."*

By the President of the United States of America: A Proclamation.

Whereas, in and by the Constitution of the United States, it is provided that the President "shall have power to grant reprieves and pardons for offences against the United States, except in cases of impeachment;" and

Whereas a rebellion now exists whereby the loyal State governments of several States have for a long time been subverted, and many persons have committed and are now guilty of treason against the United States; and

Whereas, with reference to said rebellion and treason, laws have been enacted by Congress declaring forfeitures and confiscation of property and liberation of slaves, all upon terms and conditions therein stated, and also declaring that the President was thereby authorized at any time thereafter, by proclamation, to extend to persons who may have participated in the existing rebellion, in any State or part thereof, pardon and amnesty, with such exceptions and at such times and on such conditions as he may deem expedient for the public welfare; and

Whereas the congressional declaration for limited and conditional pardon accords with well-established judicial exposition of the pardoning power; and

Whereas, with reference to said rebellion, the President of the United States has issued several proclamations, with provisions in regard to the liberation of slaves; and

Whereas it is now desired by some persons heretofore engaged in said rebellion to resume their allegiance to the United States, and to reinaugurate loyal State governments within and for their respective States; therefore,

I, Abraham Lincoln, President of the United States, do proclaim, declare, and make known to all persons who have, directly or by implication, participated in the existing rebellion, except as hereinafter excepted, that a full pardon is hereby granted to them and each of them, with restoration of all rights of property, except as to slaves, and in property cases where rights of third parties shall have intervened, and upon the condition that every such person shall take and subscribe an oath, and thenceforward keep and maintain said oath inviolate; and which oath shall be registered for permanent preservation, and shall be of the tenor and effect following, to wit:

"I, ____, do solemnly swear, in presence of Almighty God, that I will henceforth faithfully support, protect and defend the Constitution of the United States, and the union of the States thereunder; and that I will, in like manner, abide by and faithfully support all acts of Congress passed during the existing rebellion with reference to slaves, so long and so far as not repealed, modified or held void by Congress, or by decision of the Supreme Court; and that I will, in like manner, abide by and faithfully support all proclamations of the President made during the existing rebellion having reference to slaves, so long and so far as not modified or declared void by decision of the Supreme Court. So help me God."

The persons excepted from the benefits of the foregoing provisions are all who are, or shall Have been, civil or diplomatic officers or agents of the so-called confederate government; all who have left judicial stations under the United States to aid the rebellion; all who are, or shall have been, military or naval officers of said so-called confederate government above the rank of colonel in the army, or of lieutenant in the navy; all who left seats in the United States Congress to aid the rebellion; all who resigned commissions in the army or navy of the United States, and afterwards aided the rebellion; and all who have engaged in any way in treating colored persons or white persons, in charge of such, otherwise than lawfully as prisoners of war, and which persons may have been found in the United States service, as soldiers, seamen, or in any other capacity.

And I do further proclaim, declare, and make known, that whenever, in any of the States of Arkansas, Texas, Louisiana, Mississippi, Tennessee, Alabama, Georgia, Florida, South Carolina, and North Carolina, a number of persons, not less than one-tenth in number of the votes cast in such State at the Presidential election of the year of our Lord one thousand eight hundred and sixty, each having taken the oath aforesaid and not having since violated it, and being a qualified voter by the election law of the State existing immediately before the so-called act of secession, and excluding all others, shall re-establish a State government which shall be republican, and in no wise contravening said oath, such shall be recognized as the true government of the State, and the State shall receive thereunder the benefits of the constitutional provision which declares that "The United States shall guaranty to every State in this union a republican form of government, and shall protect each of them against invasion; and, on application of the legislature, or the executive, (when the legislature cannot be convened,) against domestic violence."

And I do further proclaim, declare, and make known that any provision which may be adopted by such State government in relation to the freed people of such State, which shall recognize and declare their permanent freedom, provide for their education, and which may yet be consistent, as a temporary arrangement, with their present condition as a laboring, landless, and homeless class, will not be objected to by the national Executive. And it is suggested as not improper, that, in constructing a loyal State government in any State, the name of the State, the boundary, the subdivisions, the constitution, and the general code of laws, as before the rebellion, be maintained, subject only to the modifications made necessary by the conditions hereinbefore stated, and such others, if any, not contravening said conditions, and which may be deemed expedient by those framing the new State government.

To avoid misunderstanding, it may be proper to say that this proclamation, so far as it relates to State governments, has no reference to States wherein loyal State governments have all the while been maintained. And for the same reason, it may be proper to further say that whether members sent to Congress from any State shall be admitted to seats, constitutionally rests exclusively with the respective Houses, and not to any extent with the Executive. And still further, that this proclamation is intended to present the people of the States wherein the national authority has been suspended, and loyal State governments have been subverted, a mode in and by which the national authority and loyal State governments may be re-established within said States, or in any of them; and, while the mode presented is the best the Executive can suggest, with his present impressions, it must not be understood that no other possible mode would be acceptable.

> Given under my hand at the city, of Washington, the 8th. day of December, A.D. one thousand eight hundred and sixty-three, and of the independence of the United States of America the eighty-eighth.

By the President: ABRAHAM LINCOLN
WILLIAM H. SEWARD, Secretary of State.

"Do Not Let Him Be Executed"

Letter to General Stephen A. Hurlbut

DECEMBER 17, 1863

Lincoln's record as a great pardoner has assumed legendary propor-
tions. The records are indeed filled with evidence of his frequent in-
tervention to prevent executions; this is one of them. In the case of this
old acquaintance, General Stephen A. Hurlbut replied that the accused
"tall old man," Henry F. Luckett, was undoubtedly "guilty of smuggling
percussions caps to the enemy" but that the testimony of some friends
indicated he might be insane. In March Lincoln pardoned him, and
Luckett wrote to thank him for his clemency, noting that "it has been by
your grace that I have been delivered from the Lions Paw."

Major General Hurlbut

I understand you have, under sentence of death, a tall old man, by
the name of Henry F. Luckett. I personally knew him, and did not
think him a bad man. Please do not let him be executed, unless upon
further order from me, and, in the mean time, send me a transcript
of the record.

A. LINCOLN

"DEMONSTRATED IN BLOOD"

Letter to General James S. Wadsworth

JANUARY 1864

Although the original handwritten copy of this statement has never been found—its recipient was killed at the Battle of the Wilderness in May—it has long been accepted as a reliable expression of Lincoln's growing determination to enfranchise African American veterans. It was first published in 1865.

You desire to know, in the event of our complete success in the field, the same thing followed by a loyal and cheerful submission on the part of the South, if universal amnesty should not be accompanied with universal suffrage.

Now, since you know my private inclinations as to what terms should be granted to the South in the contingency mentioned, I will here add, that if our success should thus be realized, followed by such desired results, I cannot see, if universal amnesty is granted, how, under the circumstances, I can avoid exacting in return universal suffrage, or at least suffrage on the basis of intelligence and military service.

How to better the condition of the colored race has long been a study which has attracted my serious and careful attention; hence I think I am clear and decided as to what course I shall pursue in the premises, regarding it as a religious duty, as the nation's guardian of these people, who have so heroically vindicated their manhood on the battle-field, where, in assisting to save the life of the Republic, they have demonstrated in blood their right to the ballot, which is but the humane protection of the flag they have so fearlessly defended.

The restoration of the Rebel States to the Union must rest upon the principle of civil and political equality of both races; and it must be sealed by general amnesty.

"GIVEN TO THE SOLDIERS"

Letter to Esther Stockton

JANUARY 8, 1864

Lincoln was always appreciative of efforts by women on the home front to contribute to the war effort—he thought their tireless work deeply patriotic. Here he expressed his thanks to an elderly Pittsburgh widow who had knitted hundreds of socks for the troops. "I have endeavored to do what I could for those who battle to crush this wicked rebellion," she modestly replied to the president, adding her "earnest prayer" that he "may long be spared to enjoy the blessing of a grateful nation."

Madam:

Learning that you who have passed the eighty-fourth year of life, have given to the soldiers, some three hundred pairs of stockings, knitted by yourself, I wish to offer you my thanks. Will you also convey my thanks to those young ladies who have done so much in feeding our soldiers while passing through your city?

Yours truly,

A. LINCOLN

"REMOVE UNDER-WATER OBSTRUCTIONS"

Letter to Admiral John A. Dahlgren

JANUARY 9, 1864

Letters from Lincoln on naval issues are rare. But he was no less fascinated by naval technology than by ground technology, as reflected in this note to the commander of the Washington Navy Yard. Admiral John A. Dahlgren gave New York sea captain Lavender (whose full name is unknown) "a trial of his project" to sweep mines, but nothing more was heard of it.

My dear Sir

Capt. Lavender wishes to show you a contrivance of his for discovering, and aiding to remove, under-water obstructions to the passage of vessels, and has sufficiently impressed me to induce me to send him to you. He is sufficiently vouched to me as a worthy gentleman; and this known, it needs not my asking for you to treat him as such.

Yours truly

A. LINCOLN

"MAKE A TRIAL"

Letter to Major Theodore Laidley

JANUARY 13, 1864

Always disposed to grant a hearing—and a trial run—for new weaponry, Lincoln here instructed an officer to test a so-called elongated projectile. The more powerful the proposed weapon, the greater the president's interest. The Lincoln archive is filled with such messages. His assistant private secretary, John Hay, remembered that the president "would sometimes go out into the waste fields that then lay south of the Executive Mansion to test an experimental gun or torpedo" himself.

Major Laidley

Please make a trial of the Absterdam projectile, and report to the Secretary of War.

Yours truly

A. LINCOLN

"I WILL NOT HAVE CONTROL OF ANY CHURCH ON ANY SIDE"

Letter to Secretary of War Edwin M. Stanton

FEBRUARY 11, 1864

On November 30, 1863, Stanton had ordered Union generals in the Departments of the Missouri, the Tennessee, and the Gulf to place "all houses of worship belonging to the Methodist Episcopal Church" under control of the pro-Union Reverend Edward Raymond Ames to "foster the loyal sentiment of the people." Having previously made clear he did not want churches to be politicized ("Is this supposed order genuine?" he wondered at first), Lincoln here adroitly quoted several of his own early statements on the subject to express his indignation. It was later explained to Lincoln that the order only applied to areas still in rebellion—where it really could not readily be enforced. Stanton obliged the President by modifying his order to exclude Missouri.

My dear Sir

In January 1863, the Provost-Marshal at St. Louis, having taken the control of a certain church from one set of men and given it to another, I wrote Gen. Curtis on the subject, as follows:

"The U.S. Government must not, as by this order, undertake to run the churches. When an individual, in a church or out of it, becomes dangerous to the public interest, he must be checked; but the churches, as such, must take care of themselves. It will not do for the U.S. to appoint trustees, Supervisors, or other agents for the churches."

Some trouble remaining in this same case, I, on the 22nd. of Dec. 1863, in a letter to Mr. O. D. Filley, repeated the above language; and, among other things, added "I have never interfered, nor thought of interfering as to who shall or shall not preach in any church; nor have I knowingly, or believingly, tolerated any one else to so interfere by my authority. If any one is so interfering by color of my authority, I would like to have it specifically made known to me. . . . I will not have control of any church on any side."

After having made these declarations in good faith, and in writing, you can conceive of my embarrassment at now having brought to me what purports to be a formal order of the War Department, bearing date Nov. 30th. 1863, giving Bishop Ames control and possession of all the Methodist churches in certain Southern Military Departments, whose pastors have not been appointed by a loyal Bishop or Bishops, and ordering the Military to aid him against any resistance which may be made to his taking such possession and control. What is to be done about it?

Yours truly
A. LINCOLN

"A VIEW OF LOYALTY . . . DIFFICULT TO CONCEIVE"

From a Letter to Mrs. J. J. Neagle

[FEBRUARY 13, 1864]

Lincoln did not always excuse and pardon soldiers—or civilians—accused of disloyalty. Here he let off steam about an Iowa man (Mrs. Neagle's husband) charged with a serious crime. But a month later, at the request of Senator John Harlan—whose daughter would later marry the president's son—Lincoln ordered the man paroled after all. The original has never been located; this is a published extract.

I have carefully read your letter, herewith returned. As I understand it your husbands offense was that he knowingly and willfully helped a rebel to get out of our lines to the enemy to join in fighting and killing our people, and that he did this for love of you. You pretend, nevertheless, that you and he are loyal, and you may really think so, but this is a view of loyalty which it is difficult to conceive that any sane person could take, and one which the government may not tolerate and hope to live—And even now, what is the great anxiety of you and your husband to get to Washington but to get into a better position to repeat this species of loyalty? There is certainly room enough North of the Susquehanna for a great variety of honest occupations.

"THIS EXTRAORDINARY WAR"

Remarks at Christian Commission Sanitary Fair

MARCH 18, 1864

Together with Mrs. Lincoln, the president attended the closing night of the Christian Commission Fair—an exposition organized to raise money for the benefit of soldiers in the field—at the Patent Building not far from the White House. He offered these remarks to the crowd gathered there.

Ladies and Gentlemen:

I appear to say but a word. This extraordinary war in which we are engaged falls heavily upon all classes of people, but the most heavily upon the soldier. For it has been said, all that a man hath will he give for his life; and while all contribute of their substance the soldier puts his life at stake, and often yields it up in his country's cause. The highest merit, then, is due to the soldier. [Cheers.]

In this extraordinary war extraordinary developments have manifested themselves, such as have not been seen in former wars; and amongst these manifestations nothing has been more remarkable than these fairs for the relief of suffering soldiers and their families. And the chief agents in these fairs are the women of America. [Cheers.]

I am not accustomed to the use of language of eulogy; I have never studied the art of paying compliments to women; but I must say that if all that has been said by orators and poets since the creation of the world in praise of woman were applied to the women of America, it would not do them justice for their conduct during this war. I will close by saying God bless the women of America! [Great applause.]

"Life and Limb Must Be Protected"

Letter to Albert G. Hodges

APRIL 4, 1864

During a visit to the White House, Kentucky newspaperman Albert G. Hodges told the president that "much dissatisfaction" continued in Lincoln's native state over the enlistment of black soldiers. It was a complaint Lincoln had addressed earlier for his adopted state, Illinois, with his Conkling letter. After giving Hodges a spirited reply on the spot, Lincoln provided him with this written version at the editor's request. Hodges later reported that he showed the text to several "prominent men" and "have met but one as yet who dissents."

My dear Sir:

You ask me to put in writing the substance of what I verbally said the other day, in your presence, to Governor [Thomas E.] Bramlette [named military governor by Lincoln] and Senator [Archibald] Dixon [former U.S. Senator who had once held the seat of Lincoln's political hero, Henry Clay]. It was about as follows:

"I am naturally anti-slavery. If slavery is not wrong, nothing is wrong. I can not remember when I did not so think, and feel. And yet I have never understood that the Presidency conferred upon me an unrestricted right to act officially upon this judgment and feeling. It was in the oath I took that I would, to the best of my ability, preserve, protect, and defend the Constitution of the United States. I could not take the office without taking the oath. Nor was it my view that I might take an oath to get power, and break the oath in using the power. I understood, too, that in ordinary civil administration this oath even forbade me to practically indulge my primary abstract judgment on the moral question of slavery. I had publicly declared this many times, and in many ways. And I aver that, to this day, I have done no official act in mere deference to my abstract judgment and feeling on slavery. I did understand however, that my oath to preserve the constitution to the best of my ability, imposed upon me the duty of preserving, by every indispensable means, that government—that nation—of which that constitution was the organic law. Was it possible to lose the nation, and yet preserve the constitution? By general law life *and* limb must be protected; yet often a limb must be amputated to save a life; but a life is never wisely given to save a limb. I felt that measures, otherwise unconstitutional, might become lawful, by becoming indispensable to the preservation of the constitution, through the preservation of the nation. Right or wrong, I assumed this ground, and now avow it. I could not feel that, to the best of my ability, I had even tried to preserve the constitution, if, to save slavery, or any minor matter, I should permit the wreck of government, country, and Constitution all together. When, early in the war, Gen. Fremont attempted military emancipation, I forbade it, because I did not then think it an indispensable necessity. When a little later, Gen. Cameron, then Secretary of War, suggested the arming of the blacks, I objected, because I did not yet think it an indispensable necessity. When, still later, Gen. Hunter attempted military emancipation, I again forbade it, because I did not yet think the indispensable necessity had come. When, in March, and May, and July 1862 I made earnest, and successive appeals to the border states to favor compensated emancipation, I believed the indispensable necessity for military emancipation, and arming the blacks would come, unless averted by that measure. They declined the proposition; and I was, in my best judgment, driven to the alternative of either surrendering the Union, and with it, the Constitution, or of laying strong hand upon the colored element. I chose the latter. In choosing it, I hoped for greater gain than loss; but of this, I was not entirely confident. More than a year of trial now shows no loss by it in our foreign relations, none in our home popular sentiment, none in our white military force,—no loss by it any how or any where. On the contrary, it shows a gain of quite a hundred and thirty thousand soldiers, seamen, and laborers. These are palpable facts, about which, as facts, there can be no cavilling. We have the men; and we could not have had them without the measure.

["]And now let any Union man who complains of the measure, test himself by writing down in one line that he is for subduing the rebellion by force of arms; and in the next, that he is for taking these hundred and thirty thousand men from the Union side, and placing them where they would be but for the measure he condemns. If he can not face his case so stated, it is only because he can not face the truth.["]

I add a word which was not in the verbal conversation. In telling this tale I attempt no compliment to my own sagacity. I claim not to have controlled events, but confess plainly that events have controlled me. Now, at the end of three years struggle the nation's condition is not what either party, or any man devised, or expected. God alone can claim it. Whither it is tending seems plain. If God now wills the removal of a great wrong, and wills also that we of the North as well as you of the South, shall pay fairly for our complicity in that wrong, impartial history will find therein new cause to attest and revere the justice and goodness of God.

Yours truly

A. LINCOLN

"SOMETHING TO DEFINE LIBERTY"

Address at Maryland Sanitary Commission Fair, Baltimore

APRIL 18, 1864

Despite his reputation as a great orator, Lincoln made surprisingly few speeches as president, but on a visit to Baltimore he summoned all his powers to again defend black enlistment and threaten retaliation for the recent Confederate massacres of black troops at Fort Pillow. Above all, Lincoln seemed to exult in simply returning in triumph to a city where assassination threats had compelled him to cancel a public appearance three years earlier as president-elect. In a fragment he drafted for the speech but omitted, he rationalized this history to some degree, contending: "I take it to be unquestionable that what happened here three years ago, and what happens here now, was contempt of office then, and is purely appreciation of merit now."

Ladies and Gentlemen—

Calling to mind that we are in Baltimore, we can not fail to note that the world moves. Looking upon these many people, assembled here, to serve, as they best may, the soldiers of the Union, it occurs at once that three years ago, the same soldiers could not so much as pass through Baltimore. The change from then till now, is both great, and gratifying. Blessings on the brave men who have wrought the change, and the fair women who strive to reward them for it.

But Baltimore suggests more than could happen within Baltimore. The change within Baltimore is part only of a far wider change. When the war began, three years ago, neither party, nor any man, expected it would last till now. Each looked for the end, in some way, long ere to-day. Neither did any anticipate that domestic slavery would be much affected by the war. But here we are; the war has not ended, and slavery has been much affected—how much needs not now to be recounted. So true is it that man proposes, and God disposes.

But we can see the past, though we may not claim to have directed it; and seeing it, in this case, we feel more hopeful and confident for the future.

The world has never had a good definition of the word liberty, and the American people, just now, are much in want of one. We all declare for liberty; but in using the same *word* we do not all mean the same *thing*. With some the word liberty may mean for each man to do as he pleases with himself, and the product of his labor; while with others the same word may mean for some men to do as they please with other men, and the product of other men's labor. Here are two, not only different, but incompatable things, called by the same name—liberty. And it follows that each of the things is, by the respective parties, called by two different and incompatable names—liberty and tyranny.

The shepherd drives the wolf from the sheep's throat, for which the sheep thanks the shepherd as a *liberator*, while the wolf denounces him for the same act as the destroyer of liberty, especially as the sheep was a black one. Plainly the sheep and the wolf are not agreed upon a definition of the word liberty; and precisely the same difference prevails to-day among us human creatures, even in the North, and all professing to love liberty. Hence we behold the processes by which thousands are daily passing from under the yoke of bondage, hailed by some as the advance of liberty, and bewailed by others as the destruction of all liberty. Recently, as it seems, the people of Maryland have been doing something to define liberty; and thanks to them that, in what they have done, the wolf's dictionary, has been repudiated.

It is not very becoming for one in my position to make speeches at great length; but there is another subject upon which I feel that I ought to say a word. A painful rumor, true I fear, has reached us of the massacre, by the rebel forces, at Fort Pillow, in the West end of Tennessee, on the Mississippi river, of some three hundred colored soldiers and white officers, who had just been overpowered by their assailants. There seems to be some anxiety in the public mind whether the government is doing it's duty to the colored soldier, and to the service, at this point. At the beginning of the war, and for some time, the use of colored troops was not contemplated; and how the change of purpose was wrought, I will not now take time to explain. Upon a clear conviction of duty I resolved to turn that element of strength to account; and I am responsible for it to the American people, to the christian world, to history, and on my final account to God. Having determined to use the negro as a soldier, there is no way but to give him all the protection given to any other soldier. The difficulty is not in stating the principle, but in practically applying it. It is a mistake to suppose the government is indiffe[re]nt to this matter, or is not doing the best it can in regard to it. We do not to-day *know* that a colored soldier, or white officer commanding colored soldiers, has been massacred by the rebels when made a prisoner. We fear it, believe it, I may say, but we do not *know* it. To take the life of one of their prisoners, on the assumption that they murder ours, when it is short of certainty that they do murder ours, might be too serious, too cruel a mistake. We are having the Fort-Pillow affair thoroughly investigated; and such investigation will probably show conclusively how the truth is. If, after all that has been said, it shall turn out that there has been no massacre at Fort-Pillow, it will be almost safe to say there has been none, and will be none elsewhere. If there has been the massacre of three hundred there, or even the tenth part of three hundred, it will be conclusively proved; and being so proved, the retribution shall as surely come. It will be matter of grave consideration in what exact course to apply the retribution; but in the supposed case, it must come. [Lincoln occasionally threatened, but never ordered, eye-for-an-eye retribution for such atrocities.—ed.]

"Hold a Leg"

Remarks to General Ulysses S. Grant

APRIL 20, 1864

The president made this quaint remark to General Grant when they met at the White House, after the newly commissioned lieutenant general told Lincoln he believed that even defensive troops must always advance to better position themselves for offensive movements.

Oh, yes! I see that. As we say out West, if a man can't skin he must hold a leg while somebody else does.

"Not a Specially Brave Man"

Remarks to Assistant Private Secretary John Hay

APRIL 28, 1864

Nearly two years after General George B. McClellan had abandoned his Peninsula Campaign, Lincoln remembered a late-night visit to the Soldiers' Home by Quartermaster General Montgomery Meigs, who urged Lincoln to approve the killing of the army's horses if they could not be evacuated with the troops. This is how Lincoln recalled those events.

Thus often, I who am not a specially brave man have had to sustain the sinking courage of these professional fighters in critical times.

"You Are Vigilant and Self-Reliant"

Letter to General Ulysses S. Grant

APRIL 30, 1864

Much pleased with the aggressive and recently promoted lieutenant general, Lincoln wrote this unsolicited letter of commendation, although Ulysses S. Grant had been general-in-chief of all federal armies with

his new rank only since March 10. Perhaps it represented tacit approval
of Grant's decision to cease prisoner exchanges with the Confederacy;
but possibly, with the Republican presidential convention approaching,
Lincoln wanted to keep Grant happy in the military—and out of the
race for the nomination. Lincoln was renominated in June.

Lieutenant General Grant.

Not expecting to see you again before the Spring [military] campaign opens, I wish to express, in this way, my entire satisfaction with what you have done up to this time, so far as I understand it. The particulars of your plans I neither know, or seek to know. You are vigilant and self-reliant; and, pleased with this, I wish not to obtrude any constraints or restraints upon you. While I am very anxious that any great disaster, or the capture of our men in great numbers, shall be avoided, I know these points are less likely to escape your attention than they would be mine. If there is anything wanting which is within my power to give, do not fail to let me know it.

And now with a brave Army, and a just cause, may God sustain you.

Yours very truly
A. LINCOLN

"THE 'HEAVENS ARE HUNG IN BLACK'"

From a Speech at Great Central Sanitary Fair,
Philadelphia, Pennyslvania

JUNE 16, 1864

Now officially a candidate for reelection to the presidency, Lincoln went
into the same campaign mode he had assumed four years earlier during his initial run for the White House: declining nearly all invitations
to make personal appearances and deliver speeches. He thought it "not
customary for one holding the office." But he made an exception when
invited to yet another major war charity fair, this one at Philadelphia.

I suppose that this toast was intended to open the way for me to say something. [Laughter.] War, at the best, is terrible, and this war of ours, in its magnitude and in its duration, is one of the most terrible. It has deranged business, totally in many localities, and partially in all localities. It has destroyed property, and ruined homes; it has produced a national debt and taxation unprecedented, at least in this country. It has carried mourning to almost every home, until it can almost be said that the "heavens are hung in black."

"ALL WELL"

Telegram to Mary Lincoln

JUNE 24, 1864

The president gave this assessment after returning to the White House from a refreshing visit to General Grant and his army at City Point, Virginia. Arriving in camp, Lincoln refused a glass of champagne, pointing out that too many men get "seasick ashore from drinking that very stuff." The original handwritten draft for the telegram was discovered missing from the National Archives in 2006.

Mrs. A. Lincoln

All well, and very warm—Tad and I have been to Gen. Grant's army. Returned yesterday safe and sound.

A. LINCOLN

"I NEED NO ESCORT"

Comments about Having a Military Guard

JULY 4, 1864

Lincoln scribbled this note on an invitation that had arrived the day before from the headquarters of General Christopher C. Augur: "If his Excellency the president of the U.S. wishes an escort, Lt. [James B.] Jameson will furnish it." At the time, assassination threats were not unfamiliar to the president, but he regarded them fatalistically, saying once he believed no enemy would sacrifice his own life to take his. As Lincoln later put it to his private secretary John Nicolay: "To be absolutely safe I should lock myself up in a box."

I believe I need no escort, and unless the Sec. of War directs, none need attend me.

A. LINCOLN

"BE VIGILANT BUT KEEP COOL"

Reply to a Plea to Reenforce Baltimore

JULY 10, 1864

In July 1864, Baltimore and Washington were menaced by a surprise raid by Confederate general Jubal Early. This is Lincoln's reply to a telegram from frantic Baltimore residents who feared their city was "in great peril" and begged the president to send "large re-enforcements" at once. In the end, Early was repulsed.

Yours of last night received. I have not a single soldier but whom is being disposed by the Military for the best protection of all. By latest account the enemy is moving on Washington. They can not fly to either place. Let us be vigilant but keep cool. I hope neither Baltimore or Washington will be sacked.

A. LINCOLN

"DESTROY THE ENEMIE'S FORCE"

Letter to General Ulysses S. Grant

JULY 10, 1864

The day after writing this letter reminding General Grant of Jubal Early's threat to the capital, Lincoln ventured out to Fort Stevens near his summer residence at the Soldiers' Home and himself came under

enemy fire. He later visited a Washington wharf to personally welcome
reenforcements that arrived in time to repel the Confederates.

Lieut. Gen. Grant

Your despatch to Gen. Halleck, referring to what I may think in
the present emergency, is shown me. Gen. Halleck says we have absolutely no force here fit to go to the field. He thinks that with the
hundred day-men, and invalids we have here, we can defend Washington, and scarcely Baltimore. Besides these, there are about eight
thousand not very reliable, under [Brigadier General Albion] Howe
at Harper's Ferry, with [General David] Hunter approaching that
point very slowly, with what number I suppose you know better than
I. [General Lew] Wallace with some odds and ends, and part of what
came up with [Brigadier General James B.] Ricketts, was so badly
beaten yesterday at Monocacy [a federal defeat in Maryland that
opened the way for Early to advance toward Washington—ed.], that
what is left can attempt no more than to defend Baltimore. What we
shall get in from Penn. & N.Y. will scarcely [be] worth counting, I
fear. Now what I think is that you should provide to retain your hold
where you are certainly, and bring the rest with you personally, and
make a vigorous effort to destroy the enemie's force in this vicinity. I think there is really a fair chance to do this if the movement is
prompt. This is what I think, upon your suggestion, and is not an
order.

A. LINCOLN

"THE LORD'S SIDE"

Remark to a Clergyman

CA. SUMMER 1864

Visiting artist Francis B. Carpenter overheard Lincoln making this
comment to a clergyman who told the president "he hoped the LORD
was on our side." In Carpenter's opinion: "No nobler reply ever fell from
the lips of a ruler."

I am not at all concerned about that, for I know that the LORD is *always* on the side of the *right*. But it is my constant anxiety and prayer that *I* and *this nation* should be on the LORD's *side*.

"THE EFFORT SHALL NOT BE DESPERATE"

Telegram to General Ulysses S. Grant

JULY 17, 1864

General Grant had the reputation of willingness to endure huge casualties if it brought victory; critics labeled him a butcher. Lincoln insisted: "It is the dogged persistence of Grant that wins." Nevertheless, when the commander-in-chief learned that Grant had advised Sherman he would "make a desperate effort" to secure his position in Virginia, Lincoln sent the following message—hoping for success, of course, but without too many casualties.

Lieut. Gen. Grant

In your despatch of yesterday to Gen. Sherman, I find the following, towit: "I shall make a desperate effort to get a position here which will hold the enemy without the necessity of so many men."

Pressed as we are by lapse of time, I am glad to hear you say this; and yet I do hope you may find a way that the effort shall not be desperate in the sense of great loss of life.

A. LINCOLN

"THE INTEGRITY OF THE WHOLE UNION"

Statement on Acceptable Peace Terms

JULY 18, 1864

With many exhausted Unionists desperate for a negotiated peace, Lincoln decided to set terms for such discussions—terms he knew would not be acceptable to the Confederates. Nine days earlier, he wrote New

York Tribune *editor Horace Greeley: "If you can find, any person any-where professing to have any proposition of Jefferson Davis in writing, for peace, embracing the restoration of the Union and abandonment of slavery, what ever else it embraces, say to him he may come to me with you." This same day, however, Lincoln issued a proclamation calling for five hundred thousand volunteers.*

To Whom it may concern:

Any proposition which embraces the restoration of peace, the integrity of the whole Union, and the abandonment of slavery, and which comes by and with an authority that can control the armies now at war against the United States will be received and considered by the Executive government of the United States, and will be met by liberal terms on other substantial and collateral points; and the bearer, or bearers thereof shall have safe-conduct both ways.

ABRAHAM LINCOLN

"WITH MY COLORS FLYING"

Remark to Commissioner for Indian Affairs William P. Dole

CA. SUMMER 1864

Commissioner William P. Dole was one of many political allies who thought Lincoln's proclamation calling for five hundred thousand new volunteers would put the final nail in his political coffin, guaranteeing his defeat for re-election, and told him so at the White House. This was Lincoln's reply to him.

It matters not what becomes of me, we must have the men! If I go down, I intend to go like the *Cumberland*, with my colors flying! [The *Cumberland* was a wooden Union warship rammed and sunk by the CSS *Virginia* at Hampton Roads, Virginia, on March 8, 1862—ed.]

"NECESSARY TO PREVENT ASSASSINATION AND INCENDIARISM"

Unfinished Letter to General Benjamin F. Butler

AUGUST 9, 1864

Lincoln drafted this opinion after learning that General Benjamin F. Butler was weighing whether to allow martial law to continue in occupied Norfolk, Virginia, or to permit civilian authorities to reassume control of the city. The president delayed a response on this subject until December.

Major General Butler:

Your paper of the   about Norfolk matters is received, as also was your other, on the same general subject dated, I believe, some time in February last. This subject has caused considerable trouble, forcing me to give a good deal of time and reflection to it. I regret that crimination and recrimination are mingled in it. I surely need not to assure you that I have no doubt of your loyalty and devoted patriotism; and I must tell you that I have no less confidence in those of Gov. [Francis] Pierpoint [actually *Peirpont*, Governor of West Virginia—ed.] and the Attorney General. The former, at first, as the loyal governor of all Virginia, including that which is now West-Virginia; in organizing and furnishing troops, and in all other proper matters, we as earnest, honest, and efficient to the extent of his means, as any other loyal governor. The inauguration of West-Virginia as a new State left to him, as he assumed, the remainder of the old State; and the insignificance of the parts which are outside of the rebel lines, and consequently within his reach, certainly gives a somewhat farcical air to his dominion; and I suppose he, as well as I, has considered that it could be useful for little else than as a nucleous to add to. The Attorney General only needs to be known to be relieved from all question as to loyalty and thorough devotion to the national cause; constantly restraining as he does, my tendency to clemency for rebels and rebel sympathizers. But he is the Law-Officer of the government, and a believer in the virtue of adhering to law.

Coming to the question itself, the Military occupancy of Norfolk is a necessity with us. If you, as Department commander, find the cleansing of the City necessary to prevent pestilence in your army—street lights, and a fire department, necessary to prevent assassinations and incendiarism among your men and stores—wharfage necessary to land and ship men and supplies—a large pauperism, badly conducted, at a needlessly large expense to the government, and find also that these things, or any of them, are not reasonably well attended to by the civil government, you rightfully may, and must take them into your own hands. But you should do so on your own avowed judgment of a military necessity, and not seem to admit that there is no such necessity, by taking a vote of the people on the question. Nothing justifies the suspending of the civil by the military authority, but military necessity, and of the existence of that necessity the military commander, and not a popular vote, is to decide. And whatever is not within such necessity should be left undisturbed. In your paper of February you fairly notified me that you contemplated taking a popular vote; and, if fault there be, it was my fault that I did not object then, which I probably should have done [Butler had allowed Norfolk to conduct a civil election, but then made its newly chosen civil authority subservient to his military authority—ed.], had I studied the subject as closely as I have since done. I now think you would better place whatever you feel is necessary to be done, on this distinct ground of military necessity, openly discarding all reliance for what you do, on any election. I also think you should so keep accounts as to show every item of money received and how expended [Butler was long rumored to have profited from his military occupancy of New Orleans—ed.].

The course here indicated does not touch the case when the military commander finding no friendly civil government existing, may, under the sanction or direction of the President, give assistance to the people to inaugerate one.

"Why Should They Give Their Lives for Us"

Letter to Charles D. Robinson

AUGUST 17, 1864

Charles D. Robinson, editor of a Democratic newspaper in Green Bay, Wisconsin, wrote Lincoln on August 7 to protest the president's refusal to negotiate on emancipation in return for armistice and reunion. "This," Robinson insisted, "puts the whole war question on a new basis, and takes us War Democrats clear off our feet, leaving us no ground to stand upon." This was Lincoln's reply, in which he quoted his earlier speeches and again passionately defended black recruitment.

My dear Sir:

Your letter of the 7th. was placed in my hand yesterday by Gov. [Alexander W.] Randall.

To me it seems plain that saying re-union and abandonment of slavery would be considered, if offered, is not saying that nothing *else* or *less* would be considered, if offered. But I will not stand upon the mere construction of language. It is true, as you remind me, that in the Greeley letter of 1862, I said: "If I could save the Union without freeing any slaves I would do it; and if I could save it by freeing all the slaves I would do it; and if I could save it by freeing some, and leaving others alone I would also do that." I continued in the same letter as follows: "What I do about slavery and the colored race, I do because I believe it helps to save the Union; and what I forbear I forbear because I do not believe it would help to save the Union. I shall do less whenever I shall believe what I am doing hurts the cause; and I shall do more whenever I shall believe doing more will help the cause." All this I said in the utmost sincerity; and I am as true to the whole of it now, as when I first said it. When I afterwards proclaimed emancipation, and employed colored soldiers, I only followed the declaration just quoted from the Greeley letter that "I shall do *more* whenever I shall believe *doing* more will help the cause[.]" The way these measures were to help the cause, was not to be by magic, or miracles, but by inducing the colored people to come bodily over from the rebel side to ours. On this point, nearly a year ago, in a letter to Mr. Conkling, made public at once, I wrote as follows: "But negroes, like other people, act upon motives. Why should they do anything for us if we will do nothing for them? If they stake their lives for us they must be prompted by the strongest motive—even the promise of freedom. And the promise, being made, must be kept." I am sure you will not, on due reflection, say that the promise being made, must be *broken* at the first opportunity. I am sure you would not desire me to say, or to leave an inference, that I am ready, whenever convenient, to join in re-enslaving those who shall have served us in consideration of our promise. As matter of morals, could such treachery by any possibility, escape the curses of Heaven, or of any good man? As matter of policy, to *announce* such a purpose, would ruin the Union cause itself. All recruiting of colored men would instantly cease, and all colored men now in our service, would instantly desert us. And rightfully too. Why should they give their lives for us, with full notice of our purpose to betray them? Drive back to the support of the rebellion the physical force which the colored people now give, and promise us, and neither the present, nor any coming administration, *can* save the Union. Take from us, and give to the enemy, the hundred and thirty, forty, or fifty thousand colored persons now serving us as soldiers, seamen, and laborers, and we can not longer maintain the contest. The party who could elect a President on a War & Slavery Restoration platform, would, of necessity, lose the colored force; and that force being lost, would be as powerless to save the Union as to do any other impossible thing. It is not a question of sentiment or taste, but one of physical force, which may be measured, and estimated as horsepower, and steam power, are measured and estimated. And by measurement, it is more than we can lose, and live. Nor can we, by discarding it, get a white force in place of it. There is a witness in every white mans bosom that he would rather go to the war having the negro to help him, than to help the enemy against him. It is not the giving of one class for another. It is simply giving a large force to the enemy, for *nothing* in return.

In addition to what I have said, allow me to remind you that no one, having control of the rebel armies, or, in fact, having any influence whatever in the rebellion, has offered, or intimated a willingness to, a restoration of the Union, in any event, or on any condition whatever. Let it be constantly borne in mind that no such offer has been made or intimated. Shall we be weak enough to allow the enemy to distract us with an abstract question which he himself refuses to present as a practical one? In the Conkling letter before mentioned, I said: "Whenever you shall have conquered all resistance to the Union, if I shall urge you to continue fighting, it will be an apt time *then* to declare that you will not fight to free negroes." I repeat this now. If Jefferson Davis wishes, for himself, or for the benefit of his friends at the North, to know what I would do if he were to offer peace and re-union, saying nothing about slavery, let him try me.

"CHEW & CHOKE"

Telegram to General Ulysses S. Grant

AUGUST 17, 1864

General Grant had expressed concern that any attempt to divert his troops to enforce the draft or protect the integrity of the forthcoming election would harm his effort "to suppress the rebellion in the disloyal states." Shown the dispatch, Lincoln promptly wired back to express agreement and urged Grant to remain relentless.

Lieut. Gen. Grant

I have seen your dispatch expressing your unwillingness to break your hold where you are. Neither am I willing., Hold on with a bulldog gripe [*sic*], and chew & choke, as much as possible.

A. LINCOLN

"THIS ADMINISTRATION WILL NOT BE RE-ELECTED"

Memorandum on His Likely Defeat

AUGUST 23, 1864

Convinced he was about to lose his bid for a second term, Lincoln drafted this mysterious pledge, signed it, sealed it shut—and then asked the members of his cabinet to sign it as well, sight unseen. At around the same time, the president began working closely with black leader Frederick Douglass on a plan to spread word of emancipation to as many enslaved people as possible—before the Democratic presidential candidate, former general George B. McClellan, defeated him and, as widely expected, rescinded the freedom order. Even as Lincoln was preparing himself to surrender the presidency, he was clearly hoping to widen the reach of freedom.

This morning, as for some days past, it seems exceedingly probable that this Administration will not be re-elected. Then it will be my duty to so co-operate with the President elect, as to save the Union between the election and the inauguration; as he will have secured his election on such ground that he can not possibly save it afterwards.

A. LINCOLN

"OBTAIN . . . A CONFERENCE FOR PEACE"

Letter to Henry J. Raymond

AUGUST 24, 1864

In desperation over his reelection prospects, Lincoln drafted this note instructing his campaign manager, New York Times *editor Henry J. Raymond, to seek peace terms from Confederate president Jefferson Davis—with no precondition on accepting emancipation (but with no explicit abandonment of the policy, either). The letter was doubtless inspired by Raymond's blunt and dispiriting assessment that "[t]he tide is setting strongly against us" and that "[n]othing but the most resolute and decided action on the part of the government and its friends, can save the country from falling into hostile hands." But Lincoln never sent the letter, instead summoning Raymond to Washington and convincing him that a peace overture would be "worse than losing the Presidential contest—it would be ignominiously surrendering in advance." Yet this draft, which he preserved, shows how close Lincoln came to suing for peace.*

Sir:

You will proceed forthwith and obtain, if possible, a conference for peace with Hon. Jefferson Davis, or any person by him authorized for that purpose.

You will address him in entirely respectful terms, at all events, and in any that may be indispensable to secure the conference.

At said conference you will propose, on behalf [of] this government, that upon the restoration of the Union and the national authority, the war shall cease at once, all remaining questions to be left for adjustment by peaceful modes. If this be accepted hostilities to cease at once.

If it be not accepted, you will then request to be informed what terms, if any embracing the restoration of the Union, would be accepted. If any such be presented you in answer, you will forthwith report the same to this government, and await further instructions.

If the presentation of any terms embracing the restoration of the Union be declined, you will then request to be informed what terms of peace would, be accepted; and on receiving any answer, report the same to this government, and await further instructions.

"Stand Fast to the Union and the Old Flag"

Speech to an Ohio Regiment

AUGUST 31, 1864

Lincoln overcame his political despair to thank—and offer inspiration to—a regiment of Ohio soldiers visiting the White House en route home after honorable service. Perhaps convinced he was soon to leave the White House himself, Lincoln reminded the men that they were fighting for the right to aspire to live there themselves.

Soldiers of the 148th Ohio:

I am most happy to meet you on this occasion. I understand that it has been your honorable privilege to stand, for a brief period, in the defense of your country, and that now you are on your way to your homes. I congratulate you, and those who are waiting to bid you welcome home from the war; and permit me, in the name of the people, to thank you for the part you have taken in this struggle for the life of the nation. You are soldiers of the Republic, everywhere honored and respected. Whenever I appear before a body of soldiers, I feel tempted to talk to them of the nature of the struggle in which we are engaged. I look upon it as an attempt on the one hand to overwhelm and destroy the national existence, while, on our part, we are striving to maintain the government and institutions of our fathers, to enjoy them ourselves, and transmit them to our children and our children's children forever.

To do this the constitutional administration of our government must be sustained, and I beg of you not to allow your minds or your hearts to be diverted from the support of all necessary measures for that purpose, by any miserable picayune arguments addressed to your pockets, or inflammatory appeals made to your passions or your prejudices.

It is vain and foolish to arraign this man or that for the part he has taken, or has not taken, and to hold the government responsible for his acts. In no administration can there be perfect equality of action and uniform satisfaction rendered by all. But this government must be preserved in spite of the acts of any man or set of men. It is worthy [of] your every effort. Nowhere in the world is presented a government of so much liberty and equality. To the humblest and poorest amongst us are held out the highest privileges and positions. The present moment finds me at the White House, yet there is as good a chance for your children as there was for my father's.

Again I admonish you not to be turned from your stern purpose of defending your beloved country and its free institutions by any arguments urged by ambitious and designing men, but stand fast to the Union and the old flag. Soldiers, I bid you God-speed to your homes.

"SIGNAL SUCCESS"

Statements on the Union Victories at Atlanta and Mobile

SEPTEMBER 3, 1864

Lincoln's political fortunes—and the prospects for Union victory— rebounded dramatically when General William T. Sherman captured Atlanta on September 1. An exultant commander in chief promptly issued a celebratory order along with a public note of thanks to the general (and Admiral David G. Farragut for his own recent triumphs) and a proclamation of thanksgiving. All three are presented below.

Ordered, September 3d, 1864.

First.—That on Monday, the 5th. day of September, commencing at the hour of twelve o'clock noon, there shall be given a salute of one hundred guns at the Arsenal and Navy Yard at Washington, and on Tuesday September 6th., or on the day after the receipt of this order, at each Arsenal and Navy Yard in the United States, for the recent brilliant achievements of the fleet and land forces of the United States in the harbor of Mobile and in the reduction of Fort

Powell, Fort Gaines, and Fort Morgan [three forts on Mobile Bay—ed.]. The Secretary of War and Secretary of the Navy will issue the necessary directions in their respective Departments for the execution of this order.

Second.—That on Wednesday, the 7th. day of September, commencing at the hour of twelve o'clock noon, there shall be fired a salute of one hundred guns at the Arsenal at Washington, and at New York, Boston, Philadelphia, Baltimore, Pittsburg, Newport, Ky. and St. Louis, and at New Orleans, Mobile, Pensacola, Hilton Head & Newberne, the day after the receipt of this order, for the brilliant achievements of the army under command of Major General Sherman, in the State of Georgia, and the capture of Atlanta. The Secretary of War will issue directions for the execution of this order.

ABRAHAM LINCOLN

The national thanks are herewith tendered by the President to Major General William T. Sherman, and the gallant officers and soldiers of his command before Atlanta, for the distinguished ability, courage, and perseverance displayed in the campaign in Georgia, which, under Divine favor, has resulted in the capture of the City of Atlanta. The marches, battles, sieges, and other military operations that have signalized this campaign must render it famous in the annals of war, and have entitled those who have participated therein to the applause and thanks of the nation.

ABRAHAM LINCOLN

The signal success that Divine Providence has recently vouchsafed to the operations of the United States fleet and army in the harbor of Mobile and the reduction of Fort Powell, Fort-Gaines, and Fort-Morgan, and the glorious achievements of the Army under Major General Sherman in the State of Georgia, resulting in the capture of the City of Atlanta, call for devout acknowledgement to the Supreme Being in whose hands are the destinies of nations. It is therefore requested that on next Sunday, in all places of public worship in the United-States, thanksgiving be offered to Him for His mercy in preserving our national existence against the insurgent rebels who so long have been waging a cruel war against the Government of the United-States, for its overthrow; and also that prayer be made for the Divine protection to our brave soldiers and their leaders in the field, who have so often and so gallantly perilled their lives in battling with the enemy; and for blessing and comfort from the Father of Mercies to the sick, wounded, and prisoners, and to the orphans and widows of those who have fallen in the service of their country, and that he will continue to uphold the Government of the United-States against all the efforts of public enemies and secret foes.

ABRAHAM LINCOLN

"SOME GREAT GOOD TO FOLLOW THIS MIGHTY CONVULSION"

Letter to Eliza P. Gurney

SEPTEMBER 4, 1864

No doubt feeling both relieved and vindicated by General Sherman's Atlanta triumph, Lincoln took up his pen to write for the first time in a year to the Quaker with whom he had once discussed God's mysterious purposes. Back on August 18, 1863, Eliza P. Gurney had written to express the hope "that the anger which has so long sustained this needless and cruel rebellion, may be subdued, the hearts of the insurgents changed, and the whole Nation be led, through paths of repentance and submission to the Divine will, back to the perfect enjoyment of Union and fraternal peace."

My esteemed friend.

I have not forgotten—probably never shall forget—the very impressive occasion when yourself and friends visited me on a Sabbath forenoon two years ago. Nor has your kind letter, written nearly a year later, ever been forgotten. In all, it has been your purpose to strengthen my reliance on God. I am much indebted to the good christian people of the country for their constant prayers and consolations; and to no one of them, more than to yourself. The purposes of the Almighty are perfect, and must prevail, though we erring mortals may fail to accurately perceive them in advance. We hoped for a happy termination of this terrible war long before this; but God knows best, and has ruled otherwise. We shall yet acknowledge His wisdom and our own error therein. Meanwhile we must work earnestly in the best light He gives us, trusting that so working still conduces to the great ends He ordains. Surely He intends some great good to follow this mighty convulsion, which no mortal could make, and no mortal could stay.

Your people—the Friends—have had, and are having, a very great trial. On principle, and faith, opposed to both war and oppression, they can only practically oppose oppression by war. In this hard dilemma, some have chosen one horn and some the other. For those appealing to me on conscientious grounds, I have done, and shall do, the best I could and can, in my own conscience, under my oath to the law. That you believe this I doubt not; and believing it, I shall still receive, for our country and myself, your earnest prayers to our Father in Heaven.

Your sincere friend
A. LINCOLN.

"The Whole Story of the Singing"

Comments Drafted to Defend His Alleged Insensitivity on the Battlefield

[CA. SEPTEMBER 12, 1864]

In the heat of the presidential campaign, some Democrats circulated the calumny that on a visit to the casualty-strewn Antietam battlefield two years earlier, Lincoln had asked his old friend Ward Hill Lamon, the Marshal of the District of Columbia, to sing "Picayune Butler," an untoward comic song. The Copperhead New York World *published the poem: "Abe may crack his jolly jokes / O'er bloody fields of stricken battle, / While yet the ebbing life-tide smokes / From men that die like butchered cattle." Usually thick-skinned, Lincoln was deeply upset by the rumor, and drafted the following third-person explanation, which he prepared for Lamon's signature but in the end never ordered sent. Lincoln took his visits to the troops seriously indeed, but as he admitted here, he* did *ask Lamon to sing comic songs in the vicinity of the bloodiest day's fighting in the entire Civil War—at worst, a political miscalculation.*

The President has known me intimately for nearly twenty years, and has often heard me sing little ditties. The battle of Antietam was fought on the 17th. day of September 1862. On the first day of October, just two weeks after the battle, the President, with some others including myself, started from Washington to visit the Army, reaching Harper's Ferry at noon of that day. In a short while Gen. McClellan came from his Head Quarters near the battle ground, joined the President, and with him, reviewed, the troops at Bolivar Heights that afternoon; and, at night, returned to his Head Quarters, leaving the President at Harper's Ferry. On the morning of the second, the President, with Gen. [Edwin Vose "Bull Head"] Sumner [who had accompanied then president-elect Lincoln to Washington in 1861—ed.], reviewed the troops respectively at Loudon Heights and Maryland Heights, and at about noon, started to Gen. McClellan's Head Quarters, reaching there only in time to see very little before night. On the morning of the third all started on a review of the three corps, and the Cavalry, in the vicinity of the Antietam battle ground. After getting through with Gen. Burnsides Corps, at the suggestion of Gen. McClellan, he and the President left their horses to be led, and went into an ambulance or ambulances to go to Gen. Fitz John Porter's Corps, which was two or three miles distant. I am not sure whether the President and Gen. Mc. were in the same ambulance, or in different ones; but myself and some others were in the same with the President. On the way, and on no part of the battle-ground, and on what suggestion I do not remember, the President asked me to sing the little sad song, that follows, which he had often heard me sing, and always seemed to like very much. I sang them [sic]. After it was over, some one of the party, (I do not think it was the President) asked me to sing something else; and I sang two or three little comic things of which Picayune Butler was one. Porter's Corps was reached and reviewed; then the battle ground was passed over, and the most noted parts examined; then, in succession, the Cavalry, and [William Buel] Franklin's Corps were reviewed, and the President and party returned to Gen. McClellan's Head Quarters at the end of a very hard, hot, and dusty day's work. Next day, the 4th. the President and Gen. Mc. visited such of the wounded as still remained in the vicinity, including the now lamented Gen. [Israel Bush "Fighting Dick"] Richardson [who died from wounds suffered at Antietam—ed.]; then proceed[ed] to and examined the South-Mountain battle-ground, at which point they parted, Gen. McClellan returning to his Camp, and the President returning to Washington, seeing, on the way, Gen. [George Lucas] Hartsuf, who lay wounded at Frederick Town [also wounded at Antietam—ed.]. This is the whole story of the singing and it's surroundings. Neither Gen. McClellan or any one else made any objection to the singing; the place was not on the battle field, the time was sixteen days after the battle, no dead body was seen during the whole time the president was absent from Washington, nor even a grave that had not been rained on since it was made.

"THROW IT AWAY AND THE UNION GOES WITH IT"

Campaign Statement Prepared for Isaac M. Schermerhorn

SEPTEMBER 12, 1864

Aware that swing states like New York might yet go against him because of their strong yearning for armistice, Lincoln broke his campaign silence to draft this impassioned defense of his position on peace talks for a "National Union mass ratification meeting"—in truth, a glorified campaign rally for the Republicans—in Buffalo.

My dear Sir.

Yours inviting me to attend a Union Mass Meeting at Buffalo is received. Much is being said about peace; and no man desires peace more ardently than I. Still I am yet unprepared to give up the Union for a peace which, so achieved, could not be of much duration. The preservation of our Union was *not* the sole avowed object for which the war was commenced. It was commenced for precisely the reverse object—*to destroy our Union.* The insurgents commenced it by firing upon the Star of the West [a supply ship—ed.], and on Fort Sumpter [*sic*], and by other similar acts. It is true, however, that the administration accepted the war thus commenced, for the sole avowed object of preserving our Union; and it is not true that it has since been, or will be, prossecuted by this administration, for any other object. In declaring this, I only declare what I can know, and do know to be true, and what no other man can know to be false.

In taking the various steps which have led to my present position in relation to the war, the public interest and my private interest, have been perfectly paralel [*sic*], because in no other way could I serve myself so well, as by truly serving the Union. The whole field has been open to me, where to choose. No place-hunting necessity has been upon me urging me to seek a position of antagonism to some other man, irrespective of whether such position might be favorable or unfavorable to the Union.

Of course I may err in judgment, but my present position in reference to the rebellion is the result of my best judgment, and according to that best judgment, it is the only position upon which any Executive can or could save the Union. Any substantial departure from it insures the success of the rebellion. An armistice—a cessation of hostilities—is the end of the struggle, and the insurgents would be in peaceable possession of all that has been struggled for. Any different policy in regard to the colored man, deprives us of his help, and this is more than we can bear. We can not spare the hundred and forty or fifty thousand now serving us as soldiers, seamen, and laborers. This is not a question of sentiment or taste, but one of physical force which may be measured and estimated as horse-power and Steam-power are measured and estimated. Keep it and you can save the Union. Throw it away, and the Union goes with it. Nor is it possible for any Administration to retain the service of these people with the express or implied understanding that upon the first convenient occasion, they are to be re-inslaved. It *can* not be; and it *ought* not to be.

"LET HER SOLDIERS . . . GO HOME AND VOTE"

Letter to General William T. Sherman

SEPTEMBER 19, 1864

Lincoln believed the outcome of the approaching state and presidential elections might hinge on the soldiers' vote—which he was confident he could win, even against a former general once wildly popular with his troops but now saddled with an antiwar platform. But could soldiers find the time—and a place—to vote? Here the president urged General William T. Sherman to furlough soldiers to go home and cast ballots in crucial Indiana. A week later, he chided General William Rosecrans for his reported reluctance to grant such furloughs "on the assumed ground," a chagrined Lincoln paraphrased, "that they [the soldiers] will

get drunk and make disturbance." Lincoln insisted: "Wherever the law
allows soldiers to vote, their officers must also allow it." From a political
standpoint, Lincoln was wise to advocate such participation. In the end,
he won more than 55 percent of the popular vote on Election Day—and
80 percent of the separately cast soldiers' vote.

Major General Sherman,

The State election of Indiana occurs on the 11th. of October, and the loss of it to the friends of the Government would go far towards losing the whole Union cause. The bad effect upon the November election, and especially the giving the State Government to those who will oppose the war in every possible way, are too much to risk, if it can possibly be avoided. The draft proceeds, notwithstanding its strong tendency to lose us the State. Indiana is the only important State, voting in October, whose soldiers cannot vote in the field. Any thing you can safely do to let her soldiers, or any part of them, go home and vote at the State election, will be greatly in point. They need not remain for the Presidential election, but may return to you at once. This is, in no sense, an order, but is merely intended to impress you with the importance, to the army itself, of your doing all you safely can, yourself being the judge of what you can safely do.

Yours truly
A. LINCOLN

"WE CAN NOT HAVE FREE GOVERNMENT WITHOUT ELECTIONS"

Response to a Victory Serenade

NOVEMBER 10, 1864

Two days after his decisive election victory, Lincoln made these appreciative remarks from a second-floor window of the White House to a group of well-wishers led by local Lincoln and Johnson clubs. No other nation had ever held a popular election in the midst of civil war, and now Lincoln wanted the credit he deserved for allowing the contest to go forward.

It has long been a grave question whether any government, not *too* strong for the liberties of its people, can be strong *enough* to maintain its own existence, in great emergencies.

On this point the present rebellion brought our republic to a severe test; and a presidential election occurring in regular course during the rebellion added not a little to the strain. If the loyal people, *united,* were put to the utmost of their strength by the rebellion, must they not fail when *divided,* and partially paralyzed, by a political war among themselves?

But the election was a necessity.

We can not have free government without elections; and if the rebellion could force us to forego, or postpone a national election, it might fairly claim to have already conquered and ruined us. The strife of the election is but human-nature practically applied to the facts of the case. What has occurred in this case, must ever recur in similar cases. Human-nature will not change. In any future great national trial, compared with the men of this, we shall have as weak, and as strong; as silly and as wise; as bad and good. Let us, therefore, study the incidents of this, as philosophy to learn wisdom from, and none of them as wrongs to be revenged.

But the election, along with its incidental, and undesirable strife, has done good too. It has demonstrated that a people's government can sustain a national election, in the midst of a great civil war. Until now it has not been known to the world that this was a possibility. It shows also how *sound,* and how *strong* we still are. It shows that, even among candidates of the same party, he who is most devoted to the Union, and most opposed to treason, can receive most of the people's votes. It shows also, to the extent yet known, that we have more men now, than we had when the war began. Gold is good in its place; but living, brave, patriotic men, are better than gold.

But the rebellion continues; and now that the election is over, may not all, having a common interest, re-unite in a common effort, to save our common country? For my own part I have striven, and shall strive to avoid placing any obstacle in the way. So long as I have been here I have not willingly planted a thorn in any man's bosom.

While I am deeply sensible to the high compliment of a re-election; and duly grateful, as I trust, to Almighty God for having directed my countrymen to a right conclusion, as I think, for their own good, it adds nothing to my satisfaction that any other man may be disappointed or pained by the result.

May I ask those who have not differed with me, to join with me, in this same spirit towards those who have?

And now, let me close by asking three hearty cheers for our brave soldiers and seamen and their gallant and skilful commanders.

"Thanks of the Republic They Died to Save"

Condolence Letter to Mrs. Lydia Bixby

NOVEMBER 21, 1864

Arguably the most famous condolence letter ever written by an American, this exquisite expression of sympathy and national purpose has nonetheless long been clouded in controversy. For one thing, as it turned out, the widow Bixby's sacrifices had been exaggerated—only two of her sons had actually been killed in action, not five, as Lincoln was told, and one had deserted. For another, the original manuscript has never surfaced, leading some historians to speculate that it was written not by Lincoln but by his able assistant private secretary, John Hay. Of course, even if Lincoln had merely signed it, the words would still belong to the presidential canon. Regardless, a new consensus is emerging among scholars that the letter—memorably read aloud in the film Saving Private Ryan—*was almost certainly composed by the president, as it was requested by a leading Massachusetts politician, the kind of favor Lincoln almost always obliged.*

Dear Madam,—

I have been shown in the files of the War Department a statement of the Adjutant General of Massachusetts, that you are the mother of five sons who have died gloriously on the field of battle.

I feel how weak and fruitless must be any words of mine which should attempt to beguile you from the grief of a loss so overwhelming. But I cannot refrain from tendering to you the consolation that may be found in the thanks of the Republic they died to save.

I pray that our Heavenly Father may assuage the anguish of your bereavement, and leave you only the cherished memory of the loved and lost, and the solemn pride that must be yours, to have laid so costly a sacrifice upon the altar of Freedom.

Yours, very sincerely and respectfully,

A. LINCOLN.

"NOT MUCH OF A JUDGE OF RELIGION"

Statement for Journalist Noah Brooks on Prisoners of War

DECEMBER 6, 1864

On the same day he submitted his enormously lengthy annual message to Congress, Lincoln wrote out this brief report of a recent encounter in his office with the stubborn wife of a Confederate prisoner. Apparently the president rather liked what he had said to her and hoped his remarks would reach a wider audience. He even headlined his note to journalist Brooks: "The President's Last, Shortest, and Best Speech."

On thursday last week two ladies from Tennessee came before the President [at one of his regular office "receptions," which Lincoln called his "public opinion baths"—ed.] asking the release of their husbands held as prisoners of war in Johnson's Island. They were put off till friday, when they came again; and were again put off to saturday. At each of the interviews one of the ladies urged that her husband was a religious man. On saturday the President ordered the release of the prisoners, and then said to the lady "You say your husband is a religious man; tell him when you see him, that I say I am not much of a judge of religion, but that, in my opinion, the religion that sets men to rebel and fight against their government, because, as they think, that government does not sufficiently help *some* men to eat their bread on the sweat of *other* men's faces, is not the sort of religion upon which people can get to heaven!"

A. LINCOLN.

"THE WAR CONTINUES"

From the Annual Message to Congress

DECEMBER 6, 1864

Lincoln's fourth "state of the union" message proudly reported on Sherman's march through Georgia and strongly advocated for passage of the Thirteenth Amendment abolishing slavery. It earned mild praise from the Northern press, the New York Tribune *calling it merely "straightforward and business-like." To some critics in Europe, however, the message seemed overly bellicose. After offering the usual detail on government revenues and other aspects of domestic and foreign policy, the president turned Congress's attention to the war. It proved the last formal update Lincoln ever provided to the House and Senate.*

The war continues. Since the last annual message all the important lines and positions then occupied by our forces have been maintained, and our arms have steadily advanced; thus liberating the regions left in rear, so that Missouri, Kentucky, Tennessee and parts of other States have again produced reasonably fair crops.

The most remarkable feature in the military operations of the year is General Sherman's attempted march of three hundred miles directly through the insurgent region. It tends to show a great increase of our relative strength that our General-in-Chief should feel able to confront and hold in check every active force of the enemy, and yet to detach a well-appointed large army to move on such an expedition. The result not yet being known, conjecture in regard to it is not here indulged.

Important movements have also occurred during the year to the effect of moulding society for durability in the Union. Although short of complete success, it is much in the right direction, that twelve thousand citizens in each of the States of Arkansas and Louisiana have organized loyal State governments with free constitutions, and are earnestly struggling to maintain and administer them. The movements in the same direction, more extensive, though less definite in Missouri, Kentucky and Tennessee, should not be overlooked. But Maryland presents the example of complete success. Maryland is secure to Liberty and Union for all the future. The genius of rebellion will no more claim Maryland. Like another foul spirit, being driven out, it may seek to tear her, but it will woo her no more.

At the last session of Congress a proposed amendment of the Constitution abolishing slavery throughout the United States, passed the Senate, but failed for lack of the requisite two-thirds vote in the House of Representatives. Although the present is the same Congress, and nearly the same members, and without questioning the wisdom or patriotism of those who stood in opposition, I venture to recommend the reconsideration and passage of the measure at the present session. Of course the abstract question is not changed; but an intervening election shows, almost certainly, that the next Congress will pass the measure if this does not. Hence there is only a question of *time* as to when the proposed amendment will go to the States for their action. And as it is to so go, at all events, may we not agree that the sooner the better? It is not claimed that the election has imposed a duty on members to change their views or their votes, any further than, as an additional element to be considered, their judgment may be affected by it. It is the voice of the people now, for the first time, heard upon the question. In a great national crisis, like ours, unanimity of action among those seeking a common end is very desirable—almost indispensable. And yet no approach to such unanimity is attainable, unless some deference shall be paid to the will of the majority, simply because it is the will of the majority. In this case the common end is the maintenance of the Union; and, among the means to secure that end, such will, through the election, is most clearly declared in favor of such constitutional amendment.

The most reliable indication of public purpose in this country is derived through our popular elections. Judging by the recent canvass and its result, the purpose of the people, within the loyal States, to maintain the integrity of the Union, was never more firm, nor more nearly unanimous, than now. The extraordinary calmness and good order with which the millions of voters met and mingled at the polls, give strong assurance of this. Not only all those who supported the Union ticket, so called, but a great majority of the opposing party also, may be fairly claimed to entertain, and to be actuated by, the same purpose. It is an unanswerable argument to this effect, that no candidate for any office whatever, high or low, has ventured to seek votes on the avowal that he was for giving up the Union. There have been much impugning of motives, and much heated controversy as to the proper means and best mode of advancing the Union cause; but on the distinct issue of Union or no Union, the politicians have shown their instinctive knowledge that there is no diversity among the people. In affording the people the fair opportunity of showing, one to another and to the world, this firmness and unanimity of purpose, the election has been of vast value to the national cause.

. . . .

The important fact remains demonstrated, that we have *more* men *now* than we had when the war *began;* that we are not exhausted, nor in process of exhaustion; that we are *gaining* strength, and may, if need be, maintain the contest indefinitely. This as to men. Material resources are now more complete and abundant than ever.

The national resources, then, are unexhausted, and, as we believe, inexhaustible. The public purpose to re-establish and maintain the national authority is unchanged, and, as we believe, unchangeable. The manner of continuing the effort remains to choose. On careful consideration of all the evidence accessible it seems to me that no attempt at negotiation with the insurgent leader could result in any good. He would accept nothing short of severance of the Union— precisely what we will not and cannot give. His declarations to this effect are explicit and oft-repeated. He does not attempt to deceive us. He affords us no excuse to deceive ourselves. He cannot volun- tarily reaccept the Union; we cannot voluntarily yield it. Between him and us the issue is distinct, simple, and inflexible. It is an issue which can only be tried by war, and decided by victory. If we yield, we are beaten; if the Southern people fail him, he is beaten. Either way, it would be the victory and defeat following war. What is true, however, of him who heads the insurgent cause, is not necessarily true of those who follow. Although he cannot reaccept the Union, they can. Some of them, we know, already desire peace and reunion. The number of such may increase. They can, at any moment, have peace simply by laying down their arms and submitting to the national authority under the Constitution. After so much, the government could not, if it would, maintain war against them. The loyal people would not sustain or allow it. If questions should remain, we would adjust them by the peaceful means of legislation, conference, courts, and votes, operating only in constitutional and lawful channels. Some certain, and other possible, questions are, and would be, beyond the Executive power to adjust; as, for instance, the admission of members into Congress, and whatever might require the appropriation of money. The Executive power itself would be greatly diminished by the cessation of actual war. Pardons and remissions of forfeitures, however, would still be within Executive control. In what spirit and temper this control would be exercised can be fairly judged of by the past.

A year ago general pardon and amnesty, upon specified terms, were offered to all, except certain designated classes; and, it was, at the same time, made known that the excepted classes were still within contemplation of special clemency. During the year many availed themselves of the general provision, and many more would, only that the signs of bad faith in some led to such precautionary measures as rendered the practical process less easy and certain. During the same time also special pardons have been granted to individuals of the excepted classes, and no voluntary application has been denied. Thus, practically, the door has been, for a full year, open to all, except such as were not in condition to make free choice—that is, such as were in custody or under constraint. It is still so open to all. But the time may come—probably will come—when public duty shall demand that it be closed; and that, in lieu, more rigorous measures than heretofore shall be adopted.

In presenting the abandonment of armed resistance to the national authority on the part of the insurgents, as the only indispensable condition to ending the war on the part of the government, I retract nothing heretofore said as to slavery. I repeat the declaration made a year ago, that "while I remain in my present position I shall not attempt to retract or modify the emancipation proclamation, nor shall I return to slavery any person who is free by the terms of that proclamation, or by any of the Acts of Congress." If the people should, by whatever mode or means, make it an Executive duty to re-enslave such persons, another, and not I, must be their instrument to perform it.

In stating a single condition of peace, I mean simply to say that the war will cease on the part of the government, whenever it shall have ceased on the part of those who began it.

"BUT WHAT NEXT?"

Letter to General William T. Sherman

DECEMBER 26, 1864

On December 25, emerging triumphantly from his long march through Georgia, Sherman wired Lincoln: "I beg to present you as a Christmas gift the city of Savannah with 150 heavy guns & plenty of ammunition & also about 25,000 bales of cotton." The president replied with the following congratulatory letter, brimming with gratitude and admiration, admitting characteristically that his general was right and he wrong, but then ending with a question about what Sherman's next effort might be.

My dear General Sherman.

Many, many thanks for your Christmas-gift—the capture of Savannah.

When you were about leaving for Atlanta for the Atlantic coast, I was *anxious*, if not fearful; but feeling that you were the better judge, and remembering that "nothing risked, nothing gained" I did not interfere. Now, the undertaking being a success, the honor is all yours; for I believe none of us went farther than to acquiesce. And, taking the work of Gen. [George H.] Thomas into the count, as it should be taken, it is indeed a great success. Not only does it afforded the obvious and immediate military advantages; but, in showing to the world that your army could be divided, putting the stronger part to an important new service, and yet leaving enough to vanquish the old opposing force of the whole—[John Bell] Hood's army—it brings those who sat in darkness, to see a great light. But what next? I suppose it will be safer if I leave Gen. Grant and yourself to decide.

Please make my grateful acknowledgments to your whole army, officers and men.

Yours very truly

A. LINCOLN

"MY SON . . . WISHES TO SEE SOMETHING OF THE WAR"

Letter to General Ulysses S. Grant

JANUARY 19, 1865

For many months, Lincoln's eldest boy, Robert, had badgered his parents for permission to volunteer for the military. But Mary Lincoln, who had already lost two young sons to childhood disease, remained equally adamant that he not be allowed to join up. Her husband, increasingly fearful for her mental health, was reluctant to challenge her, even as public criticism mounted about the young man's seemingly privileged civilian status. Finally, the president hit on the solution he proposed in this letter to General Grant. Robert not only joined Grant's staff as a captain February 11, he was there to witness Lee's surrender two months

later. Although Lincoln offered in this letter to bear the financial burden
of his son's commission, an unprecedented and impractical suggestion,
the president was never required to pay for him out of his own pocket.

Lieut. General Grant:

Please read and answer this letter as though I was not President, but only a friend. My son, now in his twenty second year, having graduated at Harvard, wishes to see something of the war before it ends. I do not wish to put him in the ranks, nor yet to give him a commission, to which those who have already served long, are better entitled, and better qualified to hold. Could he, without embarrassment to you, or detriment to the service, go into your Military family with some nominal rank, I, and not the public, furnishing his necessary means? If no, say so without the least hesitation, because I am as anxious, and as deeply interested, that you shall not be encumbered as you can be yourself.

Yours truly
A. LINCOLN

"WITH MALICE TOWARD NONE"

Second Inaugural Address

MARCH 4, 1865

Perhaps the greatest of all his speeches (Lincoln himself thought it would
"wear as well—perhaps better than—any thing I have ever produced"),
his canonical second inaugural was delivered to a massive, racially
integrated throng outside the U.S. Capitol. When the president began
speaking, the clouds that had blanketed Washington for much of the
day suddenly parted, sending an "electric thrill" through the plaza. The
oration is best remembered for its pacific conclusion, but Lincoln de-
voted far more time to a ringing, Old Testament justification for the
long and bloody war.

Lincoln, standing behind the small podium at center, reads his second inaugural
address, calling for "malice toward none" and "charity for all," from outside the U.S.
Capitol on March 4, 1865, in a photograph by Alexander Gardner. *(Library of Congress)*

[Fellow Countrymen:]

At this second appearing to take the oath of the presidential office,
there is less occasion for an extended address than there was at the
first. Then a statement, somewhat in detail, of a course to be pursued, seemed fitting and proper. Now, at the expiration of four years,
during which public declarations have been constantly called forth
on every point and phase of the great contest which still absorbs the
attention, and engrosses the enerergies [*sic*] of the nation, little that
is new could be presented. The progress of our arms, upon which
all else chiefly depends, is as well known to the public as to myself;
and it is, I trust, reasonably satisfactory and encouraging to all. With
high hope for the future, no prediction in regard to it is ventured.

On the occasion corresponding to this four years ago, all thoughts
were anxiously directed to an impending civil-war. All dreaded it—
all sought to avert it. While the inaugeral address was being delivered

from this place, devoted altogether to *saving* the Union without war, insurgent agents were in the city seeking to *destroy* it without war— seeking to dissol[v]e the Union, and divide effects, by negotiation. Both parties deprecated war; but one of them would *make* war rather than let the nation survive; and the other would *accept* war rather than let it perish. And the war came.

One eighth of the whole population were colored slaves, not distributed generally over the Union, but localized in the Southern part of it. These slaves constituted a peculiar and powerful interest. All knew that this interest was, somehow, the cause of the war. To strengthen, perpetuate, and extend this interest was the object for which the insurgents would rend the Union, even by war; while the government claimed no right to do more than to restrict the territorial enlargement of it. Neither party expected for the war, the magnitude, or the duration, which it has already attained. Neither anticipated that the *cause* of the conflict might cease with, or even before, the conflict itself should cease. Each looked for an easier triumph, and a result less fundamental and astounding. Both read the same Bible, and pray to the same God; and each invokes His aid against the other. It may seem strange that any men should dare to ask a just God's assistance in wringing their bread from the sweat of other men's faces; but let us judge not that we be not judged. The prayers of both could not be answered; that of neither has been answered fully. The Almighty has His own purposes. "Woe unto the world because of offences! for it must needs be that offences come; but woe to that man by whom the offence cometh!" If we shall suppose that American Slavery is one of those offences which, in the providence of God, must needs come, but which, having continued through His appointed time, He now wills to remove, and that He gives to both North and South, this terrible war, as the woe due to those by whom the offence came, shall we discern therein any departure from those divine attributes which the believers in a Living God always ascribe to Him? Fondly do we hope—fervently do we pray—that this mighty scourge of war may speedily pass away. Yet, if God wills that it continue, until all the wealth piled by the bond-man's two hundred and fifty years of unrequited toil shall be sunk, and until every drop of blood drawn with the lash, shall be paid by another drawn with the sword, as was said three thousand years ago, so still it must be said "the judgments of the Lord, are true and righteous altogether."

With malice toward none; with charity for all; with firmness in the right, as God gives us to see the right, let us strive on to finish the work we are in; to bind up the nation's wounds; to care for him who shall have borne the battle, and for his widow, and his orphan — to do all which may achieve and cherish a just, and a lasting peace, among ourselves, and with all nations.

"OBJECTING TO REBEL PRISONERS"

Letter to General Ulysses S. Grant

MARCH 9, 1865

A day earlier, General Grant had wired the secretary of war to com-plain that the policy of allowing Rebel prisoners in the North "to take the oath of allegiance and go free" was "wrong." He added: "No one should be liberated on taking the oath . . . who has been captured while bearing arms against us, except where persons of known loyalty vouch for them." Lincoln took up the question with the following letter, taking responsibility for the policy without quite clarifying it. (Two days later, he issued a proclamation offering pardon for deserters.)

Lieut. Genl. Grant

I see your despatch to the Sec. of War, objecting to rebel prison-ers being allowed to take the oath and go free. Supposing that I am responsible for what is done in this way, I think fit to say that there is no general rule, or action, allowing prisoners to be discharged merely on taking the oath. What has been done is that Members of

Congress come to me from time to time with lists of names alleging that from personal knowledge, and evidence of reliable persons they are satisfied that it is safe to discharge the particular persons named on the lists, and I have ordered their discharge. These Members are chiefly from the border states; and those they get discharged are their neighbors and neighbors sons. They tell me that they do not bring to me one tenth of the names which are brought to them, bringing only such as their knowledge or the proof satisfies them about. I have, on the same principle, discharged some on the representations of others than Members of Congress, as, for instance, Gov. Johnson of Tennessee. The number I have discharged has been rather larger than I liked—reaching I should think an average of fifty a day, since the recent general exchange commenced. On the same grounds, last year, I discharged quite a number at different times, aggregating perhaps a thousand, Missourians and Kentuckians; and their Members returning here since the prisoner's return to their homes, report to me only two cases of proving false. Doubtless some more have proved false; but, on the whole I believe what I have done in this way has done good rather than harm.

A. LINCOLN

"WILL THE NEGRO FIGHT FOR THEM?"

Speech to an Indiana Regiment

MARCH 17, 1865

Lincoln offered this final defense of black enlistment from the balcony of a Washington Hotel, where he presented a captured Confederate flag to the governor of Indiana and offered these remarks to the state's 140th Regiment. He used the occasion to question reports that desperate Confederates were now employing black troops to fight—in essence—against their own freedom.

Fellow Citizens.

A few words only. I was born in Kentucky, raised in Indiana, re-side in Illinois, and now here, it is my duty to care equally for the good people of all the States. I am to-day glad of seeing it in the power of an Indianana [*sic*] regiment to present this captured flag to the good governor of their State. And yet I would not wish to compliment Indiana above other states, remembering that all have done so well. There are but few aspects of this great war on which I have not already expressed my views by speaking or writing. There is one—the recent effort of our erring bretheren, sometimes so-called, to employ the slaves in their armies. The great question with them has been; "will the negro fight for them?" They ought to know better than we; and, doubtless, do know better than we. I may incidentally remark, however, that having, in my life, heard many arguments,—or strings of words meant to pass for arguments,—intended to show that the negro ought to be a slave, that if he shall now really fight to keep himself a slave, it will be a far better argument why [he] should remain a slave than I have ever before heard. He, perhaps, ought to be a slave, if he desires it ardently enough to fight for it. Or, if one out of four will, for his own freedom, fight to keep the other three in slavery, he ought to be a slave for his selfish meanness. I have always thought that all men should be free; but if any should be slaves it should be first those who desire it for *themselves,* and secondly those who *desire* it for *others.* Whenever [I] hear any one, arguing for slav-ery I feel a strong impulse to see it tried on him personally.

There is one thing about the negroes fighting for the rebels [a newly proposed desperate plan by Confederates to bolster their dwindling ranks by drafting slaves—ed.] which we can know as well [as] they can; and that is that they can not, at [the] same time fight in their armies, and stay at home and make bread for them. And this being known and remembered we can have but little concern whether they become soldiers or not. I am rather in favor of the measure; and would at any time if I could, have loaned them a vote to carry it. We have to reach the bottom of the insurgent resources; and that they employ, or seriously think of employing, the slaves as soldiers, gives us glimpses of the bottom. Therefore I am glad of what we learn on this subject.

"MUST MORE BLOOD BE SHED?"

Remark to Generals Ulysses S. Grant and William T. Sherman aboard the River Queen, *Docked at City Point, Virginia*

MARCH 28, 1865

Told during their last war council that another major encounter was to be expected before General Lee gave up, Lincoln said the following, recalled General Sherman.

Must more blood be shed? Cannot this last bloody battle be avoided?

"I DISLIKE TO LEAVE"

Telegram to Secretary of War Edwin M. Stanton, Army Headquarters, City Point, Virginia

MARCH 30, 1865

During a long and eventful visit to the army in Virginia, Lincoln became something of a war correspondent, sharing news of troop movements with both the secretary of war and his wife. In this typical dispatch, which charmingly describes an experience that turned out to be exciting but indecisive, he expresses some remorse for being away from Washington so long but is thrilled to be in the midst of so much action and shows no real inclination to return home.

Hon. Secretary of War:

I begin to feel that I ought to be at home, and yet I dislike to leave without seeing nearer to the end of General Grant's present movement. He has now been out since yesterday morning, and although he has not been diverted from his programme, no considerable effect has yet been produced, so far as we know here. Last night at 10.15, when it was dark as a rainy night without a moon could be, a furious cannonade, soon joined in by a heavy musketry-fire, opened near Petersburg and lasted about two hours. The sound was very distinct here, as also were the flashes of the guns upon the clouds. It seemed to me a great battle, but the older hands here scarcely noticed it, and, sure enough, this morning it was found that very little had been done.

A. LINCOLN

"PETERSBURG COMPLETELY ENVELOPED"

Telegram to Mary Lincoln, Army Headquarters,
City Point, Virginia

APRIL 2, 1865

The first lady accompanied her husband for the initial part of his lengthy trip to see General Grant's army finish the war. But outraged to see the president reviewing the troops alongside the young wife of a general, she embarrassed the president, and herself, with a jealous public outburst so mortifying that she left for (or was sent) home to regain her emotional bearings. She would return for the final part of the trip. While they were apart Lincoln kept her fully posted on military developments, as with this update from headquarters.

Mrs. Lincoln:

At 4:30 p.m. to-day General Grant telegraphs that he has Petersburg completely enveloped from river below to river above, and has captured, since he started last Wednesday, about 12,000 prisoners and 50 guns. He suggests that I shall go out and see him in the morning, which I think I will do. Tad and I are both well, and will be glad to see you and your party here at the time you name.

A. LINCOLN.

"THANK GOD THAT I HAVE LIVED TO SEE THIS!"

Remarks on the Fall of—and His Visit to—Richmond, Army Headquarters, City Point, Virginia

APRIL 3–4, 1865

Lincoln had long before realized that the Confederate army—not its capital—should be the object of Union attack. But there was no doubting the emotional impact of the city's fall. The president expressed joy when he heard the news, but the sea voyage he undertook in order to tour Richmond the next day, which required him to change from larger to smaller boats several times, reminded him of a joke that concluded, "It is well to be humble."

Thank God that I have lived to see this! It seems to me that I have been dreaming a horrid dream for four years, and now the nightmare is gone. I want to see Richmond.

"DON'T KNEEL TO ME"

Remarks to Freed Slaves

RICHMOND, VIRGINIA, APRIL 4, 1865

According to Admiral David Dixon Porter, who accompanied the president and his son Tad to the occupied Confederate capital, African Americans greeted Lincoln with wild enthusiasm when he stepped off his boat and onto the city's shores. When several fell to their knees in gratitude, Porter recalled Lincoln saying the following (although he undoubtedly idealized, or at least edited, what he heard). Today a statue of Lincoln and Tad stands in the city, a tribute to the president's visit, not as a conqueror, but as a father.

Don't kneel to me. That is not right. You must kneel to God only and thank him for the liberty you will hereafter enjoy. I am but

Lincoln as a conquering hero, as depicted by a German lithographer
who overdramatized Lincoln's visit to the conquered Confederate capital of
Richmond, Virginia, on April 4, 1865—and then compounded the error by
suggesting the scene showed the president arriving at Union army
headquarters at City Point. (*Harold Holzer Collection*)

God's humble instrument, but you may rest assured that as long as
I live, no one shall put a shackle on your limbs, and you shall have
all the rights which God has given to every other free citizen of this
republic.

"LET 'EM UP EASY"

Remark to General Godfrey Wetzel, Richmond, Virginia

APRIL 4, 1865

---

*The president made this comment to the commander of Union forces
in occupied Richmond when asked how the local population should be
treated.*

If I were in your place, I'd let 'em up easy, let 'em up easy.

"As to Peace"

Letter to Confederate Assistant Secretary of War John A. Campbell

[APRIL 5, 1865]

Lincoln drafted this document to guide Virginians onto a path toward a speedy peace—not knowing that Lee's surrender was only days away. Campbell had resigned a seat on the U.S. Supreme Court when his state of Virginia seceded.

As to peace, I have said before, and now repeat, that three things are indispensable.

1. The restoration of the national authority throughout all the States.

2. No receding by the Executive of the United States on the slavery question, from the position assumed thereon, in the late Annual Message to Congress, and in preceding documents.

3. No cessation of hostilities short of an end of the war, and the disbanding of all force hostile to the government.

That all propositions coming from those now in hostility to the government; and not inconsistent with the foregoing, will be respectfully considered, and passed upon in a spirit of sincere liberality.

I now add that it seems useless for me to be more specific with those who will not say they are ready for the indispensable terms, even on conditions to be named by themselves. If there be any who are ready for those indispensable terms, on any conditions whatever, let them say so, and state their conditions, so that such conditions can be distinctly known, and considered.

It is further added that, the remission of confiscations being within the executive power, if the war be now further persisted in, by those opposing the government, the making of confiscated property at the least to bear the additional cost, will be insisted on; but that confiscations (except in cases of third party intervening interests) will be remitted to the people of any State which shall now promptly, and in good faith, withdraw it's troops and other support, from further resistance to the government.

What is now said as to remission of confiscations has no reference to supposed property in slaves.

"LET THE *THING* BE PRESSED"

*Telegram to General Ulysses S. Grant, Army Headquarters,
City Point, Virginia*

APRIL 7, 1865

On April 6, 1865, with General Lee and his tattered army cornered, General Philip Sheridan wired General Grant to report he had defeated the enemy at Burke's Station. "I am still pressing on with both cavalry and infantry," he added. Shown the dispatch, Lincoln forwarded to Grant his enthusiastic endorsement. Victory was only days away but the commander in chief wanted no relaxation in the pounding of the Army of Northern Virginia.

Lieut Gen. Grant.

Gen. Sheridan says "If the thing is pressed I think that Lee will surrender." Let the *thing* be pressed.

A. LINCOLN

"I HAVE ALWAYS THOUGHT 'DIXIE' ONE OF THE BEST TUNES"

Response to a Serenade

APRIL 10, 1865

A weary but exultant Lincoln, fresh from his extended visit to the troops in the field, including his tour of captured Richmond, offered these amusing remarks to a crowd of three hundred well-wishers who braved rain and mud to celebrate Lee's surrender by serenading Lincoln from the White House lawn.

Fellow Citizens:

I am very greatly rejoiced to find that an occasion has occurred so pleasurable that the people cannot restrain themselves. [Cheers.] I suppose that arrangements are being made for some sort of a formal demonstration, this, or perhaps, to-morrow night. [Cries of "We can't wait," "We want it now," &c.] If there should be such a demonstration, I, of course, will be called upon to respond, and I shall have nothing to say if you dribble it all out of me before. [Laughter and applause.] I see you have a band of music with you. [Voices, "We have two or three."] I propose closing up this interview by the band performing a particular tune which I will name. Before this is done, however, I wish to mention one or two little circumstances connected with it. I have always thought "Dixie" one of the best tunes I have ever heard. Our adversaries over the way attempted to appropriate it, but I insisted yesterday that we fairly captured it. [Applause.] I presented the question to the Attorney General, and he gave it as his legal opinion that it is our lawful prize. [Laughter and applause.] I now request the band to favor me with its performance.

"NOT IN SORROW, BUT IN GLADNESS OF HEART"

From Lincoln's Final Public Address

APRIL 11, 1865

Lincoln's last speech proved a dry report on his proposed Reconstruction policies, something of an anti-climax after so many years of soaring rhetoric. Yet in a way, no other Lincoln oration ever changed history so dramatically. For when one of the members of the audience that night heard the president propose voting rights for some African Americans, he vowed it would be the last speech Lincoln ever made. His name was John Wilkes Booth. And three nights later, the racist actor shot Lincoln at a Washington theater.

We meet this evening, not in sorrow, but in gladness of heart. The evacuation of Petersburg and Richmond, and the surrender of the principal insurgent army, give hope of a righteous and speedy peace whose joyous expression can not be restrained. In the midst of this, however, He, from Whom all blessings flow, must not be forgotten. A call for a national thanksgiving is being prepared, and will be duly promulgated. Nor must those whose harder part gives us the cause of rejoicing, be overlooked. Their honors must not be parcelled out with others. I myself, was near the front, and had the high pleasure of transmitting much of the good news to you; but no part of the honor, for plan or execution, is mine. To Gen. Grant, his skilful officers, and brave men, all belongs. The gallant Navy stood ready, but was not in reach to take active part.

By these recent successes the re-inauguration of the national authority—reconstruction—which has had a large share of thought from the first, is pressed much more closely upon our attention. It is fraught with great difficulty. Unlike the case of a war between independent nations, there is no authorized organ for us to treat with. No one man has authority to give up the rebellion for any other man. We simply must begin with, and mould from, disorganized and discordant elements. Nor is it a small additional embarrassment that we, the loyal people, differ among ourselves as to the mode, manner, and means of reconstruction.

. . . .

We all agree that the seceded States, so called, are out of their proper practical relation with the Union; and that the sole object of the government, civil and military, in regard to those States is to again get them into that proper practical relation. I believe it is not only possible, but in fact, easier, to do this, without deciding, or even considering, whether these states have even been out of the Union, than with it. Finding themselves safely at home, it would be utterly immaterial whether they had ever been abroad. Let us all join in doing the acts necessary to restoring the proper practical relations between these states and the Union; and each forever after, innocently indulge his own opinion whether, in doing the acts, he brought the States from without, into the Union, or only gave them proper assistance, they never having been out of it.

The amount of constituency, so to to [sic] speak, on which the new Louisiana government rests, would be more satisfactory to all, if it contained fifty, thirty, or even twenty thousand, instead of only about twelve thousand, as it does. It is also unsatisfactory to some that the elective franchise is not given to the colored man. I would myself prefer that it were now conferred on the very intelligent, and on those who serve our cause as soldiers. Still the question is not whether the Louisiana government, as it stands, is quite all that is desirable. The question is "Will it be wiser to take it as it is, and help to improve it; or to reject, and disperse it?" "Can Louisiana be brought into proper practical relation with the Union *sooner* by *sustaining,* or by *discarding* her new State Government?"

Some twelve thousand voters in the heretofore slave-state of Louisiana have sworn allegiance to the Union, assumed to be the rightful political power of the State, held elections, organized a State government, adopted a free-state constitution, giving the benefit of public schools equally to black and white, and empowering the Legislature to confer the elective franchise upon the colored man. Their Legislature has already voted to ratify the constitutional amendment recently passed by Congress, abolishing slavery throughout the nation. These twelve thousand persons are thus fully committed to the Union, and to perpetual freedom in the state—committed to the very things, and nearly all the things the nation wants— and they ask the nations recognition, and it's assistance to make good their committal. Now, if we reject, and spurn them, we do our utmost to disorganize and disperse them. We in effect say to the white men "You are worthless, or worse—we will neither help you, nor be helped by you." To the blacks we say "This cup of liberty which these, your old masters, hold to your lips, we will dash from you, and leave you to the chances of gathering the spilled and scattered contents in some vague and undefined when, where, and how." If this course, discouraging and paralyzing both white and black, has any tendency to bring Louisiana into proper practical relations with the Union, I have, so far, been unable to perceive it. If, on the contrary, we recognize, and sustain the new government of Louisiana the converse of all this is made true. We encourage the hearts, and nerve the arms of the twelve thousand to adhere to their work, and argue for it, and proselyte [sic] for it, and fight for it, and feed it, and grow it, and ripen it to a complete success. The colored man too, in seeing all united for him, is inspired with vigilance, and energy, and daring, to the same end. Grant that he desires the elective franchise, will he not attain it sooner by saving the already advanced steps toward it, than by running backward over them? Concede that the new government of Louisiana is only to what it should be as the egg is to the fowl, we shall sooner have the fowl by hatching the egg than by smashing it? Again, if we reject Louisiana, we also reject one vote in favor of the proposed amendment to the national constitution. To meet this proposition, it has been argued that no more than three fourths of those States which have not attempted secession are necessary to validly ratify the amendment. I do not commit myself against this, further than to say that such a ratification would be questionable, and sure to be persistently questioned; while a ratification by three fourths of all the States would be unquestioned and unquestionable.

I repeat the question. "Can Louisiana be brought into proper practical relation with the Union *sooner* by *sustaining* or by *discarding* her new State Government?

What has been said of Louisiana will apply generally to other States. And yet so great peculiarities pertain to each state; and such important and sudden changes occur in the same state; and, withal, so new and unprecedented is the whole case, that no exclusive, and inflexible plan can safely be prescribed as to details and colatterals. Such exclusive, and inflexible plan, would surely become a new entanglement. Important principles may, and must, be inflexible.

In the present "*situation*" as the phrase goes, it may be my duty to make some new announcement to the people of the South. I am considering, and shall not fail to act, when satisfied that action will be proper.

"THE WAR, HAS COME TO A CLOSE"

Remarks to Mary Lincoln

APRIL 14, 1865

The president and first lady took a carriage ride together on this, the last afternoon of Lincoln's life. Mary Lincoln recalled being startled by her husband's "great cheerfulness" as he made the following comments and talked about traveling to California and Palestine in the future. A few hours later, they set off together for their very last trip: to Ford's Theatre.

I consider *this day*, the war, has come to a close . . . . We must *both*, be more cheerful in the future—between the war & the loss of our darling Willie—we have both, been very miserable.

ACKNOWLEDGMENTS

THIS BOOK EVOLVED over a long period of gestation, during which my editor, Amy Gash, showed her usual monumental patience without ever losing her enthusiasm for what became an entirely new project. I am grateful as well to publisher Elisabeth Scharlatt, managing editor Brunson Hoole, and the entire team at Algonquin Books, as well as to my superb and ever-encouraging agent Geri Thoma.

Thanks go to my able and thorough research assistant, Avi Mowshowitz, and to my assistants Kraig Smith and Rebecca Schear, for their after-hours help.

No book should be read by the public before it is read by the experts, and I am extremely grateful to my friend and colleague, Lincoln Prize–winning historian Craig L. Symonds, for subjecting these texts to his expert eye and broad knowledge. He made countless inspired suggestions and saved me from many an error, though I take sole responsibility for all that remain. I am also grateful to my friends Frank J. Williams and Richard Dreyfuss for taking time over dinner in Los Angeles in 2009 to talk through—and debate—the finer points of Lincoln's attitudes toward war.

For generously consenting to the use of the definitive Lincoln texts from *The Collected Works of Abraham Lincoln,* the author is especially grateful to the Abraham Lincoln Association of Springfield, Illinois, which sponsored the original eight-volume publication some sixty years ago and is now researching and creating a long-needed online update. I particularly thank ALA president Robert Lenz of Bloomington, Illinois, and Thomas F. Schwartz, the executive director and state historian. And for an expert job of copyediting these especially complex texts for *Lincoln on War,* I thank Jude Grant.

Special and sincerest thanks go to my family: Edith, for reading the texts and tolerating the time it took to assemble them, and my daughters Meg and Remy, son-in-law Adam Kirsch, and grandson Charlie, for making everything I do seem worthwhile.

INDEX

HAROLD HOLZER is chairman of the Abraham Lincoln Bicentennial Foundation. One of the country's foremost authorities on Lincoln and the Civil War era, Holzer is the author of *Lincoln at Cooper Union: The Speech That Made Abraham Lincoln President, Lincoln President-Elect: Abraham Lincoln and the Great Secession Winter 1860–1861, Lincoln on Democracy,* and many other award-winning titles. He lectures throughout the country, appears often on PBS, C-SPAN, the History Channel, the Discovery Channel, and the BBC, and has written for the *New York Times, American Heritage,* and *America's Civil War,* among other publications. Holzer and actor Sam Waterston have performed their program "Lincoln Seen and Heard" for three American presidents, including a performance at the White House. The recipient of research, writing, and lifetime achievement awards from the Illinois State Historical Society, the Manuscript Society, the Victorian Society, the Civil War Round Tables of New York and Chicago, and the Lincoln Groups of New York and the District of Columbia, Holzer was awarded the National Humanities Medal in 2008 by the president of the United States. He and his wife, Edith, who live in Rye, New York, have two grown daughters and a grandson. Holzer's Web site is www.haroldholzer.com.